ARCHIE COCHRANE:
BACK TO THE FRONT

Special edition for the XI Cochrane Colloquium
celebrated in Barcelona, Spain, October 2003
supported by an unrestricted educational grant from:

www.msd.es

F. XAVIER BOSCH

ARCHIE COCHRANE: BACK TO THE FRONT

© FRANCESC XAVIER BOSCH, 2003

EDITORS:
F. XAVIER BOSCH
RICARD MOLAS

COCHRANE COLLABORATION CONSULTANT:
XAVIER BONFILL

ASSISTANT EDITOR:
CRISTINA RAJO

ENGLISH PROOF-READER:
MARY SINCLAIR

TRANSLATION:
JOELLEN KLAUSTERMEIER

DESIGN:
RICARD MOLAS

DESIGN ASSISTANT:
SEBASTIÁN MACIÀ

FIRST EDITION: OCTOBER 2003

PRINTED IN BARCELONA 2003

DEPÓSITO LEGAL:
B-40550-2003

ISBN:
84-607-8958-6

This book cannot be reproduced in total or in part by any editorial means, including electronic. Reproduction is strictly forbidden without the explicit written permission of the editors and are subject to legal prosecution under the law.
All rights reserved.

TABLE OF CONTENTS

Preface: *Joan Clos* — 14
Do you know Grañén?..: *F. Xavier Bosch* — 16

ARCHIE COCHRANE, THE MAN

Sir Richard Doll on Archie Cochrane — 26
Archie Cochrane and politics: *Julian Tudor Hart* — 38
Archie Cochrane: man of vision with feet of clay: *Peter Elwood* — 44
Remembering Archie Cochrane: *Rolando Armijo* — 52
The international profile: *Devra and Lester Breslow* — 58
Archie in a hundred words: *Sir Sandy Macara* — 62
A long time friend: *Bill Miall* — 64
Archie and Barcelona: *Josep M. Anto* — 72
Epidemiology and Health Services Research: *Archie Cochrane* — 77
Student memories of Archie Cochrane: *Susana Sans,* — 82
Daan Kromhout — 84

A sensible man:
  The artistic taste: *Peter and Annie Nicholas* — 90
  Sketches from the family: *Giles and Margaret Stalker* — 98

TABLE OF CONTENTS

ARCHIE COCHRANE, A MAN OF HIS TIME

The Spanish Civil War (1936-1939)
    The Spanish Civil War, a unique war: *Gabriel Jackson* (∗)   114
    1936, arrival in Barcelona: *George Orwell* (∗)   116
    A touch of friendship: *George Orwell* (∗)   118
    The political war: *George Orwell* (∗)   122
    The international propaganda: *George Orwell* (∗)   128
    The party militia and the popular army: *George Orwell* (∗)   130
    The International Brigades: *Josep Maria Solé i Sabaté*   134
                              Hugh Thomas (∗)   140

War Medicine: Archie Cochrane and the surgical triage
    The organization of the health services at the battle front: *Moisès Broggi*   144
    Josep Trueta: Not all cheese that smells bad is bad: *F. Xavier Bosch*   148
    Four words to win a war: *Jaume Bosch i Pardo*   152
    Archie in the Spanish Civil War: *Archie Cochrane with Max Blythe* (∗)   156
    The death of Julian Bell: *Reginald Somes Saxton*   182

Farewell to the Brigades, farewell to Spain: *George Orwell* (∗)   186

World War II. Medical care and trials at the concentration camp
    The political context: *Gabriel Jackson* (∗)   190
    Salonica: *Archie Cochrane with Max Blythe* (∗)   196

A research life in Wales
    Cohort Studies among miners   209
    Cochrane and Coal: *A. J. Newman Taylor*   212
    The aspirin trial   216
    Wine consumption: the correlation that would not go away   222
    Studies on screening   225
    Health Services Research   227

Back to the front
    Forty years back. A retrospective survey: *Archie Cochrane* (∗)   232
    A triage of travel anecdotes: *F. Xavier Bosch*   237

(∗) Selected extracts from published work.

TABLE OF CONTENTS

THE LEGACY. THE COCHRANE COLLABORATION

The pre-history of the first Cochrane Centre: *Sir Iain Chalmers*	242
The development of The Cochrane Collaboration in Spain and Latin America: *Xavier Bonfill*	254
The Cochrane Collaboration in Italy: *Alessandro Liberati* and *Gianni Tognoni*	261
The Cochrane Collaboration in Germany: *Yngve Falck-Ytter, Britta Lang, David Booker* and *Gerd Antes*	269
The Cochrane Collaboration in China. Needs, challenges, and opportunities: *Youping Li, Xin Sun* and *Jun Lu*	273
Observational reflections of a clinical pharmacologist on Archie Cochrane's legacy: *Joan Ramón Laporte*	280

EPILOGUE

Barcelona, Granollers, Gernika... the early trials of a sinister saga: *F. Xavier Bosch*	293
Barcelona remembers the Brigades and the Civil War	
Barcelona and the International Brigades, memory to the homage, 1978-2000: *Francesc Bonamusa*	296
The long lasting scars of the Civil War in Spain	
Teo, Isabel and Susanna: an International Brigadier, a Brigadier of Remembrance and a Brigadier of Peace: *Montserrat Armengou*	306
Archie Cochrane wishes you well...	
Obituary: *Sir Richard Peto* and *Sir Iain Chalmers*	315
Obituary: *King's College Annual Report*	317

PORTRAIT

F. Xavier Bosch and *Ricard Molas*	324

KEY MATERIALS & ILLUSTRATIONS

Broggi M. *Memòries d'un cirurgià (1908-1945).* Barcelona: Edicions 62. Biografies i Memòries, 2001.

Cochrane AL. *Forty years back: a retrospective survey* BMJ 1979; ii: 1662-1663.

Cochrane AL. Effectiveness and Efficiency. Random Reflections on Health Services. London: Nuffield Provincial Hospitals Trust, 1972. (Reprinted in 1989 in association with the BMJ, reprinted in 1999 for Nuffield Trust by the Royal Society of Medicine Press, London).

Cochrane AL, Blythe M. *One Man's Medicine. An Autobiography of Professor Archie Cochrane.* London: BMJ (Memoir Club), 1989.

Jackson G. *Civilization and barbarity in 20th century Europe.* New York: Humanity Books, 1999.

Maynard A, Chalmers I. *Non-Random Reflections on Health Services Research. On the 25th Anniversary of Archie Cochrane's Effectiveness and Efficiency.* London: BMJ Publishing Group, 1997.

Orwell G. *Homage to Catalonia.* London: Penguin Books, 1968.

Professor Archie Cochrane CBE (1909-1988) *in interview with Max Blythe.* Cardiff, September 1987. London: The Medical Sciences Video Archive, Oxford Brookes University, 1987 (videotape).

Thomas H. *The Spanish Civil War.* London: Penguin, 2003.

PHOTOGRAPHY

Robert Capa*, Francesc Català Roca*, Agustí Centelles*, Albert Fortuny

COLLABORATORS

Theodoros Agorastos, Gerd Antes, Josep M. Anto, Montserrat Armengou, Rolando Armijo, Juan Jose Artells, Carol Beadle, Max Blythe, Francesc Bonamusa, Xavier Bonfill, F. Xavier Bosch, Jaume Bosch i Pardo, Devra and Lester Breslow, Moisès Broggi, David Broker, Iain Chalmers, Joan Clos, Cochrane Library - Llandough Hospital, Mireia Díaz, Richard Doll, Charles du V Florey, Peter Elwood, Yngve Falck-Ytter, Albert Fortuny, Joan Josep Galve, Julian Tudor Hart, King's College - Cambridge, Joellen Klaustermeier, Daan Kromhout, Britta Lang, Dr Joan Ramón Laporte, Youping Li, Alessandro Liberati, Jun Lu, Elisabeth Luquin, Sandy Macara, Sebastián Macià, Medical Sciences Video Archive at Oxford Brookes University, Bill Miall, Rosalind Moad, Ricard Molas, Jesús Muñoz, Anthony J. Newman Taylor, Peter & Annie Nicholas, Jordi Pardo, John Pemberton, Richard Peto, Cristina Rajo, Rosaleen Ross, Susana Sans, Reginald S. Saxton, Andreu Segura, Julia Sheppard, Mary Sinclair, Josep Maria Solé i Sabaté, Rosemary Soper, Giles & Margaret Stalker, Xin Sun, Gianni Tognoni.

ILLUSTRATIONS REPRODUCED: A large number of illustrations and photographs have been generously contributed by the authors of the chapters of this book, the family and the Cochrane Lybrary in Cardiff. Efforts have been made to trace the source of all illustrations. However, for a few of them this could not be achieved on time. Correspondence to this respect would be welcome and should be addressed to Cristina Rajo: serc@ico.scs.es.

The contributions specifically requested for this work reflect the opinions of the authors.
* Historical archives of photography.

INTRODUCTORY NOTE AND ACKNOWLEDGEMENTS

Many people have volunteered their time, material and effort to make this work possible and on time. Several of those who knew and collaborated with Archie are now well into their 80's. Some, much younger, joined this commitment at their busiest times, earlier in their careers. Our first words of acknowledgement and gratitude go to them.

Special recognition should be paid to the efforts of the Epidemiology and Cancer Registration Unit at the Catalan Institute of Oncology and of The Cochrane Collaboration Centre in Barcelona, for their dedication to the compilation and editing of the materials received.

Our deepest gratitude also to the Cochrane Library in Llandough Hospital in Cardiff, to Archie's family and to Professor Max Blythe for their generous contributions. The support of the Fundación Salud Innovación y Sociedad and the creative dedication of Mary Sinclair and Cristina Rajo is recognized with gratitude.

We have made an effort to sketch some of the features of the war and the political scenario in Spain in the years 1936-1937 by using original texts written either at the time by participants or witnesses, or, later, by authorized historians. The previously-published texts have been selected by the editors in an attempt to represent fairly the opinions of the authors.

We sincerely hope that you enjoy this work dedicated to a charismatic man and to the unique, international scientific outcome initiated by his life's work. The Cochrane Collaboration is today associated with the use of unbiased, reproducible methods in the subtle interface between science, medicine and public health for the benefit of patients. Archie and The Cochrane Collaboration effort outline a challenge for an entire generation of public health professionals. Our challenge.

The editors
Barcelona, 2003

ARCHIE COCHRANE WAS A MAN OF THE 1930s.
HIS CHARACTER AND LIFELONG CONVICTIONS WERE FORMED BY
THE CATACLYSMIC EVENTS THAT BROUGHT HITLER TO POWER AND
PLUNGED THE GREATER PART OF THE WORLD INTO A DEVASTATING SIX-YEAR WAR.
IN THIS HE WAS NOT ALONE.
WHAT DISTINGUISHED HIM FROM SO MANY OTHERS OF HIS GENERATION WAS THE
DEPTH OF HIS EMOTIONAL AND INTELLECTUAL REACTION TO THESE EVENTS AND
HIS FIERY INDEPENDENCE OF MIND, WHICH PREVENTED HIM FROM ACCEPTING
ANY OF THE EASY POLITICAL SITUATIONS AND KEPT HIM A RATIONALIST TO THE
DAY OF HIS DEATH.

RICHARD DOLL, JUNE 1989*

* *Credit & Legend, see page 326.*

ARCHIE COCHRANE

Doctor
Joan Clos
Mayor of Barcelona

Joan Clos has been the mayor of Barcelona since September 1997. In 1999 he was elected for a four-year term and reelected in May 2003. Born in Parets del Vallés in 1949, he graduated in Medicine at the Autonomous University of Barcelona at the Hospital de Sant Pau. He practiced as an anaesthesiologist for some time until he decided to reorient his career towards epidemiology, community medicine and management of health resources. He took an active role in the political movements against the dictatorship towards a renewed National Health Service. In the transition to democracy he worked at the Centre d'Anàlisi i Programes Sanitaris (Centre for Health Analysis and Programs) along with colleagues in the medical community who fought for the political transformation of the country as an instrument to reinstall professional dignity.

PREFACE

Medicine is a social science, and politics is nothing else but medicine on a large scale. RUDOLF VIRCHOW

I was studying Community Medicine in Edinburgh when the group of young democratic epidemiologists first invited Archie Cochrane to Sant Pau's hospital in Barcelona. At the time I was reading *Effectiveness and Efficiency* up in the north. When I came back to Barcelona we invited him again. We were delighted to learn that he had been a freedom fighter in the International Brigades. We liked his critical approach to conventional medicine. We sensed that, in some way, he belonged to the generation of '68 (he was one of us) only with a few more years on his shoulders.

He liked to be different. We discovered with some astonishment that Archie smoked a little and enjoyed it. He gave a night-time conference beginning a little after 10 p.m., and he came down from his room very excited with a face full of joy. He told me that it was the first time he was to give a lecture like this one. It also happened to be his birthday and he was delighted to have the opportunity to try out new things at his time in life. Therefore, he wanted to celebrate with a couple of whiskies beforehand! He gave an excellent talk, explaining the case of vitamin B12 to us, but even more importantly, we were listening to a founder of epidemiology who was also in love with the Spanish republican democracy and in the very same city that George Orwell (another British republican fighter) had described so well in *Homage to Catalonia*. How far away was all of it from our conventional technocratic talks at medical school! We were enjoying the knowledge of a Brigadier and a caring soul, marked by an exuberant capacity for 'joie de vivre'.

The generation of young democratic epidemiologists learnt a lot from Archie Cochrane and the founders of the new epidemiology: Rose, Susser, Doll, Shapiro, Breslow, McKeown, Morris (every one of us could add a name or two more to this list). We were able to build a bridge between clinical medicine, then the model followed by our post-democracy university, towards community, social and preventive medicine. Some of us went into politics which, according to Virchow, is 'medicine on a large scale'.

We had the great opportunity of personally knowing the fathers of our discipline and discovering such a remarkable man as Archie. Truly a privilege.

Doctor
F. Xavier Bosch
Epidemiologist

Periodically, Archie helps me to refresh my emotional ties with the Spanish Civil War. It happened at the time I first met him in Los Angeles, at the time of our journey back to the front, and whenever Archie comes into the conversation or a Cochrane review crosses my desk.

DO YOU KNOW GRAÑÉN?...

In the hills surrounding Los Angeles, in the Westwood and Bel-Air canyons, the Breslows were hosting a party to welcome a distinguished visitor: Archibald L. Cochrane, commonly known as Archie. It was nearly summer and we all enjoyed a beautiful day back then in 1978. Lester Breslow was, at the time, the Dean of the Public Health School at the University of California in Los Angeles (UCLA) and Devra Breslow, the editor of the UCLA newsletter, was taking care of most of the significant social events around the university. Archie was a prominent epidemiologist and a passionate promoter of the concept of the Randomized Controlled Trial. He was persuaded that this method was the correct way to evolve towards evidence-based medicine. He was also an interesting character, a fine mind and a politically determined gentleman. Another guest at the party was Rolando Armijo, a professor of epidemiology at UCLA, from Chile, still under the shock of the military coup and the distressing news from his home country. At the time, I was completing my post graduate studies at UCLA and had developed a personal and long lasting friendship with Rolando, his wife Fanny and the Breslows. When Archie realized I was from Barcelona, his first words after greeting me were plain and to the point:

Do you know Grañén? ... and this book was on.

Aidez l'Espagne, 1937 by Joan Miró.

Poster displayed at the Republican Pavilion at the International exhibit in Paris in 1937.

DANS LA LUTTE ACTUELLE JE VOIS DU CÔTÉ FASCISTE LES FORCES PÉRIMÉES, DE L'AUTRE CÔTÉ LE PEUPLE DONT LES IMMENSES RESSOURCES CRÉATRICES DONNERONT À L'ESPAGNE UN ÉLAN QUI ÉTONNERA LE MONDE

MIRÓ

In 1937, an international militia, known as The International Brigades, was raised and sent to Spain to fight for the Republic against a military coup by the army who had the support of the growing fascist movement in Europe.

Archie was part of the English brigade that underwent some of the most fierce combat in the central part of Spain, Brunette and the Jarama, and in the front line in Aragon, near Huesca, where Grañén, at that time a small village, is located. Archie had spent some time in Grañén and its surroundings as a member of one of the medical units supporting the Brigades. Archie was still a medical student, and he was required to triage patients as they arrived straight from the battle front. Triage on the war-front is an intuitive, on-the-spot, decision-making procedure in which a wounded person is classified by urgency of need into a prognostic group. That inspection reflected the wounded's estimated probability of surviving his or her injuries. Medical effort was limited to those who had a reasonable chance of survival. The experience probably had an influence on his future view of the cost-effectiveness of medical decisions and the chances of medical error.

Although he did make some short visits, Archie had no desire to return to Spain while the dictatorship was in place. However, from his reaction to the suggestion

Archie in Spain in 1937 with a republican soldier.

of returning to the scenes of his time during the Civil War, it was obvious that he had had this trip in mind ever since he had left.

The story fascinated me. After Spain, Archie had embarked on the European war, in which he had spent a great deal of time as a prisoner of war, first in Greece, and then in Germany. I was astonished at his story of attempting a randomized trial in a concentration camp to test the hypothesis that a nutritional supplement could solve an outbreak of oedema in malnourished prisoners. I admired his simplicity in describing complex political and medical situations in the most conventional and, at the time, dispassionate manner.

Our conversation then evolved in a number of ways but the fishhook was in the right place. As a student, I had been intensively involved in the students' union movement at the University of Barcelona. The International Brigades were a part of the legend that shaped the fate and the destiny of most families in Spain, including my own. Here was an opportunity to pay a debt of gratitude to one of the militiamen and a wonderful chance to get to know a man who was close to the work I respected and hoped to practise in my own medical career.

Archie wandering a ruin in El Escorial, 1978. The building hosted a hospital during the Battle of Brunete in 1937.

Not long after this encounter at the Breslows, we organized a trip in 1978 to revisit the places where the English hospitals (locally called the Blood Hospital) had been set up. Archie first came to Barcelona where he gave a seminar at the Hospital de Sant Pau, possibly on randomized trials involving the evaluation of Health Services. The room was full and the expectation was high. I was glad that my colleagues appreciated his presence and his talk. The next day we were on the road for a unique experience.

Travelling with Archie was a pleasure and an intellectual challenge. He was keen to find the houses where the hospitals had been located, as well as tracking down more difficult targets such as the tomb of a British pilot whose name he only vaguely remembered. We developed a search strategy: on arrival in a village, we went to the local coffee shop, bar or central plaza if the sun was out, and introduced ourselves to friendly-looking elderly people. We told our story and, soon after the introductions and greetings were over, it was clear who from the audience would be our contact.

We were then escorted to the relevant sites, which generally included a large mansion or its remains. Over and over again, amazing scenes from the past were

Near El Escorial in 1978. Archie interacted with many who knew or collaborated in the activities of the English hospital.

recreated. Archie wandered about the place trying to recall past events, while our contact repeated for him names and places. We were listening to the stories and living through some very emotional experiences.

On returning to Barcelona, it was clear that Archie had accomplished what he had wanted to do and did not attempt further travelling. He published a travel report in the *British Medical Journal* (see section *Back to the Front*). We corresponded regularly. He became an honourable member of the Spanish Epidemiological Society and participated at several scientific events.

Visiting Archie at Rhoose Farm in Wales was a rare pleasure. On two occasions, I spent time with him there while becoming acquainted with the Medical Research Council Unit in Cardiff, driving along the Rhonda Fach and visiting epidemiologists in the UK. Over the weekend, Archie would keep an interested eye on the news but never left the TV set on beyond the news. Visitors were received constantly and conversation never stalled. Occasionally, Archie smoked cigarettes. His argument was that for a late starter, the time interval to lung cancer easily overlapped his life expectancy. With time, that proved to be true.

Archie in Grañen, near Huesca in 1978. Grañen was one of the first places in Spain where Archie spent some time in 1937.

I saw him for the last time in 1986 during a brief stop-over in Rhonda. He was as cheerful as ever and keenly interested in my research projects. He kept me up to date on the latest analyses and publications of the data from the cohort of miners in the Rhonda valley that had occupied him for several decades. We touched only briefly on his health.

Twenty-five years after sharing with Archie his journey back to the front line, we had the opportunity to put together this small homage to a great man. We hoped to show his commitment to the anti-fascist movement by compiling descriptions and images of some of the events from that unfortunate period in Spain. Several of Archie's friends have generously contributed memories, pictures and anecdotes and we are grateful to them.

We have also wanted to pay homage to the International Brigades and to the city and population of Barcelona. The city, like other cities in Europe later on, suffered some of the first aerial bombardments in history. Barcelona will always keep the memory alive of those volunteers who tried to help and of the victims of the madness.

Xavier and Archie in Rhoose in 1986 in front of "La Cocarde". This superb painting had pride of place on a wall, in the room where Archie spent most of his time working and entertaining visitors.

We also want to recognize the work and the contribution of The Cochrane Collaboration, a considerable organisation that involves the generous work of hundreds of scientists throughout the world. They have fulfilled the most ambitious dreams of the founders of the randomized trial philosophy by taking the organisation worldwide. Archie would probably have been pleased. We can speculate that, if he was alive today, he would be promoting a critical evaluation of the impact of the Cochrane reviews on the quality of care delivered at the bedside of patients.

On behalf of the many authors, I sincerely hope that you enjoy this collection of memories and tributes.

F. Xavier Bosch
Barcelona 2003

IN ONE OF THE VILLAGES, AN OLD FELLOW VOLUNTEERED TO SHOW US THE HOUSE
WHERE THE ENGLISH HOSPITAL HAD BEEN LOCATED.
ON OUR WAY, HE EXPLAINED THAT, IN 1937, HIS SON HAD BEEN AMONG THE
WOUNDED. HE WAS DEEPLY GRATEFUL BECAUSE HIS SON HAD BEEN ABLE TO KEEP
HIS LEG AFTER AN OPERATION. THE VILLA WAS A RUIN, WITH THE REMAINING
WALLS STILL SHOWING PAST SPLENDOUR. ARCHIE FELT THAT IT WAS INDEED THE
RIGHT PLACE AND CLIMBED INSIDE. ON HIS WAY OUT,
THE OLD MAN OFFERED HIM A HANDFUL OF WILD FLOWERS
THAT HE HAD PICKED FROM THE GARDEN.
THEY HUGGED EACH OTHER IN A MOMENT OF INTENSE EMOTION.
I COULD NOT SEE A TEAR IN ARCHIE'S OR THE OLD MAN'S EYES.

F. XAVIER BOSCH, JUNE 2003

* *Credit & Legend, see page 326.*

Emeritus Professor Sir Richard Doll
Epidemiologist

Sir Richard Doll deserves a chapter in the history of modern epidemiology. In the 1950s, he first reported the association between cigarette smoking and lung cancer, alerting the world to what has turned out to be the major human-driven epidemic of the last century. His work is associated with many of the major pieces of research leading to the identification of environmental carcinogens: asbestos, hormones, viruses and nutritional factors. In 1981, he was a co-author, with Sir Richard Peto, of one of the most influential publications in the field: The Causes of Human Cancer. *Sir Richard and Archie had been colleagues since the time of the students' political movement of the 1930s and maintained a fruitful scientific dialogue and friendship from that time on.*

SIR RICHARD DOLL ON ARCHIE COCHRANE

Sir Richard, we would like to thank you very much for your presence in this little homage to Archie Cochrane. With your help and the contribution of many of his colleagues, family and friends, we are trying to describe Archie's presence in the Spanish Civil War and the World War as well as providing a brief glance to some of his principal contributions to epidemiology and Health Services Research.

Q   *What was the feeling among university students of the time about the Spanish Civil War?*

A   It certainly was a major issue for those of us who had any interest in politics. We saw it as a testing-ground for the spread of fascism. We were very antagonistic towards Mussolini's regime and therefore to the idea that a similar regime might come to Spain. We believed it would strengthen the German position for a future war, which many young people saw as inevitable.

We tried to persuade our government of this, for its policy of so-called non-intervention was a farce. What it meant was that nothing was allowed to go to the legal Spanish government, not just military support, but also medical aid and supplies for the civilian population. There were many protest marches and people tried in all sorts of ways to get publicity about the seriousness of the issue. I cannot say that the majority of students was involved because the majority of students was not politically minded, but those that were were deeply involved. Nearly all supported the Spanish government and there was no significant support at all for the right-wing rebels among the students.

In support of the government, there was unity of all political groups although Labour party members were not supposed to associate with communists. In fact everybody worked together to emphasise the seriousness of the situation, while the medical students specifically tried to raise money to send medical aid.

Q   *What was the feeling at university about students who, like Archie, had decided to go to Spain and get actively involved? Were they considered as not being dedicated to their studies?*

A   Certainly not. The majority of students greatly admired them. It is difficult to say what the thinking of the teachers was, but I can give you an indication of the general sentiment by explaining what happened when Archie came back. He had just started his clinical work in the hospital wards at University College Hospital in London when the war broke out and he gave it up to go to Spain. He was away for over a year and when he came back he wondered how he would be received by his teachers. When he turned up in the ward for his first medical rounds, the consultant said: Oh, hello Cochrane, had a good weekend? So there was no criticism from anybody. There was just admiration.

Q   *Were there many other medical students who went to Spain?*

A   No, I am aware of only one other.

Q   *He mentioned in his autobiography that he met you in the army during the Second World War going to Egypt. Did you meet him there for the first time?*

A   Oh no. I had met him as a student in the Spanish Medical Aid movement. He was never a member of my political party; as I am sure you know. He was the only member of the Ambulance Unit who went to Spain, who was neither a member of a political party nor of a religious group. Whether I had met him before he went to Spain, I am not sure, but I met him frequently after he returned in the Spanish Medical Aid movement and later in agitating for proper air-raid precautions and a national blood transfusion service in preparation for the war against Hitler, which he saw as inevitable.

Photographic portrait of Archie.

Q   *Was your involvement with the army during the Second World War compulsory or did you all join voluntarily?*

A   As far as I was concerned, I had joined what was called the Supplementary Reserve Unit in the army. Immediately following the Munich Agreements in September 1938, it was quite clear to me that a war was going to come and I wanted to play my part in it. So, being in the Reserves, I was called-up a few days before the war began to be a medical officer in a regular army battalion. As a result, I went to France at the beginning of September 1939.

Q   *Can you remind us of what the Munich Agreements were?*

A   The Munich agreements took place in 1938 between Hitler, Mussolini and the British Prime Minister, Chamberlain, to allow Hitler to take over part of Czechoslovakia (the Sudetenland) in order to stop him from further revisions to Versailles. Chamberlain came back from Munich waving a piece of paper and saying it was peace in our time. But it was quite obvious to many of us, who thought we had a better understanding of the nature of the Hitler movement, that it was far from "peace in our time". It merely gave Hitler a much stronger position from which to walk in and annex the rest of Czechoslovakia a few months later. I joined the army Reserve Unit then.

Archie (second row, second L to R) with some comrades.

Q   *Do you know whether Archie had also joined at that moment? Did you plan to go together or was it just by chance that you met on the way to Egypt?*

A   It was entirely by chance. We were both sent out as members of a group of 50 medical people as medical reinforcements to Egypt, and to our great pleasure, we met on the boat. As far as I could make out we were the only two officers who were trying to learn Arabic. Archie was learning it from a very big book which began with the Arabic alphabet. I was studying it from a very small one "Teach yourself Arabic in three months". Archie was a good linguist and did learn some of it. I was not and never learnt more than a few phrases.

Q   *He spoke several (eight or nine) languages, didn't he?*

A   Yes, I am not sure if it was as many as that, but he certainly spoke several languages fluently. And, of course, the reason, as you know, he was captured in Crete was because there was a battalion of Spanish volunteers with the British army in Crete and he was sent to them because he was the only available British doctor who could speak Spanish. I was fortunately sent to the Island of Cyprus, which was not invaded.

Q	*Did you correspond with him during his imprisonment?*
A	Oh yes! I wrote to him regularly.

Q	*Have you kept the letters?*
A	No, I didn't keep copies.

Q	*I mean, did you receive letters from him?*
A	I am just trying to think. It's a long time ago and I can't honestly remember whether I ever got any letters from him.

Q	*Do you think that his experience there in his prison camp triggered his interest in the conduct of trials later on?*
A	I have to think about that. I don't think so. He described his "first and worst experiment" as having been carried out there, but I don't think it was this particular experience that made him think of applying scientific methods to trials in general. I think it came from his understanding of scientific medicine and, in particular, from his dissatisfaction with the evidence for psychoanalysis, which he had encountered in Germany while still a student.

Q	*With respect to his relationship with Sir Austin Bradford Hill, do you think that Hill influenced him a lot?*
A	Well, Bradford Hill's teaching did influence very many people in England and certainly influenced Archie who attended his course in medical statistics shortly after the war, but I thing he was already mentally prepared for the need to eliminate bias from the conduct of trials.

Q	*Many years later in 1972 he became the first President of the Faculty of Community Medicine of the Royal College of Physicians of the United Kingdom for which I believe you had been invited to be President but you decided not to accept. Why didn't you accept the position?*
A	Well, I was invited to be the first President but I had just taken on a very big administrative job in Oxford, as Regius Professor of Medicine, and I didn't

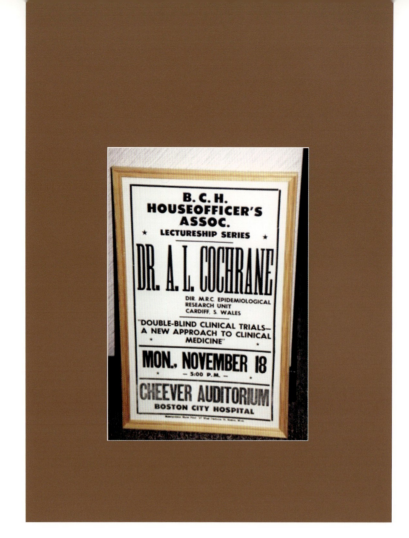

want to take on another big administrative job as well. I just didn't think I could manage the two jobs properly.

Q   *Which do you think were Archie's most important and original contributions to epidemiology in general and to clinical trial methodology in particular?*

A   Archie was, towards the end of his life, a little disappointed that he was just regarded as someone interested in controlled trials, and not as a general epidemiologist. He liked to think that much of his best work was straightforward epidemiology. The most original and most potentially important study that he ever did was the one he designed to find out whether tuberculosis was necessary for the production of the disabling pneumoconiosis of miners. The study which he designed for the Pneumoconiosis Research Unit in Cardiff sought to eliminate tuberculosis in the usual way from one of the Welsh industrial valleys, while intensive efforts were made to detect and treat all case of tuberculosis in another Welsh valley. He might have had an interesting result if streptomycin had not just been introduced, which successfully treated tuberculosis in both valleys. That design was typical of Archie's way of thinking on a large scale and dealing with whole populations. Later, of course, he carried out many surveys of the frequency of conditions in whole populations.

Q   *Do you think the Rhonda Fach study was revolutionary for that time?*

A   It was imaginative (I wouldn't say it was revolutionary) to think that you could conduct a study on such a large scale. It was, of course, particularly appropri-

Portrait that signals original text from Archie.

ate in south Wales where the population was sharply divided up in the different valleys, unlike the population mixtures that you have in big towns. Your were able then to make a comparison of independent groups that were not mixing with each other.

Q   *Do you think that he had always been interested in science even from a very young age or did his interest in science develop as a consequence of his experience of politics?*

A   No, he was primarily interested in science. After he got his degree in Cambridge he started doing a research degree and it was only because of the way that the work developed that he changed to practical medicine. He found the topic he was working on would not produce any outcome of practical value and he voluntarily abandoned it; but he certainly set out after obtaining his medical qualification to be a research worker.

Q   *Was the idea behind the Streptomycin Trial, that interventions needed to be tested in controlled trials, generally accepted by the medical community or was there resistance to the introduction of such trials in a systematic way?*

A   There was resistance, but there was a number of scientifically-minded professors in the country who recognised the importance of the idea and started carrying out such trials. So the resistance was gradually broken down but certainly there was quite a large number of physicians who criticized the concept of the controlled trial, because they said that the results were meaningless because people were treated who were not going to respond. What you have to do, they said, is to treat only people who are going to respond to the treatment. Bradford Hill used to respond to this argument by saying: "You just tell me which patients will respond and we will recruit them into the trial."

Q   *Do you think this resistance is returning today with the increasing popularity of genetic screening or testing that enables those who are going to respond to treatment, to be identified thus making randomized trials unnecessary?*

A   Well, of course as Hegel pointed out, the same ideas do come back at a different level. No, this search for characterization of people who will or will not respond to a specific treatment is a perfectly reasonable idea. People who are keen to do that are not saying that there shouldn't be controlled trials, but that contemporary knowledge should be such to make them more efficient. Indeed there is an example of this that has already happened. There is a drug called Imanitib Mesylate, which has just been introduced for the treatment of chronic myeloid leukaemia. This drug was designed specifically to affect the abnormal enzymes produced by the disease and it was so effective that a controlled trial has not been necessary. From preliminary studies to determine the appropriate dose, the effect was sufficiently clear. So, this is a perfectly reasonable objective to have. But it's going too far to say that we shall have no need for clinical trials.

Q   *How do you value the current contribution of The Cochrane Collaboration in doing systematic reviews of trials?*

A   I think it is one of the most important contributions to medicine in my lifetime.

Q   *How do you envision the future of the Collaboration? Is there still a lot to do?*

A   No, I am sorry, I am too old. I do not envisage the future at all. The present is more than enough for me.

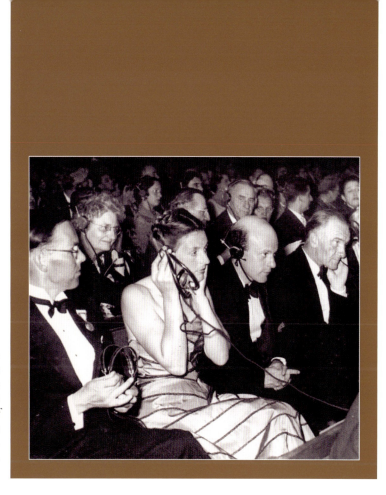

L to R: *Bill Miall, Mary Miall, Stewart Kilpatrick, Archie Cochrane, Jopin Crofton at the plenary session of the Meeting of American Chest Physicians. Barcelona 1954.*

Q   *What is the current appreciation of Archie's contribution to the medical culture in the UK?*

A   Probably, if anything, it is over appreciated because he is identified so closely with controlled trials that it is forgotten that other people introduced them. But there is no question, his role is greatly appreciated.

Q   *What was his relation to Green College? Why did he leave so much to Green College?*

A   That I can tell you very simply because I am one of only two people that know. Archie approached me one day and said that he realised that some of the art works he had bought when young were extremely valuable and that when he died there would be a very big inheritance tax to pay on them. He would like the money they raised to be used for research, without a deduction for tax. At that time he was particularly interested in the epidemiology of AIDS, even before it became clear what the causes of AIDS were. I told him that all he had to do was leave the art works to a charity with the instruction that the money they raised was to be used for the the epidemiology of AIDS and I added that he could for example, leave them to Green College. I assured him that Richard Peto, who was a friend of Archie's, and I would see that the money was spent in the way he wanted. I heard no more about it until after he died, when the epidemiology of AIDS was well known. We found he had left a share of the money to Green College, without indicating any specific purpose for it.

Archie at a conference.

Q *Do you think Archie missed having a family?*

A Yes, I think he was. I wrote his biography for our dictionary of National Biography and the editors returned it to me and asked why he had not married and whether or not he was a homosexual. To my knowledge, he was not a homosexual. He had had sexual experiences in his youth with women, which were unsatisfactory and were, as it eventually turned out, probably due to his porphyria and he didn't want to repeat them, but I did not want to say that in his biography. He had many friends of both sexes. Later in life, he certainly had many young male friends, but I do not think it was because he was homosexual; but rather because of the lack of a family.

NOTE FROM EDITORS: Sir Richard Doll was interviewed by Juan J. Artells and Susana Sans with a briefing prepared by the editors. Sir Richard personally edited the transcripts of the recorded conversation.

Eleventh Scientific Meeting of the International Epidemiological Association, Helsinki, Finland, August 1987.

L to R: *Professor John Pemberton, Dr Joan Faulkner (Lady Doll) and Professor Sir Richard Doll attended the first meeting in 1957.*

Doctor Julian Tudor Hart
General Practitioner

Dr Julian Tudor Hart's father, Alex, was a Major in the Spanish Republican Army specialising in traumatic surgery, in the same unit as Archie Cochrane. Julian qualified in medicine in 1952, and served an apprenticeship first with Richard Doll, and later with Archie in south Wales. In 1961, he left Archie's unit to work for 30 years as a general practitioner in the mining village of Glyncorrwg, where he undertook epidemiological research supported by the Medical Research Council (MRC).

ARCHIE COCHRANE AND POLITICS

We need to remember that, during his year in the Spanish Civil War, Archie was only a student. He had little clinical experience even as an undergraduate, so however well he worked, he could not actually do very much. However, even allowing for that, he was a minor player, and sometimes an irritant to those who had to get serious work done.

Archie was always a dissident, protected from much of reality by exceptional inherited wealth, but too imaginative to share the complacency of most of his class in 1936. Despite the largely successful efforts of conservative historians to erase our national memory, aid to the Spanish republic quickly became a huge force in Britain.[1] At the same time, the British government was providing intelligence to Franco through the Royal Navy, which later assisted the German and Italian fleets in blockading all seaborne assistance to the Republic, while Hitler's Condor Legion gained the experience used later to bomb Warsaw, Amsterdam and London.[2] Like his friends and medical school contemporaries, George Pickering and Stan Peart, he recognised that Spain offered the first apparent opportunity for material resistance to Fascism. According to Stan, the three of them met in 1936 to discuss what they might do. Alone of these three, Archie had enough money not only to run his own private sports car (a rare privilege in those days, even for a medical student) but even to take a year off his studies. So the other two stayed behind.

When he returned to University College Hospital (UCH) after his year with the International Brigades, Len Crome, his commanding officer, summed him up with a simple conclusion: *Archie is hostile.* Coming from Len, respected by all who served with him whatever their political orientation, this judgement was serious. His hostility, not towards the Republic, but to communists precluded any effective work with them. Communist Parties throughout the world were in fact the principal organisers of aid for the Republic, just as the USSR, with the sole excep-

"Come to Holland for a free holiday." The Christmas card Archie sent out to commemorate his first experience of prison life.

(...) He had lent his car to a friend who had lent it to a communist who had left it, full of subversive literature, outside the Parliament buildings in The Hague on the night before Queen Wilhemina was due to open a new session. (...)*

tion of Mexico, was its only supplier of arms. As in the Second World War from 1941 to 1945, whether people liked communists or not, when the house is on fire you don't ask for character references from the best firemen available. Even in the middle of a war, Archie could never accept that.

Despite this ambiguity, the mere fact of Archie's participation in Spain became, for him as for many others, far more important than what he actually did there. It acquired huge symbolic and romantic significance, which he wished to retain, even while distancing himself from its reality.

This ambiguity was, I think, echoed later in his historical role as a pioneer of British social medicine. He undoubtedly introduced and vigorously campaigned for more rational approaches to clinical medicine. He made important contributions to its transition from a quasi-religious institution based more on faith than on evidence, to the beginnings of serious health care, with measurable inputs and outputs. On the other hand, together with Tom McKeown, he also prepared the ideological ground for medical care as commodity production, legitimising the present worldwide retreat from public service to corporate marketing. I don't think he could have imagined medical care as social production, but then who even tries to do that today?

* Cohen D. Introduction. In: Cochrane AL, Blythe M. One Man's Medicine. An Autobiography of Professor Archie Cochrane. London: BMJ (Memoir Club), 1989.

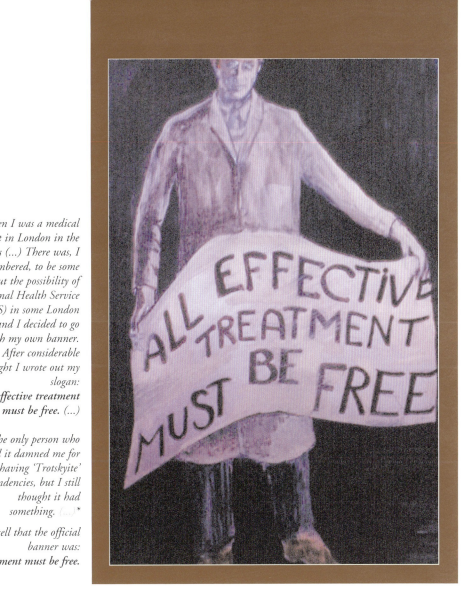

(...) When I was a medical student in London in the 1930s (...) There was, I remembered, to be some rally about the possibility of a National Health Service (NHS) in some London suburb, and I decided to go alone with my own banner. (...) After considerable thought I wrote out my slogan: **All effective treatment must be free.** *(...)*

(...) The only person who noticed it damned me for having 'Trotskyite' tendencies, but I still thought it had something. (...)*

Stories tell that the official banner was: **All treatment must be free.**

The ambiguity was also reflected in his research. Above all, his success was based on high participation rates, seldom less than 90%. This high participation rate in population studies was an immense achievement, particularly if we recall that before 1950, response rates of 60% were regarded as excellent. These rates were achieved in the special circumstances of the first years following the Second World War, coinciding with the birth of a nationalised coal industry, a National Health Service, and exceptional optimism about the construction of a new social order in which human needs would at last take priority over the rights of property. The high response rates in the Rhondda Fach[3] depended to a large degree on the active and generous support of the National Union of Mineworkers, which mobilised whole communities to support the first Rhondda Fach research studies as an act of social solidarity, a collective investment in knowledge for a more human future.

Archie certainly recognised this aspect of his research in the 1950s, but by the time I worked with him in 1960, he was turning to other sources of power. These precluded any further development of epidemiology as a means toward mass participation in research, mass understanding of science, and mass application of human rather than business priorities. Of course, he was not alone in this development.

* Cochrane AL. Effectiveness and Efficiency. Random Reflections on Health Services. London: Nuffield Provincial Hospitals Trust, 1972. (Reprinted in 1989 in association with the BMJ, reprinted in 1999 for Nuffield Trust by the Royal Society of Medicine Press, London).

Reproduced with permission from the BMJ Publishing Group and the Royal Society of Medicine Press

1

Within ten years, social medicine had become epidemiology, epidemiology was becoming methodology, and the world was being returned as far as possible to its pre-war state.

I miss him, and realise that from my point of view, I expected too much. I wish very much that he was still alive to argue with. For me, 'homage' is not quite the right word*. I no longer want to pay homage to anyone, except perhaps to the patient collective endurance of our species. What about evaluation and celebration? There would be many points of view, but providing they can be expressed honestly and compassionately, we could all celebrate a great man.

REFERENCES:

1. Fyrth J. The signal was Spain: the Spanish aid movement in Britain, 1936-1939. London: Lawrence and Wishart, 1986.
2. Beevor A. The Spanish Civil War. London: Cassell, 1982.
3. Hart JT, Smith GD. Response rates in south Wales 1950-1996: changing requirements for mass participation in human research. In: Chalmers I, Maynard A (eds), Non Random Reflections on Health Services Research: on the 25th Anniversary of Archie Cochrane's Effectiveness & Efficiency. London: BMJ Publishing Group, 1997, pp. 31-57.

* NOTE FROM EDITORS: The initial correspondence in the preparation of this book requested contributions to "a modest homage to Archie Cochrane".

2

The mining valleys in Wales became natural observatories for epidemiological studies on respiratory diseases, notably tuberculosis and massive lung fibrosis.

3

4

Photos 1, 2, 3 & 4: Source unknown

Honorary Professor
Peter Elwood
Epidemiologist

On Archie's retirement, I was appointed Director of the Epidemiology Unit in Cardiff. There followed some charmed years. Archie managed to work on in the unit without causing any embarrassment, or any difficulty in any way. He attended meetings and events only if invited, and he was slow to comment on anything, until asked.

ARCHIE COCHRANE: MAN OF VISION WITH FEET OF CLAY

I owe an enormous debt to Archie. My first job in epidemiology was with John Pemberton in Belfast and at the end of a three-year fellowship John suggested that I should write to Archie in Cardiff. I spent two days with Archie: certainly the longest, but at the same time, the most pleasant interview I have ever had. We talked about everything, except politics, about which I had almost no opinion. We even talked about religion, but Archie explained that he cared so little about this that he would not even bother to argue with me!

Undoubtedly, what warmed Archie towards me at that time was the fact that I had just completed both a population-based survey with a 98% participation rate, and a six-month randomized-controlled feeding trial.

I joined Archie in 1963. I cannot say that we worked closely together. I was a hands-on worker, always anxious to get into the field and work alongside my team. In my time with him, I never saw Archie involved at this level. He was a great stimulator and encourager, but more and more he was away on committee work, or lecturing, and often abroad. In fact, we used to say that we did the work, he did the talking, and how he could talk!

I very quickly set up a number of studies, at first on iron deficiency anaemia, but then on child growth, lead pollution, heart disease, stroke, cognitive function and other topics. Those were great days. Resources were almost unlimited, and others who later joined the unit broadened the work of the unit further on migraine (Estlin Waters), gastro-intestinal disease (David Bainton), asthma, infant feeding and the health of the elderly (Michael Burr) and so on. Archie was especially proud of the unit's work in collaboration with the local ophthalmologists. He helped to

Archie's interest in the Times' crossword never waned while he was at the unit, and he showed special favor to those members of the unit who could help him with the clues. I used to walk through the rooms of the unit at fairly frequent intervals. Often, when I entered the attic room, Archie would be doing the crossword, and he would slide his newspaper quickly under his desk and look up at me with a rather guilty expression!

set up the surveys and trials, but then, characteristically, he encouraged younger men to develop the work and he himself withdrew.

Archie loved his unit, and he exaggerated scandalously when talking about our work. At intervals he would walk round the building, asking each of us in turn what we were working on. Then, with great skill he would make a suggestion about this study, or point to a weakness in that study, and at times he would suggest a completely new line of investigation.

It is appropriate therefore that Archie is best remembered for the work others did at his suggestion. There is no better example than The Cochrane Collaboration. The idea had been Archie's, but the initiative should perhaps have been called The Chalmer's Collaboration. At the same time, Archie had little interest, and not a lot of respect, for technology. I am sure therefore that he would have been delighted to learn that one writer has stated that the Collaboration, in its potential effect upon clinical practice, is likely to be as important as the human genome project!

And what about the feet of clay? The randomized controlled trial (RCT) became almost a religion with Archie. He talked about it, lectured on it and promoted it

I gave Archie a desk in an attic room, together with several young researchers. He loved it and he was a great encouragement to them. His main occupation was the following of several old cohorts of miners, though most of the work was actually done by Fred Moore, Archie's long standing assistant and critic! As time passed Archie became less active, but only gradually so, and it was only very shortly before his death that I received a letter from his niece asking me not to send Archie any more drafts of papers as he was to ill to read them.

whenever possible. I well remember the consternation at meetings in my early years with him, when, a senior clinician having given a talk about a condition and its treatment, relying heavily upon experience of course, Archie would jump up and ask: "Why did you not randomise?" I would duck, but later I would be asked to explain what had been meant by the single word: randomized!

On the other hand, Archie was delighted when I told him that I had purchased tropical fish for my children. I explained that I had prepared two tanks. I had filled one with hard water and the other with soft water, and I had instructed my children to record mortality in the two tanks. Archie was intrigued and he insisted on paying for the tanks! When I told him later that the population density was steadily increasing in the soft water tank, while remaining static in the hard tank, he became excited and he raised the possibility that hard water might be contraceptive! His hopes were dashed however when I told him that the children had known all along that there happened to be a cannibal fish in the hard water tank!

Despite his enthusiasm for the RCT, Archie never conducted one. His nearest approach was a trial of yeast in the alleviation of starvation oedema. The story is most moving, but the background to its telling is also of interest. I had organised a meeting in Cardiff with a preparatory dinner for the speakers and unit staff. I asked Archie if he would give an after-dinner talk and I suggested that he tell us some of his prisoner-of-war experiences. He agreed, though with obvious reluctance. After the dinner, he spoke at length of his attempts to do medical work in a POW camp in Salonica. He almost broke down during the telling, but afterwards he thanked me and said that talking about his experiences had helped him come to terms with them. Very shortly after this he wrote up the story and his account was published in the British Medical Journal.

Only a man with feet of clay could lecture on the role of tobacco in respiratory disease and smoke before, during and after the lecture! One of the photographs of himself that Archie liked, and has been reproduced all over the world, shows him with a very prominent index finger under his chin. The finger is heavily stained with nicotine. I don't think that Archie noticed, and he certainly would not have cared!

Archie could have been termed a self-contained man. He lived alone, attended by a non-resident butler, he travelled extensively, he read widely, he collected pictures, he supported the Arts and had the outhouses of his residence, Rhoose Farm House, adapted to accommodate a sculptor, Peter Nicholas. Yet he was a very lonely man. Upstairs in his unit he talked nothing but science, but below stairs the girls cleaned his glasses for him, polished his shoes and straightened his tie, as he told, or heard, the latest gossip!

On Archie's retirement I was appointed Director of the unit. I asked Archie to continue to work in the unit and none of us ever regretted that decision. He maintained a very low profile, he would come to unit meetings only if specifically invited, and he commented on research studies only when asked. He had a desk in an attic room together with some young workers and he loved it. He contributed to the tea money, but pleaded for a reduction on the grounds that he was an old age pensioner. He brought in the Times' crossword each day and he showed special favour to the few who could help him solve the clues. On occasions however, when I walked into the room, he would quickly slide the newspaper under his desk and look up at me with embarrassment.

Together with Fred Moore, Archie's assistant over thirty and more years, Archie continued to work on his follow-up studies of coal miners. As time passed he became less active and eventually he went to live with his niece some distance away. He continued to correspond with us, and it was only very shortly before his death that I received a letter asking that we send him no more data or drafts of papers.

Perhaps the final evidence of his feet of clay was the fact that, despite having written his own obituary and leaving directions for a totally religion-free memorial service, his niece said that shortly before his death Archie had called her into his room and asked that she ensure that he was given a Christian burial. So may he rest in peace, his memory treasured and revered by many.

The photographs enclosed all come from a delightful album which was prepared by a distinguished US scholar who worked with us for a year, Michael Lichtenstein. Michael made a facetious comment under most of the photographs and under two of those I enclose were amusing comments relating to Archie and the Time's crossword.

Archie was a colorful character and stories about him must be endless. He enjoyed a joke, and on the whole he accepted jokes against himself but not always. Shortly after I joined the unit I set up a most ambitious study in which we screened 3000 women in the Rhondda Fach for iron deficiency anaemia, and then, for four years, we supplied a selected sample of 300 with their daily bread, half of which was fortified with iron. While this trial was running, a team under Archie conducted a fairly simple follow-up of who had been seen in an early study. Archie was proud of his study and he hired a film crew to make a documentary of the work. (This film is still available, and I later had it transferred to video). Archie was somewhat annoyed when he discovered that I had referred to his team as the B team and that the term that caught on and became widely used at the time!

Around the time of his retirement Archie sat for the sculptor, Peter Nicholas, who resided in the barn at Rhoose Farm House. Despite the encouragement of many, the bust has no cigarette dangling from the mouth! Two copies were cast. I presented one to the Faculty of Community Medicine (now the Faculty of Public Health Medicine) in London. The other I presented to the Cochrane Centre in Oxford at its formal opening.

(...) In his fieldwork among the mining communities of the Rhondda Valley, whom he came to respect so deeply, he aimed at response rates of never less than 90% and by driving himself and others to the limits of endurance, even in the bitterest weather, regularly obtained such figures, or better, and showed that in survey work on populations it was possible to make measurements with an accuracy previously thought possible only in laboratory research. It was an astonishing achievement. Making the fullest use of representative population samples was to remain his dominant scientific interest for the rest of his life.(...)*

Richard Cohen, June 1989

The high response rate of subjects involved in Archie's studies has been the envy of many. Archie was always given credit for this and he took it happily. The truth is rather different! Towards the end of a survey, Archie would arrive at the field centre in his gleaming silver Daimler limousine. He would chat to the person in charge of the visiting of subjects and would ask for a bundle of visiting cards, saying: *Give me the most resistant subjects.* He would take the bundle of cards, select one of these and drive to the address on the card. He would park his car prominently outside the door of the house, and as most of the houses in the Rhondda open directly onto the street, with no garden, the car was exceedingly obvious to whoever opened the door. He would announce himself as Professor Cochrane and ask for the person named in the card. He would invite this person (he almost always selected a male) to come with him in his car (emphasized) to the clinic.
As soon as the person was delivered and safely inside the clinic, Archie would suddenly remember an important engagement back in Cardiff and would hand back the bundle of cards to someone in the field centre, saying:

I've got to go, you finish them off.

* Cohen D. Introduction. Cochrane AL, Blythe M. One Man's Medicine. An Autobiography of Professor Archie Cochrane. London: BMJ (Memoir Club), 1989.

(...) It was in the Pneumoconiosis Research Unit, too, that he developed his great interest in observer error, reproducability and bias. Bias, indeed, in all its forms, scientific or otherwise, became almost a personal enemy and once it was detected he was ruthless in exposing it. Later, when he had become something of a pundit, I used to enjoy watching him at meetings reacting to some over-authoritative subjective judgement from some overconfident pillar of the Establishment; first he would bristle, then proceed to dissect his opponent's argument with the air of a plumber looking for an escape of gas which his nose assures him must exist somewhere. He had always been keenly interested in his own character and as he grew older he more and more relished and embellished his idiosyncrasies even to the point of parody. (...)

Richard Cohen, June 1989*

(...) In 1976 Archie and I were guests at several institutions in New Zealand and on one occasion we both addressed a meeting at Wellington Hospital. Not wishing to startle unduly the staid group of white coated clinicians I tempered my message slightly by stating, instead of 10-15%, that only between 15-20% of physicians' interventions were supported by objective evidence that they did more good than harm. In mid-sentence Archie suddenly called out: *Kerr, you're a damned liar, you know perfectly well that it isn't more than 10%!* We were probably both correct and may well have used the same study for our observations (funded, I believe, by Gordon McLachlan and the NPHT). My figures came from a two week survey in 1963 by 19 general practitioners 'representing almost every partnership and practice in a northern (British) industrial town'. All recorded the 'intent' of each prescription written. Those for proprietary drugs with 'specific' benefit were 9.3%. Another 22.8% were considered to be of 'probable' benefit, 27.2% of 'possible' benefit, 28.2% were 'hopeful', and 8.9% were regarded as a placebo; 3.6% were 'not stated'. Distributions for non-proprietary drugs were similar.[1] (...)

Kerr L White, 1997**

1. Silcock B. The wishful thinking that guides doctors. The Sunday Times, 19 March 1972.

(...) "Archie had a great desire to stimulate and challenge others. He was a delightful conversationalist", recalls Dr Elwood, a former colleague and friend, who succeeded Archie as Director of the MRC Epidemiology Unit in Penarth, Wales.
Sometimes, that desire backfired. "At meetings he would occasionally attack a clinician, asking: *Why did you not randomize?* Dr Elwood says. This often irritated the speaker rather than stimulating discussion. "Whenever Archie indicated that he wanted to ask a question, I would duck!" (...) ***

* Cohen D. Introduction. In: Cochrane AL, Blythe M. One Man's Medicine. An Autobiography of Professor Archie Cochrane. London: BMJ (Memoir Club), 1989.

** White KL. Archie Cochrane's legacy: an American perspective. In: Maynard A, Chalmers I. Non-Random Reflections on Health Services Research. On the 25th Anniversary of Archie Cochrane's Effectiveness and Efficiency. London: BMJ Publishing Group, 1997.
Reproduced with permission from the BMJ Publishing Group.

*** Culp K. History, Archie Cochrane. Scottish Medical Journal. August 2002.
Reproduced with permission from the Scottish Medical Journal.

Professor
Rolando Armijo
Epidemiologist

I first met him in Chile in 1960 when he came to visit the School of Public Health, while I was teaching epidemiology. We had a number of lengthy, enjoyable and very interesting talks. He wanted to see what the country that Lord Cochrane had helped to liberate from Spain in 1818 looked like, pretending to be an illegitimate descendant of the famous Admiral. There is no town in Chile, even small villages, that do not have a distinguished Cochrane Street.

REMEMBERING ARCHIE COCHRANE

Sir Thomas Cochrane was the tenth Count of Dunbonald, born in Annsfield, Lanarkshire, Scotland, on the 14th of December 1775. At the age of 43, being an outstanding Admiral, he undertook the incredible adventure of travelling from England to Chile, at the request for help of the weak Chilean government. Historians depict him as astute and bad-tempered. However, he was to organize the first Chilean navy, consisting of four ships with 31 officers (four Chileans and 27 Britons), plus 589 sailors from all parts who perhaps communicated in Spanglish. Our first Admiral, after a year, destroyed the Spanish navy. Lord Cochrane then continued his fight for the liberation of Brazil and Greece!

These two Cochrane men separated by more than 150 years seem to share several characteristics. Both are valiant, generous and keen to struggle for freedom and justice. The similarities make one wonder whether Archie's claim of being a relative has any merit!

A boat trip in Korçula in September 1961.
L to R: *Archie and Rolando Armijo. Second row, the president of the Epidemiological Association in Korçula who lost his leg in World War II, after having spent ten years in exile in Chile. Next to him, with a hat, a former Auschwitz prisoner of war, who survived by working in the slaughterhouse and drinking animal blood.*

In August 1960, we both attended the International Epidemiological Association meeting in Korçula, Jugoslavia. One afternoon, exploring the islands on a small boat with one ex-prisoner of war and one Auschwitz survivor, we stopped at a house on Archie's request to talk to the people as he liked to do. Surprisingly, he started talking fluent Serbo-Croatian. We were flabbergasted. He simply explained that, as a prisoner of war, he had been assigned to care for several hundreds of Jugoslav prisoners. The first month he managed with two words: *bolye* (better) and *boli* (pain) – his charm and warmth did the rest. I can think of no better example than those two magic words to describe the doctor-patient relationship in simplified primary health care.

Fragment of the family photograph at the IEA meeting in Princeton in 1964. In the middle row, Rolando Armijo, Peter Elwood and Archie Cochrane.

He was gifted in languages. His aristocratic German became a strong tool to persuade Nazi officers to provide minimum standards of care to sick prisoners, during the four years of an "ordeal of the severest kind," as Richard Cohen points out.

During the IEA meeting of 1964 in Princeton, a group photograph was taken and published by John Pemberton recently in the International Journal of Epidemiology. The last time Archie attended the IEA meeting was in Helsinki in 1987. As always, Archie was lucid and in good humor, so as to exclaim aloud *I am still alive!*. That was one year before his death in 18 June 1988.

Drawing of Rhoose Farm House by Rolando Armijo.

For years we had numerous opportunities to continue our conversations. During the winter of 1961, I had the privilege of staying at his lovely Rhoose Farm House in Cardiff for a week, visiting the Rhondda Valley and a coal mine which was similar to our mines in Chile.

Corner of the garden at Rhoose Farm House.
Archie devoted considerable efforts and took great pleasure at taking care of the garden and the green house. Often, guests were offered to participate in the cleaning and arranging of the grass, flowers or to pick tomatoes. The choice of plants in the garden was greatly inspired in the local flora. It received some attention (and a price) by a specialized journal and was open for visitors to stimulate interest in gardening.
The garden is now a settlement of buildings.

Miner at work. Saarland (Germany), September 1934.

ARCHIE FACING AN ANGRY COAL MINER

The incident occurred in about 1960, in the realm of his huge community studies in the Rhondda Fach, where he was handling large samples and even total communities. One coal miner made himself known by complaining rather violently and refusing to participate, on the grounds that he had been selected for a fifth time during a short period. Archie was interested to meet this chap, and invited him to his office to discuss his case. Archie found himself confronted with an irate coal miner. He revealed his best smile and overwhelming charm, in order to convince this coal miner of the importance of his collaboration in randomized controlled trials. He started with the easiest example that came to his mind:

Let us suppose I have a hat, into which I toss ten thousand names printed on tiny pieces of paper. One carries your name. Then I blindly pick one piece of paper out of the hat. It happens to be yours – a one in ten thousand chance! That is what I mean by random, and the probability of picking your name is one in ten thousand. Your case is unusual because you have been selected five times. We are all very interested to meet you, for being such an extraordinary person. Now, what do you think?

And the miner responded slowly with his cavernous voice: *I think Doctor, that you have got a bloody funny hat!*

Devra Breslow

Professor Lester Breslow
Epidemiologist

LESTER:
I knew Archie Cochrane best from the early days of the International Epidemiological Association (IEA) when we both attended the founding meeting (then called the International Corresponding Club in Social Medicine). In the IEA Archie was regarded as an original thinker, often "out-of-the-box", always a bright light.

DEVRA:
I have just used the search engine, Google, on The Cochrane Collaboration. Archie, a truly humble man, with positive attitudes toward human beings, would have been as astonished as I was at the breadth and depth of The Cochrane Collaboration's work worldwide. The numbers of investigators involved must be close to 1000 by now and I can appreciate your eagerness to finish your tribute to Archie.

THE INTERNATIONAL PROFILE

I believe that Archie's major contribution was to advance and popularize the use of Randomized Controlled Trials (RCT), an effort that was later on amplified through The Cochrane Collaboration and for which he is still commemorated, at least in the USA. Devra, my wife, remembers Archie for his explanation of how to conduct a randomized trial. He said that in the case of myocardial thrombosis (in those days) he carried slips of paper in his coat pocket, on equal numbers of which he had written *hospital* or *home*. Experience indicated that in those days home care was as effective as hospital care. When he encountered a case, he would simply reach in and pull out a slip which would direct him to the proper intervention for that patient!

The medical community in the USA has adopted the RCT as the standard method of evaluating proposed new therapies. I don't recall any particular US landmark test of the concept though there may have been one. The RCT has restrained, though by no means completely, the tendency in this country to market new drugs and procedures of little or no greater value than those already in use. Judgement must still be made concerning data which indicate greater health value in relation to cost.

I greatly admired him not only for his epidemiological brilliance but also for his having served in the International Brigades defending the Spanish Republic against Franco, something that I almost but didn't do. For me, he was a hero who showed political understanding, commitment and fearlessness.

Lester Breslow and Archie. The sculpture is from Barbara Hepworth and is located at the UCLA Sculpture Garden.

During the Spanish Civil War, the USA contributed by sending an International Corps named the Lincoln Brigade. That was well known in left-wing circles in the USA but I'm not sure whether the American people as a whole knew much about it. Its existence was certainly no secret and recruitment on college campuses was not uncommon though not publicized. The US policy, it seemed to me, was to try to stay neutral, but those tending toward the left politically were definitely anti-Franco. Those who joined the Lincoln Brigade I think were generally regarded as passionately anti-fascist. You will recall, however, that even Roosevelt was not able to bring the USA openly into the struggle until the Pearl Harbor attack by the Japanese in 1941.

Devra & Lester Breslow

Jamaica, 1968.
IEA Council Meeting &
Caribbean Seminar.

Puerto Rico, 1977
ISM/IEA
"Survivors" present at first
(Noordwijk) ISM meeting.

Edinburgh, 1981
IEA Scientific Meeting.

DEVRA:

Clearly this book is engaging so many people who are equally passionate about remembering Archie and especially his commitment to resistance to oppression. Archie, in his modest way, would say the book is not necessary. But we know better. I remember his talking in detail about the impact of imprisonment and what he was able to contribute to help his fellow prisoners. My recollection is that he acquired tuberculosis in prison. What his biography does not say is how devoted he was to his family and colleagues. We never visited him in Wales. But we know he had a magnificent rose garden and sculpture collection. He knew Barbara Hepworth and others, like Henry Moore, perhaps David Hockney, Lucien Freud and Francis Bacon. He was a man of great taste and culture, a man who kept his own counsel, but was quite capable of having a good time with friends he trusted. I imagine he was an attentive host. He certainly was a fabulous guest (...). Archie seemed different to others. I always felt he was humble (...). He could be confident and diffident, but to be as influential as he became, worldwide, he had to be touched by modesty and humility.

e-mail extracts, 2003.

Sir Sandy Macara
Public Health Physician

There is always something reassuring about a doctor who speaks on the radio or television with a Scottish accent. Sandy Macara hails from the west of Scotland and has devoted his life to community medicine and public health, with the result that he has a wider interest in medicine than most family doctors or hospital specialists. Nowhere has this concern been seen better than in his role as chairman of the Council of the British Medical Association, where he has been an outspoken and effective advocate for the National Health Service.

ARCHIE IN A HUNDRED WORDS

There are few individuals who can truly be described as unique but Archie Cochrane certainly was, not least in reconciling all manner of paradoxes in his personal and professional life. He was blessed with wit and a substantial private income from his family business in the Scottish Borders. The driving force behind all his activities was an abiding concern for the poor and disadvantaged in society. A life-long rebel in the pursuit of innovative epidemiological approaches, notably randomized controlled clinical trials (RCTs) against his profession's own establishment, he nevertheless became the first President of the new Faculty of Community Medicine of the Royal College of Physicians in the United Kingdom (now the Faculty of Public Health Medicine) which was established in the early 1970s to promote the practice of public health in the United Kingdom and beyond. No-one could doubt the sincerity with which he resolved such paradoxes especially when, with a glittering professional career in prospect, he served as a volunteer against the forces of fascism in the Spanish Civil War. His last pioneering activity was to pen his own obituary in the British Medical Journal.

It is essential to know the paradoxical personality of the man to understand the reaction of his profession to the single-minded zeal with which he promoted his gospel of the RCT within the context of a sustained attack upon the sloppy thinking and even sloppier research methods with which most of his contemporaries were engaged. Nevertheless, the strength of his conviction, and the quality of his work, won him influential friends including the editorial board of the Nuffield Provincial Hospitals Trust which awarded him the Rock Carling Fellowship in 1971. The outcome was his *Effectiveness and Efficiency: random reflections on health services* book with its compelling autobiographical account of his harrowing experience as a German prisoner of war in Greece for four years, where for much of the time he was the only doctor to care for 20 000 prisoners. To read, as the preface to his book, the poem which he wrote on "superfluous doctors" is to understand what drove his passion to match the human instinct for survival with competent health care.

Doctor
Bill Miall
Epidemiologist

Bill Miall joined the Research Unit in Cardiff 1952 where he was principal investigator in the studies of blood pressure. Bill spent some time at the MRC Research Unit in Jamaica where he was involved in the discussions on the sculpture "The Savacou". On return to the UK Bill was responsible of a large trial on the treatment of slightly raised blood pressure.

A LONG TIME FRIEND

I first met Archie Cochrane in 1941 when we were both prisoners of war in Salonica. He had been taken prisoner in Crete where, as a medical officer in the Commandos and a good linguist, he had been involved in the surrender of the island to the Germans. I had been captured in Kalamata, in Southern Greece, a few weeks earlier where I was a member of a Quaker field ambulance unit.

We were in the transit camp for allied prisoners in Salonica. At that time, Archie sported an impressive auburn beard and a large Viking moustache. He was a Captain and one of the doctors in charge of the 200-bed hospital in that dreadful German camp. Otherwise the hospital was staffed by medical orderlies-Australians, New Zealanders, Britons, and Jugoslavs. Archie was a very good mixer and seemed to get on well with all nationalities, perhaps even including the German troops who guarded the place and with whom he had to negotiate on behalf of the prisoners, sometimes with success. Although I didn't know about it then, it was at that time that he carried out what he describes in *One Man's Medicine* as his first, worst and most successful randomized controlled trial – a trial of the effects of yeast on protein-deficiency oedema.

In that camp, the main medical conditions were infections, sandfly fever, diphtheria, malaria, typhoid, hepatitis and later beri-beri. I remember having hepatitis myself and how ill I felt with it. The irritation from bed bugs was quite enough without the itching of jaundice as well. There were about equal numbers of surgical patients, mostly walking wounded with amputations. The main meal of the day provided by the Germans for the ten thousand prisoners was often a dead donkey, made into a watery stew by the army cooks. I can confirm most of the appalling things Archie recounts in his autobiography about that period. It must have been a depressing situation for him, with very ill patients and virtually no effective treatments to give them.

British prisoner, giving the sign of victory. The photo was taken in Salonica by a German photographer. 30 April 1941.

Archie, as one of the camp doctors, had one of the very few single rooms in the camp and let some of us use it. It was the one place where there was peace and quiet and I remember how much I appreciated it at the time. It was a manifestation of his generosity and kindness that I got to know so well in later years.

In 1951, ten years after that first meeting, I heard of a job vacancy in the Medical Research Council's Pneumoconiosis Research Unit (PRU). By then I had qualified in medicine and knew that Archie was working there. I became his assistant and was soon involved with him in the very early days of chronic disease epidemiology in South Wales. It was stimulating and fun. From then on until his death in 1988, we worked together and were close friends.

Archie was an interesting but complicated Scot. In the early 1950s, he shared his house in South Wales with two PRU colleagues. He had a large house, a lovely garden, a Jaguar (of which he was very proud) and a husband and wife, the Barlows, who looked after him. He had lots of friends, some living locally, some in London, many among the miners and ex-miners of Welsh mining valleys and he was very hospitable. There were many parties, often rather too alcoholic. Archie was a

Rhoose Farm House garden. "Meridian", bronze by Barbara Hepworth.

wealthy bachelor with good artistic taste. At that time he was buying pictures and sculpture by artists who hadn't yet made their reputations. After his death, some of these works had to be valued and a Ben Nicholson abstract and a Fergusson portrait each fetched many thousands of pounds. During his terminal illness, a fine Barbara Hepworth sculpture was left for some months unattended in his garden and fortunately survived.

Archie was a well liked and a much respected character but in many ways rather odd and certainly neurotic. Sometimes I found myself irritated by his inclination to overdo the prima-donna role. In those early days at PRU, one of the important contributions made by the unit was a series of studies of medical error and the measurement of observer variation between doctors. The medical profession didn't like such studies. It was at about this time that Archie, tongue-in-cheek, started to speak of clinical delinquency, a concept that was made in fun but maybe lost him some friends among clinicians. Soon after I started at PRU a senior colleague wrote to me advising: *You have a big job in helping Archie through the emotional contortions with which he tortures himself.* How very true! But he was an amusing, delightful chap and wonderful company.

Archie Cochrane and Bill Miall

(...) As a young man Archie had always comported himself as a man of means (...) but it was not until well in his time at Cambridge that he inherited from his grandfather, who had become wealthy in the family business of Scotch Tweed (...), a small entirely independent private income which was greatly to influence his life from them on. (...)

D. Cohen, June 1989*

I was involved when Archie got worried about some epitheliomata which were developing on one of his hands. He thought they might have been caused by his X-ray screening of tuberculous prisoners in Germany. He had someone do a biopsy; the site of the biopsy became infected, he developed swollen axillary lymph nodes which he took to be evidence of malignancy and this led on to a radical clearance of his axillary glands on that side and the removal of one of his pectoralis muscles (the histology showed infective changes only). He had a tendency to get himself over-doctored.

Emotional contortions or not, we became very fond of him and he was extremely generous and kind to us as a family. Although a bachelor, he was fond of, and good with children but had a habit of visiting us every Sunday evening just at their bed time, exciting them and then leaving us as parents to cope with the chaos he had caused.

Over the years we had a number of overseas holidays with him; some were linked with medical meetings. One of the early ones was to Barcelona in 1954 for a meeting

---

* Cohen D. Introduction. In: Cochrane AL, Blythe M. One Man's Medicine. An Autobiography of Professor Archie Cochrane. London: BMJ (Memoir Club), 1989.

Archie and his colleagues motored down to Barcelona for a cardiology conference in 1954. Many remembered the jaguar, in which Archie drove and taxied colleagues during the Rhonda surveys.

L to R: *Mary Miall, Archie, Stewart Kilpatrick. ALC's Jaguar, in route to Barcelona, 1954.*

of the American Association of Chest Physicians. Archie decided to take his Jaguar and combine the meeting with a few days on the Costa Brava. Stewart Kilpatrick, my wife, Mary, and I motored down with him, calling on Rocamadour and the Lascaux caves on the way. My most vivid memory of that trip is of the start of the first plenary session of the conference when a technician on the stage took hold of a microphone in each hand and was almost electrocuted. He was unable to drop either of them. This happened in front of an audience of about a thousand physicians and their wives who could do little more than shout to someone to switch off the current. It was nearly a very embarrassing, and tragic occasion.

Archie wrote his own obituary for the British Medical Journal. It finished with these words:

> *He was a man with severe porphyria who smoked too much and was without the consolation of a wife, a religious belief or a merit award but he didn't do so badly.*
>
> *ALC**

* Cochrane AL. A L Cochrane [obituary]. BMJ 1988;297:63.
  Reproduced with permission from the BMJ Publishing Group.

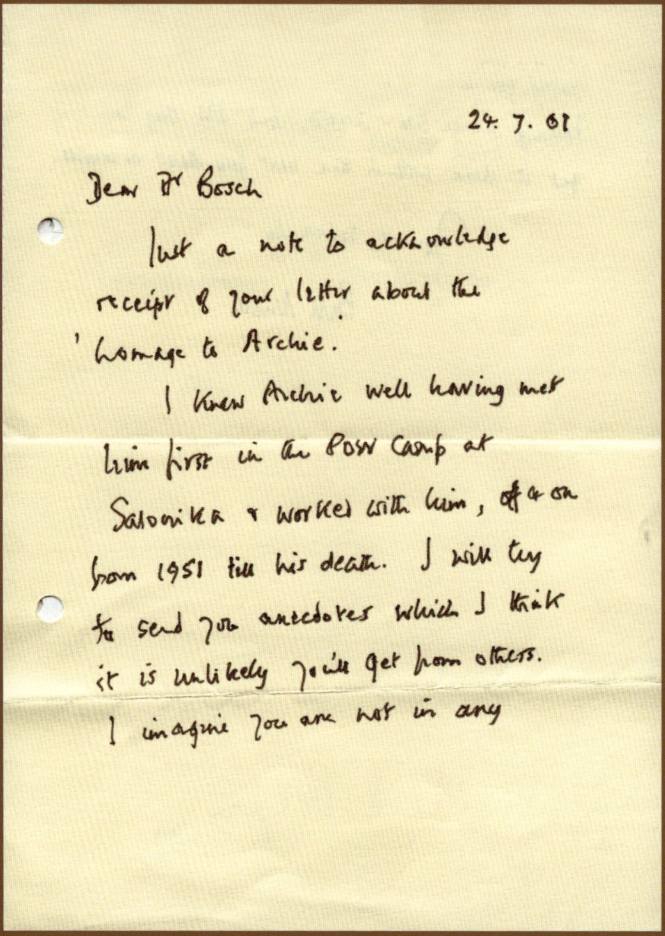

BILL MIALL

24. 7. 01

Dear Dr Bosch

Just a note to acknowledge receipt of your letter about the 'Homage to Archie.'

I knew Archie well having met him first in the POW Camp at Salonika & worked with him, off & on from 1951 till his death. I will try to send you anecdotes which I think it is unlikely you'll get from others.

I imagine you are not in any

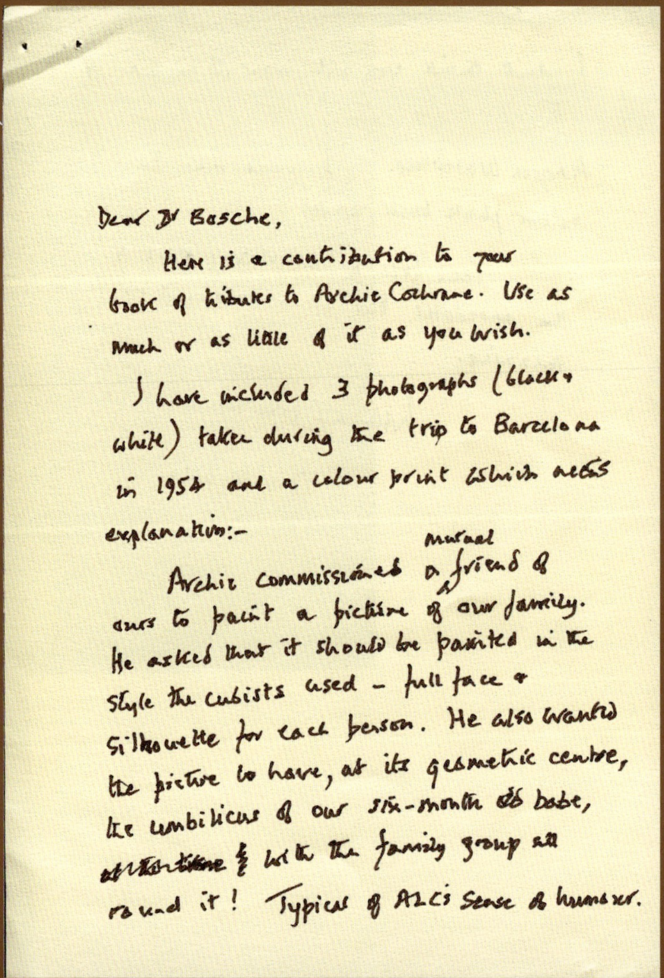

Dear Dr Bosche,

Here is a contribution to your book of tributes to Archie Cochrane. Use as much or as little of it as you wish.

I have included 3 photographs (black & white) taken during the trip to Barcelona in 1954 and a colour print which needs explanation:—

Archie commissioned a mural friend of ours to paint a picture of our family. He asked that it should be painted in the style the cubists used – full face & silhouette for each person. He also wanted the picture to have, at its geometric centre, the umbilicus of our six-month old babe, at that time & with the family group all round it! Typical of Archie's sense of humour.

Correspondence from Bill Miall to Dr F. X. Bosch.

BILL MIALL

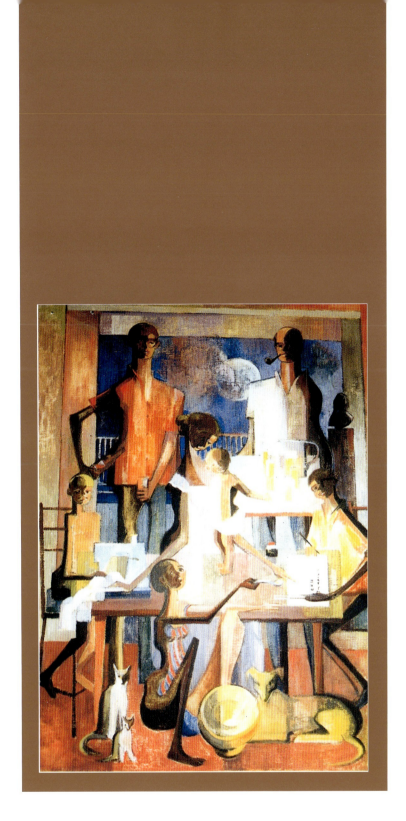

A FRAGMENT OF THE LETTER

Archie commissioned a mutual friend of ours to paint a picture of our family. He asked that it should be painted in the style the cubists used - full face of silhouette for each person. He also wanted the picture to have, at its geometric centre, the umbilicus of our six-month old babe, with the family group around it! Archie's typical sense of humour.

Oil painting by Angela Waterlow.

Professor
Josep M. Anto
Epidemiologist

Degree in Medicine and Surgery (1975), specialist in respiratory medicine (Hospital Vall d'Hebron, 1976-1980) and PhD (Epidemiological Investigations of Asthma Epidemics) at the Universitat Autónoma de Barcelona. He has been at the Institut Municipal d'Investigacións Mèdiques (IMIM-IMAS) since 1986, currently as Director of the Unit of Research on Respiratory and Environmental Health. Since 1998, he has been Professor of Medicine at the Universitat Pompeu Fabra, Barcelona. His research is on the epidemiology and environmental causes of asthma and chronic obstructive pulmonary disease. Dr Anto is pioneer in Spain and one of the intellectual leaders in the efforts to integrate epidemiological research into the Health Services network.

ARCHIE AND BARCELONA

In 1981, the Centre for Health Analysis and Programs (CAPS) in Barcelona, was a think tank for health services reform. Among its priorities were public health issues with epidemiology as its centre. It should not be a surprise that its activities at that time included a series of lectures on the most prominent ideas in the international debate about health and health services. I was extremely lucky to be in charge of the coordination of this programme with invited lecturers as distinguished as Archie Cochrane and Thomas McKeown. It is difficult to state over the influence that they had on our thinking and activities. I met Archie Cochrane both at his arrival and departure, and several other times during his stay. I remember vividly the conversation we had, while waiting for his departure flight, about his activities in the UK in support of the Spanish Republic. In 1981 the Spanish transition to democracy was still weak and the memory of the military coup of 23 February still very alive. In more recent times I have also had repeated opportunities to talk with Richard Doll and his wife Joan, during our various encounters in Florence, about the energy and idealism of those young British physicians who demonstrated frequently in Trafalgar Square to support the Spanish Republic.

A few months before his visit we received the text of the lectures. We invited Archie to talk about primary health care to a wide audience including those who at that time were leading primary care reforms in Catalonia and the rest of Spain. In addition we asked him for a second lecture on health services research for a more specialised audience. His papers arrived accompanied by a short handwritten note: *I am rather alarmed at the prospects of lecturing at 10 p.m. I hope I stay awake! AC.* This was a demonstration of the sense of humour and irony of a man used to thinking in the first person about the big challenges of his time. In the following pages, there is the summary of this lecture in a direct, clear and sharp style. The other lecture about primary health care is of interest in its own right since it was like giving formal public advice to an audience closely involved in changing the health services left by the totalitarian regime. He started with a reference to the beginning of the twentieth century when the USA, and to a lesser extent the UK, lost its way in primary health care, especially after the Flexner report. Soon after he focused on several of the questions that he thought were key to a country facing the opportunity of changing its national health system. Deeply rooted in the available scientific evidence with strong emphasis on randomized trials, including several from his own unit, he suggested that the role of physicians was not as important as it is usually considered to be and that it was possible to compensate the role of physicians with a more influential role of nurses. In particular he suggested that Catalonia should not go beyond 12 physicians per 10 000 population and that no measure against private medicine was as effective as promoting high quality public services. He devoted a substantial part of his lecture to what he thought were to be taken as the priorities for the Catalan context and, among these, he recommended a strong role of primary physicians in prevention, an active policy against the consumption of unnecessary drugs with a preference for the list of essential drugs promoted by the World Health Organization (WHO).

I'm sure that during his visit most of us had the feeling of meeting one of the more prominent thinkers in health sciences. There is no doubt that our appreciation was strengthened by the affinity with his political beliefs and especially his solidarity at the time of our civil war. During the years following that visit his intellectual influence has not ceased to grow. I'm sure that we have had enormous benefit from sharing his ideas.

LEFT: *Parc Güell. Barcelona.*
RIGTH: *Barcelona. View from the Tibidabo.*

EPIDEMIOLOGY AND HEALTH SERVICES RESEARCH

*Lecture presented by Archie Cochrane
at the Medical College in Barcelona on 30 November 1981.*

Epidemiology has evolved very rapidly in the last fifty years. When I was a student it was a rather dull non-quantitative, observational branch of medicine confined to infectious diseases. Then quite suddenly, after the war, it widened its scope to include all diseases and became very statistical. (In the UK this was mainly due to the genius of Sir Austin Bradford-Hill).

At first the statistics were only applied to observational studies, such as surveys and case-control studies, but in the mid-fifties it developed an experimental technique (again with the help of Sir Austin) in the form of the Randomized Controlled Trial (RCT). Epidemiology then became a fully fledged science.

There was one further step to take and it was surprising that it took so long to develop in the UK. We had had a National Health Service, one of the biggest industries in the country, for many years, but it had never occurred to anyone that it needed an organisation to check on its effectiveness and efficiency. As the cost of the health service continued to rise, the need for this sort of research became obvious.

A start was made with 'screening' which has become almost epidemic in the early 60s. The underlying idea was that early diagnosis would lead to more effective treatment. This was a pious hope, but there was really no evidence to support it, and my old research unit put forward the idea that a proposal to screen should be treated as testing a hypothesis and that the best test would be a randomized controlled trial. Three such trials were carried out during that period for cancer of the lung[1], anaemia[2] and glaucoma.[3] All three trials showed that screening was ineffective, and this led to the end of the screening epidemic.

It became clear that epidemiological methods might be of value in improving the non-clinical aspects of medicine, in the same way as the RCT had been so important in improving clinical medicine. In this way Health Service research was born.

Most of the standard epidemiological techniques have been used in this developing field. For instance the case-control technique was used to compare out-patient surgery with in-patient surgery in Cali, Colombia, but little attention has been paid to this. There were also may publications showing how doctors differed – eg, in their average length of stay in hospital for the same disease.[4] We also, as I mentioned in my previous lecture contrasted the 'expected-observed' comparison, so common in mortality studies, to compare the expected and observed consumption of vitamin B 12.[5]

Sad to say this flood of observational studies had very little effect on medical behaviour.

We had greater success with randomized controlled trials, which are of course, more costly, take longer and are more difficult to carry out. I have already mentioned our success with screening. This was followed by a series of trials which slowly reduced the average length of stay from over 30 days to five or six days for uncomplicated ischaemic heart disease.[6-8]. This is quite an achievement.

We also had some success in randomizing 'place of treatment' i.e. in-patient / out-patient or at home. Probably the most successful was randomizing the injection treatment of varicose veins in out-patients against surgical treatment in hospital.[9, 10] This time we decided to cost the two treatments. This was one of the factors which led to economists entering Health Service research in a big way.

The economists were certainly to be welcomed as they had valuable techniques which seemed likely to be of value in the Health Service research. I am no economist, but the techniques are usually called cost-productivity, cost-effectiveness and cost-benefit. Cost-productivity simply seeks to minimise the cost per unit of service output. Cost-effectiveness goes a step further and aims to minimize the cost per unit of health outcome, while cost-benefit compares the costs and benefits of different strategies to achieve particular objectives.[11] They all sounded very promising.

However, in my opinion, much less has been achieved than was expected. Some snags have appeared. The main snag is the very real difficulty in the accurate costing of medical procedures. How for example do you cost care. The only measure available is the time devoted to it by medical staff which is a very inadequate measure. Or how do you allow for patient preference, for example, if some prefer to go into hospital or some prefer to be treated at home.

An associate problem is the cost of costing. We were amazed to find in costing the two sides of a controlled trial that the cost of the costing was nearly as great as that of the trial itself.

Another snag soon became apparent. Detailed medico-economic studies rarely led to clear-cut decisions. One was usually left with a value judgement. For instance if one shows that, by adding an additional medical investigation to a well defined group of patients, one would probably save one life per year, at an additional cost to the Health Service of £ 60 000, who decides whether the country can afford it?

Possibly the greatest contribution the medico-economists make is in educating the medical profession. They are slowly learning that the costs of the health service depend largely on their decisions. The total cost of the National Health Service. is fixed by the government, so the extravagant, inefficient doctors penalise other parts of the health service.

I must also refer here to the excellent economic work done by people like Brian Abel Smith[12] and Robert Maxwell[13] in comparing the cost of Health Services in different countries. The results are very interesting. Developed countries differ in the number of doctors, nurses, and hospital beds, and even more surprisingly none of these medical variables relate to the differing mortalities in the various countries, that is, with the exception of the prevalence of doctors, which is unfortunately positively related to mortality in the younger age groups.

Another group who have entered Health Service research is the sociologists. In general their approach has been one of 'doctor bashing' and this has had very little effect in the UK. In the USA the sociologists have been more useful particularly in evaluating social work.[14]

I would not advise Catalonia to spend too much money on Health Service research at present. I would advise them to concentrate on basics:

1. Accurate censuses and death certification.

2. Accurate figures for hospital admissions with age, sex, diagnosis, length of stay and outcome.

3. Accurate cancer registration.

4. Accurate costing of the whole health service, public and private broken down in the way suggested by Maxwell,[15] together with costs of individual hospitals.

With these data, and by comparing them with those of other countries, you should get a clear idea of the areas where improvement is possible.

REFERENCES:

1. Brett GZ. The value of lung cancer detection by six-monthly chest radiographs. Thorax 1968; 23: 414-420.
2. Elwood PC, Waters WE, Greene WJ, Wood MM. Evaluation of a screening survey for anaemia in adult non-pregnant women. BMJ 1967; 4: 714-717.
3. Graham PA. The definition of pre-glaucoma. A prospective study. Trans Ophthalmol Soc U K 1969; 88: 153-165.
4. Heasman MA, Carstairs V. Inpatient management: variations in some aspects of practice in Scotland. BMJ 1971; 1: 495-498.
5. Cochrane AL, Moore F. Expected and observed values for the prescription of vitamin B 12 in England and Wales. Br J Prev Soc Med 1971; 25: 147-151.
6. Groden BM, Allison A, Shaw GB. Management of myocardial infarction: the effect of early mobilization. Scott Med J 1967; 12: 435-440.
7. Hayes MJ, Morris GK, Hampton JR. Comparison of mobilisation after two and nine days in uncomplicated myocardial infarction. BMJ 1974; iii: 10-13.
8. West RR, Henderson AH. Randomised multicentre trial of early mobilisation after uncomplicated myocardial infarction. Br Heart J 1979; 42: 381-385.
9. Chant AD, Jones HO, Weddell JM. Varicose veins: a comparison of surgery and injection-compression sclerotherapy. Lancet 1972; 2: 1188-1191.
10. Piachaud D, Weddell JM. Cost of treating varicose veins. Lancet 1972; 2: 1191-1192.
11. Griffiths DA. Economic evaluation of health services. Concepts and methodology applied to screening programmes. Rev Epidemiol Sante Publique 1981; 29: 85-101.
12. Abel-Smith B. An international study of health expenditure. Public Health Papers. Geneva: WHO, 1967.
13. Maxwell RJ. Health and wealth : an international study of health-care spending. Published for Sandoz Institute for Health and Socio-Economic Studies by Lexington Books, 1981.
14. Cochrane AL, St Leger AS, Moore F. Health service 'input' and mortality 'output' in developed countries. J Epidemiol Community Health 1978; 32: 200-205.

Doctor
Susana Sans
Epidemiologist

Dr Susana Sans graduated in medicine from the Autonomous University of Barcelona in 1975. She first trained in respiratory diseases and after as an epidemiologist and has directed several population studies on chronic, mainly cardiovascular, diseases in Catalonia. She was Archie Cochrane's student in the Master's degree in Community Medicine course at the London School of Hygiene and Tropical Medicine in 1979-80. She visited Archie at Rhoose Farm to learn about the Pneumoconiosis Unit studies in 1979. She has helped in the collection of material and conducted the interview with Sir Richard Doll for this book.

STUDENT MEMORIES OF ARCHIE COCHRANE

I personally met Professor Cochrane when he visited Saint Paul's Hospital in Barcelona in 1978. He had been invited by Dr Xavier Bosch. It was his first return to Spain since the Spanish Civil War, when he had joined the International Brigades. I was impressed by his strong personality and his comments about the Catalan character, while Xavier and I were driving him to the renovated Hotel Colon in front of the Cathedral in the Gothic Quarter, where he had stayed in the 1930s. Later on, I had the benefit of attending his brilliant lectures as a student of the Master's in Community Medicine degree at the London School of Hygiene and Tropical Medicine in 1979-80. Then, I was privileged to visit him at his Welsh home with other colleagues from the School, and members of his team at the Pneumoconiosis Research Unit. We arrived late on a very cold and windy Friday night in the autumn of 1979, after a train journey from London. He welcomed us with great warmth in his lovely garden in Rhoose Farm House on the top of a hill near the Welsh cliffs, and offered us a hot punch to warm us up. It was his fierce critical and rebellious spirit dressed with British humour which impressed me so much, as well as his love for art, and, above all, his humanity, which has left a lasting imprint on my mind. While showing us his interesting art collection and, knowing my origin, he teased me by criticising Catalans for losing the Civil War against the fascists, but he did so with delicacy and a fine sense of humour.

Reading his book *Effectiveness and efficiency: random reflections on the health services* was undoubtedly an important moment in my career. At a time when medical dogmatism was the norm, and being at the dawn of the democratic transition in Spain, reading somebody who approached the health system with constructive criticism, scientific methodology, intellectual rigour and light-hearted creativity, was the right encouragement to look at the future with confidence.

The whole generation of remarkable public health leaders who, among other things, did a great job in eradicating endemic malaria and trachoma in Spain, had either died or emigrated to the American continent because of the Civil War. Our generation had to invent ourselves and were desperately looking for leaders. The influence Archie had in the evolution of public health in Spain was confined to a small nucleus of people who, at the end of the 1970s and beginning of the '80s, had to create almost from nothing, opportunities for the development of epidemiology and public health and the modernization of the health system in Spain. The recent boom of so-called evidence-based medicine, is the systematic application of epidemiology to clinical medicine, which has been possible thanks to the work began by Archie Cochrane during those early years.

All aspects of Cochrane's intellectual and professional legacy are of enormous value to the progress of health in the 21st century: not only his internationally recognised contribution to the evaluation of public health systems, but also other less widely known works, such as the quality of death certificates, that indirectly reflects the quality of clinical practice and the surveys of Welsh mining communities exemplifying the role of economic and social factors on the health status of populations. In all of his work, there are lessons to be learnt and actions to be started or continued. But the most important aspect of his legacy is his deep humanism expressed in the leitmotiv of his entire work: the drive to improve the human condition.

Professor
Daan Kromhout
Epidemiologist

Professor Daan Kromhout is a nutritional epidemiologist and currently Director of the Nutrition and Consumer Safety Division at the Netherlands National Institute for Public Health and the Environmental (RIVM) in Bilthoven. He was formerly Director of the Public Health Research Division at RIVM and Professor of Epidemiology at Wageningen and Leiden Universities. Professor Kromhout has published extensively on nutritional epidemiology and is the principal investigator of the Dutch contribution to the Seven Countries study on coronary heart disease. He met Archie Cochrane during his fellowship at the International Society and Federation of Cardiology Ten-Day Seminar on cardiovascular epidemiology in 1976.

STUDENT MEMORIES OF ARCHIE COCHRANE

In 1975 Professor Cochrane was a faculty member of the eighth Ten-day International Teaching Seminar of the International Society and Federation of Cardiology held in Oaxtepec close to Mexico City. This seminar is still held yearly and was at that time directed by Geoffrey Rose, Jeremiah Stamler and Rose Stamler.

Professor Cochrane presented a few lectures stressing the importance of randomized controlled trials (RCTs) in order to obtain information about the effectiveness and efficiency of treatments. He was also very critical when we held small-group discussions on the strengths and weaknesses of articles or attempted to design an epidemiological study.

After the seminar I stayed for a day in Mexico City. On Saturday morning I met Professor Cochrane at breakfast. He asked when I was leaving. I told him that I was going on Sunday morning. He said that he had a similar schedule and proposed to spend that day together. We visited several museums and markets and went out together for dinner. I had a book on visiting Mexico City for five dollars a day which recommended a restaurant with seven courses and was well known for good quality food at low prices, a very attractive offer for a young Dutch Ph.D. student with a big appetite. Professor Cochrane agreed to go to that restaurant and told the waiter that he would have one of the seven courses and would leave the other six for me!

During that day he teased me about my interest in nutritional research. He said that nutrition was not a science and that there never had been a Nobel Prize winner in nutrition. My counter argument was that there were many examples of Nobel Prize winners for the discovery of different vitamins. He disagreed because research into vitamins was biochemistry and not nutrition! I am not sure whether I influenced his thinking on nutritional research either during the seminar or in our correspondence thereafter. I was however surprised to read in 1979 the Lancet paper that he wrote together with Drs St. Leger and Moore on wine consumption and cardiac mortality in 18 developed countries. Professor Cochrane was very interested in correlates of population mortality rates. He had earlier found that health-service factors and dietary factors were of little importance in explaining differences in all-cause mortality rates between countries. Gross national product was the only (inversely) related factor with all-cause mortality.

In the Lancet paper, he showed that the per capita wine consumption was inversely associated with deaths from coronary heart disease. This association was stronger than that of any other factor. He was very much amused by this result and he concluded that this medicine is already in a highly palatable form and it is almost a sacrilege to isolate the protective component from it. During one of his talks on the results of this study, a colleague asked whether white or red wine showed the larger effect. His answer was "I prefer rosé!"

My interaction with Professor Cochrane greatly influenced my thinking on and research in nutritional epidemiology. Most of my research is based on data collected in cohort studies. Professor Cochrane taught me the necessity of carrying out RCTs in order to establish cause-and-effect relationships and to know whether a treatment does more good than harm. We are currently carrying out an RCT with a factorial design studying the health effects of the N-3 polyunsaturated fatty acids, alpha-linolenic acid (ALA, present in vegetables, soybean oil and nuts) and the N-3 polyunsaturated fatty acids eicosapentaenoic acid (EPA) and docosahexaenoic acid (DHA) present in fish. The health effects of four different margarines with either a placebo or with ALA and/or the combination of EPA and DHA will be tested in 4 000 cardiac patients. This trial would not have seen daylight if I had not met Professor Cochrane.

STUDENT MEMORIES OF ARCHIE COCHRANE

MFS writes:

Is it real that Professor Archie Cochrane (Obituary, 2 July, page 63) has died? Because of his teaching, many of his Sudanese pupils have saved millions from premature death. Archie Cochrane will remain alive and fighting so long as his boys continue his teaching. You may ask what bridges a black Moslem like me from the tropical heat with a red haired Scot from the cold. It is the love that Archie put in my heart, though the last time I saw him was 26 years ago. We will never forget him.*

* MFS. (correspondence) British Medical Journal. 1989; 298:154.

(...) BUT IF I WERE ASKED TO CHOOSE ONE SCENE THAT WOULD BEST CONVEY THE UNIQUE FLAVOUR OF ARCHIE'S PERSONALITY, IT WOULD BE NONE OF THESE BUT RATHER THE 'CURIOUS SHERRY PARTY' HE GAVE FOR ALL HIS AVAILABLE RELATIVES AT WHICH HE GAVE A SHORT LECTURE ON PORPHYRIA AND ITS IMPLICATIONS FOR THEM ALL AND FOLLOWED IT BY DISTRIBUTING DIY KITS AND REQUESTING SAMPLES OF URINE AND FAECES. IT'S SO SENSIBLE AND PRACTICAL AND AT THE SAME TIME SO TRUSTING AND SOMEHOW COMICAL. IN THE END HE SEEMS TO HAVE DISCOVERED THE GREAT GRANDFATHER WHO WAS THE ORIGINAL SOURCE AND TO HAVE TRACED AND EXAMINED BY DIY KIT 152 OUT OF HIS 153 WIDELY SCATTERED LIVING DESCENDANTS – 152 OUT OF 153 – THAT WAS THE STANDARD THAT ARCHIE HAD ALWAYS SET HIMSELF FOR ALL HIS WORK. (...)

RICHARD COHEN 1989*

* *Credit & Legend, see page 326.*

A SENSIBLE MAN

Peter Nicholas
Sculptor

Annie Nicholas
Designer

THE ARTISTIC TASTE

Collectors of visual arts are invariably obsessive - finding it difficult to quit, their acquisitions multiply with the inevitable result of storage problems and the rotation of pieces accompanied by interior design modification. Unable to rationalise why, they might discipline their collecting into conveniently boxed categories, for example, by material use, constraints of size, subject matter, market forces, and so on. I don't think Archie Cochrane approached his collection at all like this. He bought only enough work to provide conversation pieces for a minimal number of spaces inside his home. Apart from a few painters of the Scottish school, most of his collection reflected a catholic taste leavened by a token number of works by Welsh artists. It never occurred to me at the time to question why he acquired what (at this point in time it seems an interesting inquiry) but I instinctively knew he had to be with art - not of art. When people assembled at Rhoose Farm House, he enjoyed so much recounting how he purchased the works, trawling London galleries, contacting the artists directly and rarely paying more than £50.00 for a piece, the latter I suspect was a deliberate understatement to amuse. His was not a large collection, certainly for such a house, mostly the work occupied two rooms on the ground floor. In the comfortable, Heals 1930s furnished study, a Ben Nicholson still life *Lorca*, an oil painting on board, hung over the fireplace. An unusual, clinical Ceri Richards assemblage in wood titled *Adam and Eve* perched almost apologetically to one side. On the opposite wall, at the corner where Archie invariably sat to work, eat and think, hung a Peploe exuding a quiet, comfortable, timeless painterly quality which was juxtaposed with Josef Hermann's painting *Miners* posed in their now dated but frighteningly familiar crouch of resignation. On the wall facing the only window, dominating the room and the collective works, hung a masculine painting of a handsome woman wearing a wide-brimmed hat, *La Cocarde* by J.D. Ferguson.

Peter & Annie Nicholas

1968: Sometime towards the end of the year I had a brief note from Professor AL Cochrane, Rhoose Farm House, near Cardiff offering me a commission to make a very large piece of sculpture. The letter also invited me to discuss the idea over dinner at Rhoose as soon as I could manage it. My wife and I with two very young children lived sixty miles away. The proposed journey at night, in winter to meet a person I didn't know at a location I had never visited was a little daunting. I went on my own. The occasion was strangely relaxed, a very pleasant meal with plenty to drink and I think we struck a note of trust and friendship. However Archie's idea for a massive memorial to Welsh miners on the skyline above the Rhondda valleys was not at all practical and we settled for a more modest piece, in marble, for his garden, to be completed by the following summer. Three or four weeks into the job Archie turned up at my studio ostensibly to check on progress but really it was to meet the family, inspect our lifestyle and drop a bombshell: would we like to move to Rhoose and take up residence with him? If he was surprised by my reaction he certainly didn't show it and left with a cheery wave as he drove away in his ivory coloured Daimler Jaguar.

I had recently been awarded a major bursary by the Arts Council with which I rented a large studio, bought the tools and equipment to provide a professional base and already enjoyed the private patronage of a very influential and likeable man, Col. Sir Williams Crawshay for whom I had a devoted gratitude and respect. I was certainly not going to live in Rhoose.

Summer 1969 and the marble was almost complete when we had a phone call from Archie inviting me to help him choose the site for the sculpture, and, "Oh, do bring Marjorie, (my first wife now pregnant) and Ruth (daughter No. 1) and Saul (her little brother) and if the weather is fine they can have a picnic by the swimming pool". The weather was hot and sunny, the picnic was magnificent, and I was left to supervise the swimming lessons.

Archie took Majorie on a guided tour of the gardens, the studio buildings with associated newly decorated, furnished and domestically equipped flat, nothing of which I had seen on my previous visit. He again posed the same question mischievously, "Why can't you all come for six months, leave everything behind, rent the little house, it will be there for your return whenever".

Before autumn settled on his garden, the marble carving was in place, we as family were in residence, Rachel was born and I lived at Rhoose Farm House for more than twenty years.

Ceri Richards "Adam and Eve" or "Adam's apple".

Dame Barbara Hepworth "Galatea".

John Piper "Gordale Scar".

La Cocarde by J.D.Ferguson
Archie called it THE COURTESAN

This, then, was the room in which so many people gathered over the years in intellectual discussion, party mood or friendly, sometimes contentious, banter, Archie's collection used as a pivotal metaphor to illustrate his position on a rainbow of topics. I feel that the location of each work had a real if subconscious importance for Archie, not least the single, lonely, bronze sculpture of an *Acrobat* by Michael Ayrton balancing on a tall stand with its own light source.

Ben Nicholson OM Still life-Lorca. Archie was proud of having liked the painter early in his career. Later he was also proud at having purchased the painting he liked for less than 100 pounds.

Kyffin Williams "Cottage on a hill".

The dining room along the hall was home to a less significant group. Although work by some celebrated artists, they perhaps represented tokenism by Archie rather than visual stimuli. I liked the Trevelyan very much but the Ayrton *Monk* was gloomy. John Piper's *Gordale Scar* was not one of his best and *Cottage on the Hill* -another Kyffin Williams. Of the others, the anonymous Indian painting was interesting, also the Levaille which Archie decided was a "minor impressionist". It was on the dining table in this room that I modelled one of several clay portraits of Archie who admitted he liked the completed bronze but disliked the terracotta original, as the clay was too faecal. I have never used the material since. Personally I enjoyed the garden. The two Barbara Hepworth bronzes contributed enormous prestige to a sumptuous environment and of course it was the setting

Stone replica of The Lady of Llanmiangel.
The original carving is at the Manor House at Llanmiangel in the Vale of Glamorgan. Archie placed it in his garden and arranged for the sources to constantly flow water.

The legs of Rhoose by Peter Nicholas.

"Mother and child" by Peter Nicholas.

for my own contribution, a two element carved marble, the work that Archie commissioned before I was invited to live and work at Rhoose Farm House. He called it *Mother and child*.

But it was the study which I think provides a clue to Archie's psyche. Each work in the room had been positioned before I knew him. In fact the entire collection was already complete. In the twenty years I lived there, he didn't introduce a new piece; indeed only one was ever moved. The Nicholson was hidden behind suits hanging in his wardrobe when he went on trips abroad, its space taken by a very convincing copy that was so accurate that Archie could never recognise the original.

Peter & Annie Nicholas

Archie called this painting by Levaille "The minor impressionist".

My favourite memories will be of him in this room, in good form, with stimulating company, or reflective and alone, at one with art works which to him were important, essential and priceless.

Peter & Annie Nicholas

Pink roses in a blue and white vase by Samuel John Peploe. This painting was, for years, hung on the wall behind his desk.

Giles & Margaret Stalker

Between 1974 and 1977 Giles Stalker (Joe), nephew of Archie, his wife Margaret (Maggie) and their four children went to Rhoose to live in the farm. They provided for some time the family-life atmosphere that was most appreciated by Archie. In the late eighties, Archie moved into Joe and Maggies's precious house in Dorset where he spent his last days. He gave them the copy of the "Savacou" that graced the garden at Rhoose and some sculptures. A replica of part of the botanical arrangements made at Rhoose now decorates a corner of the Stalker's garden.

SKETCHES FROM THE FAMILY

Archie was very much a family man. Not only was he generous financially to his relations, but he made time for them. He had no children of his own, but called his great nephews and great niece his grandchildren. He joined many family holidays and paid for them. When his sister was very ill he spent much time travelling to Scotland to see that she was tended properly. Once, having been in London with his nephew and family, he returned to Wales by train, at that time, a three-hour journey. On arrival at his house, he heard that his nephew had collapsed. His wife, with the four small children, was distressed. As tired as he was, Archie caught the next train back to London to help.

After the war Archie lived in a large house in Wales, which he shared with various colleagues and friends. They employed a couple, the Barlows, to cook and cater for their needs. A swimming pool was built and generally, a good time was had by everyone who visited. Gradually, the other colleagues went their various ways and Archie was left owning Rhoose Farm House and being cared for very well by Mr and Mrs Barlow. Indeed, they spoiled him. Archie took a great interest in gardening and created a beautiful garden around him. He was also interested in art and managed to collect some very good paintings and sculptures. He loved the house and made many welcome there.

When she heard of Archie being 'very important', his sister thought of the photo of him in his 'sailor suit' and smiled to herself.

When his niece of six years had something in her eye, Archie volunteered to help and asked, *Has anyone a penknife?* His sister gasped and cried, *No, Archie*.

He offered his sister a sherry. She replied, *Yes please*.
Archie poured it and drank it.
Another time ...
Archie: *Would you like a drink?*
Visitor: *Yes please, I'd love a sherry*.
Archie pours a drink
Visitor: *Thanks. But this is gin and tonic!*
Archie: *Yes, but that'll be fine*.

A group of friends arrived with a nervous, middle-aged woman. Drinks were served and everyone was seated.
Archie (to start conversation): *Here is our old dog. In spite of his age, he still has an enormous appetite...*
Nervous woman (trying to contribute): *Aaah, just like me*.
Archie (continuing): *...both for food and for sex*.
Grins and embarrassment all round!

After an illness he wanted to go to Kenya to recover in the sun. He needed a companion. His great-nephew, Simon, about 17, was persuaded. Archie promised to keep him in funds but failed to do so. Although he was generous and kind he did not understand that not everyone had pocketsful of ten pound notes. Simon had to sell his jeans, which fetched a good price and allowed him to water ski.

GILES & MARGARET STALKER

Archibald Leman Cochrane was born in Galashiels, Scotland on 12 January 1909.

Archie's grandfather became wealthy in the business of tweed manufacturing in Galashiels. At the time Archie was in Cambridge, he inherited an independent private income which greatly influenced his life and made him distinct from many of his colleagues and collaborators.

Archie in a sailor suit.

LEFT: *Archie with younger brother Robert (right) at preparatory school at Rhos-on-sea in 1920.*

Copy of page 1 of handwritten summing-up notes for Archie's biography, "One Man's Medicine".

I must admit I made many mistakes when I was young, particularly in my reaction to the writings of Marx & Freud. It was however a common fault amongst the intellectuals of my generation, and my adoration to Freud, was biased by my personal handicap. I am not ashamed of having helped medically in the Spanish Civil War, although I am ashamed in retrospect of how little I knew about Spanish politics when I went there. But, I think the basic idea was sound. If Hitler, Mussolini and Franco, joined hands, France and the UK were lost.

Giles & Margaret Stalker

The atmosphere in Archie's family was one of Calvinist discipline and responsibility. In the photograph Archie (2nd right) with his beloved father, his elder sister Helen, and two young brothers, Robert and Walter.

Archie's father died when he was eight. The premature death of his brothers dramatically reduced the family and reinforced his ties with his sister Helen.

WALTER FRANCIS COCHRANE
CAPTAIN 4TH BN KINGS OWN
SCOTTISH BORDERERS OF GALASHIELS. SCOTLAND.
FELL IN ACTION AT THE SECOND BATTLE OF GAZA.
PALESTINE, 19TH, APRIL 1917.

At school Archie had been 'confirmed' into the Church of England. Later, when he had thought about it, he wrote a letter of resignation to the Archbishop of Canterbury. On his deathbed he was still annoyed that he hadn't had a reply.

In the 1940s he came on holiday with his sister's family to the north-east coast of England. He was working hard on pneumoconiosis so he spent all day speaking to the National Union of Mine workers from a pay phone. He used a nephew or niece as a runner to fetch coins from the surrounding shops. This was a popular job because there was always plenty left over.

It rained very hard that year of the holiday. Railways were washed away. Archie was resourceful. He donned his swimming trunks and went out into a downpour to wash his car.

His car was a little four-seater Vauxhall. The doors were held closed by a piece of string tied to each other across the car. He was driving with the family in squashed conditions and in heavy rain. He spied a woman with two small children struggling against the weather. He stopped immediately and offered them a lift. Not a popular idea with the rest of the family. They had wet strangers sitting on their knees. But that was Archie's way.

In the 1950s he was already questioning doctors' methods and teaching in medical schools. He gave a lecture, 'Debunking Doctors', at his nephew's school. It was very popular, except with the sons of doctors, and caused amusement and thought for a long time.

GILES & MARGARET STALKER

[...] At Cambridge, in the genial and liberating air of King's College, where I and others of his lifelong friends first got to know him, Archie blossomed. Gifted both intellectually and at sports, and with a romantic buoyancy and gaiety, he managed, until a rugger accident slowed him down in his second year, to play rugger, golf, tennis, and squash, to ride hoses and to play bridge, and to act at the Amateur Dramatic Club, without ever, so he says, missing a lecture or a laboratory session. [...] *

Helen's wedding.

Archie taking the place of his father to "give her away".

* Cohen D. Introduction. In: Cochrane AL, Blythe M. One Man's Medicine. An Autobiography of Professor Archie Cochrane. London: BMJ (Memoir Club), 1989.

Peter Reid (Margaret's brother) had been staying with Archie and accepted a lift to the station on Archie's way to the MRC. He had not reckoned on the smelly sample jar of faeces on the back seat. Almost at once, in his generosity, Archie stopped to pick up a hitchhiker. Peter was suffering in front with the window open. Would the hiker ever hitch again? Archie was not practical. Screwing on a top properly would have been difficult.

While at Cambridge he took his sister and a friend for a run in his Austin 7. To their alarm and embarrassment, he started shouting, braked hard, leapt from the car and took off his trousers. He shook them hard and explained that a wasp had gone up the leg.

Just after the war, he visited his sister's family in Galashiels, Scotland, fairly frequently. His young nephew and nieces enjoyed his presence because he played games and entertained them. Monopoly was popular. He always won, but no one knew how. Of course he was the Banker, as well as a player. It was difficult to distinguish one heap of money from another.

He fascinated his young relations by his vast amount of reading. He did this while eating chocolates, scarce though they were. It was decided that he did not notice what he was eating. A chocolate was surreptitiously refilled with mustard (or toothpaste depending on whose memory). Archie was watched by two naughty children. He ate it without flinching.

Later he arrived in Galashiels in bigger smarter cars. There were always scrapes and bashes in them. He explained, *A woman backed into me when I was parked*. He expected to be believed.
Women and dogs in the back. Archie's rule of motoring.
Some people preferred not to be driven by Archie.

GILES & MARGARET STALKER

Archie and Helen.

Archie's sister Helen remained an important referent throughout his lifetime. Diagnosed as a carrier of porphyria after an acute attack, Archie conducted a full family research. Archie himself was described in a test result as, biochemically, a severe porphyric. He loved to lecture on the point. Later in life, Maggie Stalker expressed some reasonable doubts on the severity of the case.

(Based on additional medical observations)

Giles & Margaret Stalker

With his step father, John Lock.

Archie, guide and niece, Jennifer visiting his father's grave in Gaza.

L to R: *Joe (nephew), Helen (sister), Sutcliff, George Rink, Jennifer (niece), Susan (niece), Margaret Rink, Sutcliff and Archie.*
George & Margaret Rink went skiing with Archie every year The Sutcliff boys are her sons.

During his time in Wales Archie created a garden, a shelter and a home in a property named Rhoose Farm House. In the photograph main entrance.

Dorset, is the current residency of the Stalkers where Archie spent his last days. In the photograph the Stalkers with Peter Nicholas and the author reviewing early drafts of this book.

Archie received Doctorates from York University, England and Rochester University, in the USA. He was invited to give the Dunham lectures at Harvard on "Health Services of the world". Perhaps his most famous recognition was however, the Rock Carling Fellowship named after Sir Ernest Rock Carling, for many years a Governing Trustee of the Nuffield Provincial Hospitals Trust and Chairman of the Trust's Medical Advisory Committee.

The topic reviewed by Archie in 1971 resulted in his most famous publication "Effectiveness & Efficiency Random reflections on Health Services".

In the photograph Archie with Jennifer (niece) and Helen at Buckingham Palace after receiving Commander of the British Empire.

ARCHIE WAS A STUDENT AT UNIVERSITY COLLEGE HOSPITAL
WHEN THE SPANISH CIVIL WAR BROKE OUT AND IMMEDIATELY VOLUNTEERED FOR
THE MEDICAL AID UNIT WHICH WAS BEING RAISED FOR THE REPUBLICAN CAUSE
AND WHICH, ALMOST INCREDIBLY, WAS ORGANISED AND DESPATCHED IN NOT
MUCH MORE THAN A FORTNIGHT AFTER THE START OF FRANCO'S INVASION.
HE NEVER REGRETTED THE YEAR HE SPENT IN SPAIN OR RISKING HIS LIFE FOR A
CAUSE HE DEEPLY BELIEVED IN; AND HE KNEW HE HAD BEEN VERY USEFUL AND HAD
LEARNT A LOT ABOUT HIMSELF. AND, DESPITE HAVING BEEN SICKENED AND
EXASPERATED BY THE SQUABBLES AND INTRIGUES OF THE POLITICAL FACTIONS
INSIDE AND OUTSIDE THE UNIT, AND VOWING THAT HE WOULD NEVER EVER JOIN
THE COMMUNIST PARTY IN BRITAIN, HE SEEMS TO HAVE FELT, LOOKING BACK,
THAT HIS INVOLVEMENT IN SPAIN HAD
A PURITY AND INNOCENCE THAT HE WAS NEVER AFTERWARDS TO RECAPTURE.

RICHARD COHEN JUNE 1989*

* Credit & Legend, see page 326.

ARCHIE COCHRANE

A MAN
OF
HIS TIME

(...) ON 12 APRIL 1931 MUNICIPAL ELECTIONS WEE HELD THROUGHOUT SPAIN. THE RESULTS SHOWED THAT THE LARGER CITIES, INCLUDING GRANADA, WERE OVERWHELMINGLY ANTI-MONARCHIST AND PRO-REPUBLICAN, AND TWO DAYS LATER KING ALFONSO XIII LEFT THE COUNTRY. FROM 1923 TO 1930 SPAIN HAD BEEN LABOURING UNDER THE YOKE OF AN AUTHORITARIAN REGIME IMPOSED BY THE GENIAL, ERRATIC AND PHILANDERING GENERAL PRIMO DE RIVERA, AND NOW SHE WANTED A CHANGE.
AS IS WELL KNOW, THE FIVE YEARS OF THE REPUBLIC'S SHORT LIFE WERE MARKED BY A TURBULENCE IN WHICH THE HATREDS, PASSIONS, CONTRADICTIONS, HOPES AND FEARS THAT HAD BEEN DIVIDING SPANIARDS FOR GENERATIONS CAME INEXORABLY TO A HEAD AND EXPLODED IN A FRATRICIDAL WAR THAT KILLED ABOUT 600 000 PEOPLE. (...)

IAN GIBSON, 1983*

* *Credit & Legend, see page 326.*

THE SPANISH CIVIL WAR (1936-1939)

Anti-fascist militia on departure from Barcelona to the front line. 28 July 1936.

EXTRACT FROM *CIVILIZATION AND BARBARITY IN 20TH CENTURY EUROPE* BY GABRIEL JACKSON

Gabriel Jackson

The Spanish Civil War was to be headline news for over thirty months. For almost all politically conscious people in Europe and the western hemisphere, it was seen as the critical battleground between the forces of political liberty and economic progress and the forces of reaction and traditional privilege. The defence of the Republic involved nothing less than the defence of the entire emancipatory heritage of both the French and Russian revolutions: individual liberty and constitutional, civilian government; economic reforms in favour of landless peasants and exploited industrial workers; separation of church and state; universal public education and basic medical and social services; linguistic rights and local autonomy for the minority nationalities within Spain; and acceptance of anarchist and socialist collective experiments both in agriculture and factory management. The cause of los nacionales,[1] meanwhile, was nothing less than the defence of the entire conservative heritage of Europe: the sanctity of private property and public order; hierarchical social and economic relations between the existing classes (thought of as the God-given nature of human society); centralized, authoritarian political and religious institutions, and the rejection of Marxism, atheism, universal equal suffrage, parliamentary sovereignty, and political parties.

Within Spain itself, it was a war not just of interest but of ideals. The liberal republicans and the parliamentary socialists were fighting to bring Spain into the ranks of twentieth-century democracy, to endow it with institutions like those of France, Scandinavia, and the Anglo-Saxon world. The left socialists, anarchists and various non-Stalinist Marxist parties were fighting to give Spain the revolutionary institu-

---

1. In Spanish usage *nacionalistas* generally refers to the Catalan and Basque autonomist parties and *los nacionales* to the troops under General Franco's command during the Civil War.

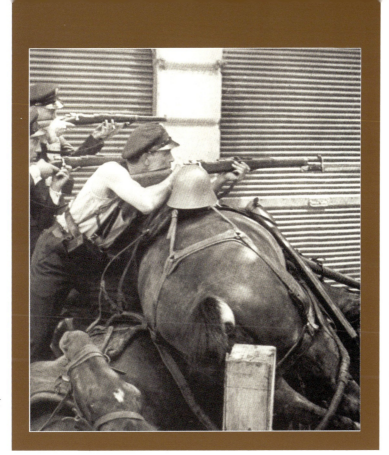

Street fighting in Barcelona. 19 July 1936.

tions which they ardently imagined had been the original intent of the Russian revolution, however much it had been deformed by Stalinist bureaucracy. The Catalan and Basque nationalists were fighting to give Spain not only a civilian democratic regime, but one which would recognize the rights of non Castilian languages and cultures.

On the side of General Franco, Catholics were fighting to defend their Church against anti-clerical outrages and to maintain Catholic education and mortality. Alphonsine monarchists were fighting for the eventual restoration of a parliamentary monarchy under the Bourbons, and Carlists were fighting for a more traditionalist authoritarian monarchy as espoused by the Carlist branch of the royal family. Middle-class conservatives were fighting to preserve the growing secular capitalist society, which they saw as the best means to improve Spain's economy and attenuate the class struggle. The Falange was fighting to establish an Italian-style fascist state, which it saw as the best means to combat the danger of atheist, materialist Marxism. General Franco was fighting to restore traditional authority and order. Also, at a time when churches were being desecrated by the anarchists, Franco felt that he had been destined to save Christian Spain from atheist, masonic, and materialistic hordes.

All wars involve a mixture of ideology and specific power interests. But in the case of Spain, the relative weight of political and moral ideals was much greater than in most wars. Hence the commitment, the heroism, the sense of universal *destiny*, the self-sacrifice, and the cruelty to opponents.*

---

* Jackson G. Civilization and barbarity in 20th century Europe. Amherst, NY: Humanity Books. Copyright © 1999 by Gabriel Jackson. Reprinted with permission.

1936: ARRIVAL IN BARCELONA

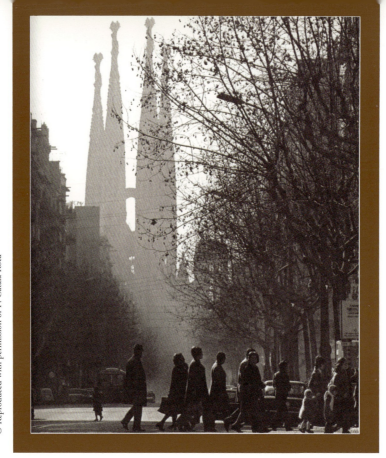

The Sagrada Familia by Antoni Gaudi, one of the symbols of Modernism in Barcelona.

EXTRACTS FROM *HOMAGE TO CATALONIA* BY GEORGE ORWELL

George Orwell

(...) This was in late December 1936, (...) I had come to Spain with some notion of writing newspaper articles, but I had joined the militia almost immediately, because at that time and in that atmosphere it seemed the only conceivable thing to do. The Anarchist were still in virtual control of Catalonia and the revolution was still in full swing.(...) But when one came straight from England the aspect of Barcelona was something startling and overwhelming. It was the first time that I had ever been in a town where the working class was in the saddle. Practically every building of any size had been seized by the workers and was draped with red flags or with the red and black flag of the Arnarchists; every wall was scrawled with the hammer and sickle and with the initials of the revolutionary parties; almost every church had been gutted and its images burnt. (...)

(...) Down the Ramblas, the wide central artery of the town where crowds of people streamed constantly to and fro, the loudspeakers were bellowing revolutionary songs all day and far into the night. And it was the aspect of the crowds that was the queerest thing of all. In outward appearance it was a town in which the wealthy classes had practically ceased to exist. Except for a small number of women and foreigners there were no "well-dressed" people at all. Practically everyone wore rough working-class clothes, or blue overalls, or some variant of the militia uniform. All this was queer and moving. There was much in it that I did not understand, in some ways I did not even like it, but I recognized it immediately as a state of affairs worth fighting for. (...)

The timeless scenery of the monument to Columbus, down the Ramblas, in the early morning light.

(...) Above all, there was a belief in the revolution and the future, a feeling of having suddenly emerged into an era of equality and freedom. Human beings were trying to behave as human beings and not as cogs in the capitalist machine. In the barber's shop were Anarchist notices (the barbers were mostly Anarchists) solemnly explaining that barbers were no longer slaves. In the streets were coloured posters appealing to prostitutes to stop being prostitutes. To anyone from the hard-boiled, sneering civilization of the English-speaking races there was something rather pathetic in the literalness with which these idealistic Spaniards took the hackneyed phrases of revolution. (...)

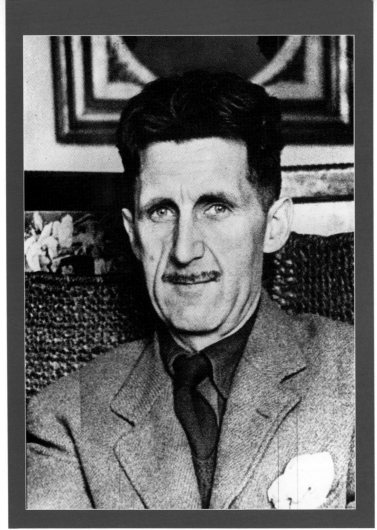

Eric Blair (George Orwell) was born in India in 1903 and educated at Eton. In 1937 he went to Spain to fight for the Republicans in the Regular Army and was wounded. Orwell died in London in 1950.
Extracts from his report on the Spanish Civil War entitled Homage to Catalonia *and first published in 1938, have been used to illustrate the scenarios that Archie also shared. They both volunteered, they were fierce independent minds strongly committed to the basic terms of reference of the war and they were both dramatically lost in the political struggle. Archie and Orwell met at least once in a bar in Barcelona.*

George Orwell

(...) All this time I was having the usual struggles with the Spanish language. Apart from myself there was only one Englishman at the barracks, and nobody even among the officers spoke a word of French. Things were not made easier for me by the fact that when my companions spoke to one another they generally spoke in Catalan. The only way I could get along was to carry everywhere a small dictionary which I whipped out of my pocket in moments of crisis. But I would sooner be a foreigner in Spain than in most countries. How easy it is to make friends in Spain! Within a day or two there was a score of militiamen who called me by my Christian name, showed me the ropes, and overwhelmed me with hospitality. (...)

(...) But I defy anyone to be thrown as I was among the Spanish working class, I ought perhaps to say, the Catalan working class, for apart from a few Aragonese and Andalusians I mixed only with Catalans - and not be struck by their essential decency; above all, their straightforwardness and generosity. A Spaniard's generosity, in the ordinary sense of the word, is at times almost embarrassing. If you ask him for a cigarette he will force the whole packet upon you. And beyond this there is generosity in a deeper sense, a real largeness of spirit, which I have met with again and again in the most unpromising circumstances. (...)

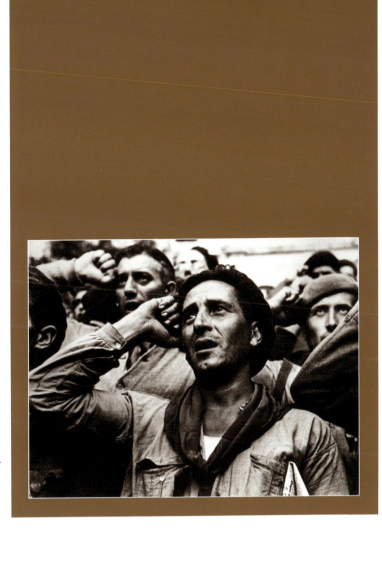

Montblanch, near Barcelona. 25 October 1938. Bidding farewell to the International Brigades, which were dismissed by the Republican government, as a consequence of Stalin's friendship with Germany.

(...) GOOD LUCK GO WITH YOU, ITALIAN SOLDIER!
BUT LUCK IS NOT FOR THE BRAVE;
WHAT WOULD THE WORLD GIVE BACK TO YOU?
ALWAYS LESS THAN YOU GAVE

BETWEEN THE SHADOWS AND THE GHOST,
BETWEEN THE WHITE AND THE RED,
BETWEEN THE BULLET AND THE LIE,
WHERE WOULD YOU HIDE YOUR HEAD?

(...) YOUR NAME AND YOUR DEEDS WERE FORGOTTEN
BEFORE YOUR BONES WERE DRY,
AND THE LIE THAT SLEW YOU IS BURIED
UNDER A DEEPER LIE; (...)

Biescas, a village in the Aragon front. "Al enemigo" literally "Towards the enemy".
Archie, while in Grañen, felt that there was no action for long periods of time and that consuming the limited resources and doing nothing to help represented little more than a burden and could be better spent if the Brigades were sent back home or forwarded to the front in Madrid.

George Orwell (...) Wherever the lines were within hailing distance of one another there was always a good deal of shouting from trench to trench. From ourselves: *Fascistas! Maricones!* From the Fascists: *Viva España! Viva Franco!* (...)

(...) On the Government side, in the party militias, the shouting of propaganda to undermine the enemy morale had been developed into a regular technique. (...)

(...) There is a very little doubt that it had its effect; everyone agreed that the trickle of Fascist deserters was partly caused by it. If one comes to think of it, when some poor devil of a sentry - very likely a Socialist or Anarchist trade union member who has been conscripted against his will - is freezing at his post, the slogan "Don't fight against your own class!" ringing again and again through the darkness is bound to make an impression on him. It might make just the difference between deserting and not deserting. Of course such a proceeding does not fit in with the English conception of war. I admit I was amazed and scandalized when I first saw it done. The idea of trying to convert your enemy instead of shooting him! I now think that from any point of view it was a legitimate manoeuvre. (...)

(...) If you can immobilize a certain number of men by making them desert, so much the better. (...)

Republican soldier at a check point in Barcelona on 20 July 1936.

(...) But at the beginning it dismayed all of us; it made us feel that the Spaniards were not taking this war of theirs sufficiently seriously (...)

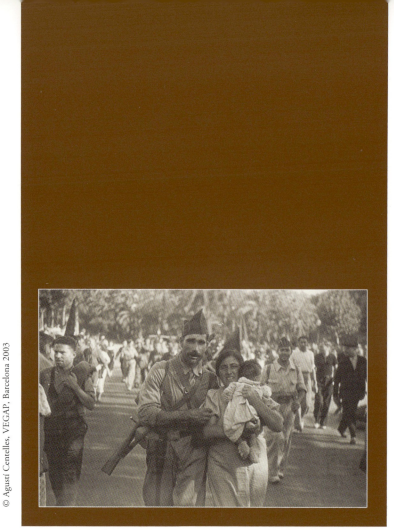

Volunteers joining the militia in Barcelona. 28 July 1936.

George Orwell

(...) When the fighting broke out on 18 July it is probable that every anti-Fascist in Europe felt a thrill of hope. For here at last, apparently, was democracy standing up to Fascism. For years past the so-called democratic countries had been surrendering to Fascism at every step. The Japanese had been allowed to do as they liked in Manchuria. Hitler had walked into power and proceeded to massacre political opponents of all shades. Mussolini had bombed the Abyssinians while fifty-three nations (I think it was fifty-three) made pious noises "off". But when Franco tried to overthrow a mildly Left-wing Government the Spanish people, against all expectation, had risen against him. It seemed - possibly it was - the turning of the tide. (...)

(...) More important than this was the fact that the Spanish working class did not, as we might conceivably do in England, resist Franco in the name of "democracy" and the status quo; their resistance was accompanied by - one might almost say it consisted of - a definite revolutionary outbreak. (...)

(...) Even if one had heard nothing of the seizure of the land by the peasants, the setting up of local soviets, etc., it would be hard to believe that the Anarchists and Socialists who were the backbone of the resistance were doing this kind of thing for the preservation of capitalist democracy, which especially in the Anarchist view was no more than a centralized swindling machine. (...)

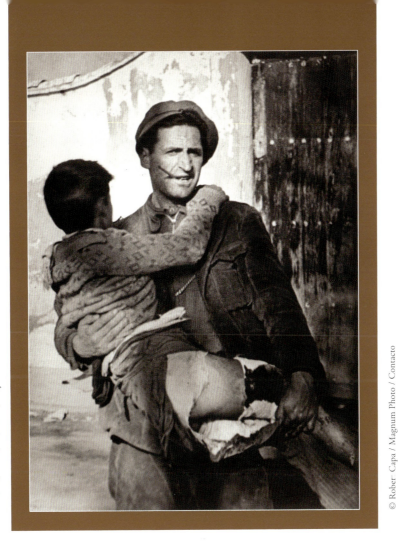

Aragon front. Battle of Teruel. 21 December 1937. When Republican soldiers first entered this strategically located hilltop town after a hard siege, they found many civilian casualties.

(...) The thing that had happened in Spain was, in fact, not merely a civil war, but the beginning of a revolution. It is this fact that the anti-Fascist press outside Spain has made it its special business to obscure. The issue has been narrowed down to "Fascism versus democracy" and the revolutionary aspect concealed as much as possible. In England, where the Press is more centralized and the public more easily deceived that elsewhere, only two versions of the Spanish war have had any publicity to speak of: the Right-wing version of Christian patriots versus Bolsheviks dripping with blood, and the Left-wing version of gentlemanly republicans quelling a military revolt. The central issue has been successfully covered up. (...)

(...) And since the revolution had got to be crushed, it greatly simplified things to pretend that no revolution had happened. In this way the real significance of every event could be covered up. (...)

(...) Outside Spain few people grasped that there was a revolution; inside Spain nobody doubted it. (...)

THE POLITICAL WAR...

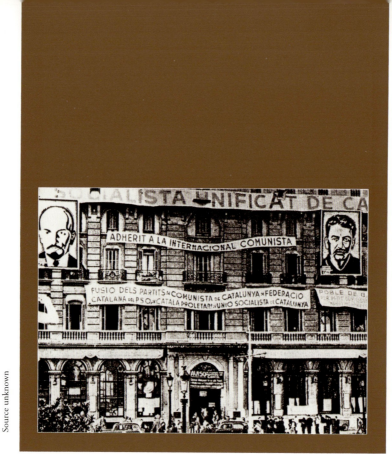

Source unknown

Hotels were often the headquarters of the political parties and a centre of interest for journalists and the secret police.

COMUNISM

George Orwell

(...) The Partit Socialista Unificat de Catalunya (PSUC, Catalan Unified Socialist Party) line which was preached in the Communist and pro-Communist press throughout the world, was approximately this:

> At present nothing matters except winning the war; without victory in the war all else is meaningless. Therefore this is not the moment to talk of pressing forward with the revolution (...)

(...) At this stage we are not fighting for the dictatorship of the proletariat, we are fighting for parliamentary democracy. Whoever tries to turn the civil war into a social revolution is playing into the hands of the Fascists and is in effect, if not in intention, a traitor. (...)

All public transport was collectivized in the populations with organized unions. Barcelona 1937.

DISSIDENT COMUNISM

(...) The Partido Obrero de Unificación Marxista (POUM, Workers Party of Marxist Unification) was one of those dissident Communist parties which have appeared in many countries in the last few years as a result of the opposition to *Stalinism*. (...)

(...) The POUM line was approximately this:

It is nonsense to talk of opposing Fascism by bourgeois *democracy*. Bourgeois *democracy* is only another name for capitalism, and so is Fascism; to fight against Fascism on behalf of *democracy* is to fight against one form of capitalism on behalf of a second which is liable to turn into the first at any moment. The only real alternative to Fascism is workers' control. (...)

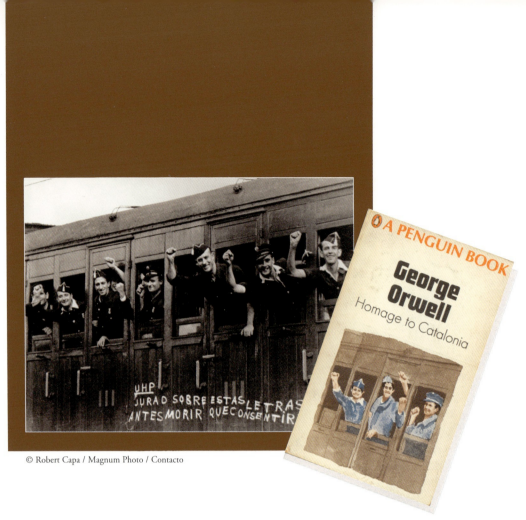

Barcelona. August, 1936. Republican soldiers leaving for the Aragon front. The sentence written on the train means "UHP (Union of Proletariat Brothers) swear upon these fraternal letters that you will sooner dye than live under tyranny".

The photograph taken by Robert Capa probably inspired the artist who draw the cover page of the publication "Homage to Catalonia" in the edition of 1968 by Penguin Books RIGHT.

© Robert Capa / Magnum Photo / Contacto

ANARCHISM

George Orwell

(...) The Anarchist's view point is less easily defined. In any case the loose term "Anarchism" is used to cover a multitude of opinions. The huge block of unions making up the Confederación Nacional de Trabajadores (CNT, the Anarcho Syndicalist Trade Union Confederation), with round about two million members in all, had for its political organ the Federación Anarquista Ibérica (FAI, Iberian Anarchist Federation), an actual Anarchist organization. (...)

(...) Roughly speaking, the CNT-FAI stood for:

1. Direct control over industry by the workers engaged in each industry, e.g. transport, the textile factories, etc.;
2. Government by local committees and resistance to all forms of centralized authoritarianism;
3. Uncompromising hostility to the bourgeoisie and the Church. (...)

(...) The Communist's emphasis is always on centralism and efficiency, the Anarchist's on liberty and equality. Anarchism is deeply rooted in Spain and is likely to outlive Communism when the Russian influence is withdrawn. (...)

(...) What was more important was that once the war had been narrowed down to a "war for democracy" it became impossible to make any large-scale appeal for working-class aid abroad. If we face facts we must admit that the working class of the world has regarded the Spanish war with detachment. Tens of thousands of individuals came to fight, but the tens of millions behind them remained apathetic. (...)

Coffee shops were often the social meeting spots. Archie and George Orwell met at least once in a bar in Barcelona. The photograph corresponds to the Café de la Opera in The Ramblas, in front of the Opera House El Liceu, not far from the Poliorama Hotel that hosted the headquarters of the POUM. Orwell stayed on continuous duty on the roof of the Hotel Colon during the political and military battle that initiated the disappearance of the POUM in May 1937.

© Reproduced with permission of F. Català Roca

CONTRADICTIONS IN THE BAR

(...) It is easy to see why, at this time, I preferred the Communists' viewpoint to that of the POUM. The Communists had a definite practical policy, an obviously better policy from the point of view of the common sense which looks only a few months ahead. And certainly the day-to-day policy of the POUM, their propaganda and so forth, was unspeakably bad; it must have been so, or they would have been able to attract a bigger mass-following. What clinched everything was that the Communists – so it seemed to me – were getting on with the war while we and the Anarchists were standing still. This was the general feeling at the time. The Communists had gained power and a vast increase in membership partly by appealing to the middle classes against the revolutionaries, but partly also because they were the only people who looked capable of winning the war. The revolutionary purism of the POUM though I saw its logic, seemed to me rather futile. After all, the one thing that mattered was to win the war. (...)

Orwell meets Cochrane

(...) I had one interesting meeting in a bar in Barcelona with a tall Englishman with big feet, who had been fighting with the POUM militia. In the course of the conversation I criticised the anarchist and POUM militia for not capturing Huesca and Zaragoza and linking up with the Basques. He argued fiercely that the anarchist and the POUM had been perfectly correct to consolidate their revolution before thinking of assistance for the Communists in Madrid. I later asked him why he had joined the POUM. As far as I remember he admitted it was by chance. They were the first people he met and he liked them. He said his name was Blair. I often wonder what would have happened to his literary output if he had joined the International Brigade. I later enjoyed his books more than I had that conversation. (...)*

* Cochrane AL, Blythe M. One Man's Medicine. An Autobiography of Professor Archie Cochrane. London: BMJ (Memoir Club), 1989. Reproduced by permission of Max Blythe.

...AND THE INTERNATIONAL PROPAGANDA

*A portrait of members of the International Brigades frequently used to show the ethnic diversity of the volunteers.
Archives of the International Brigades in Moscow.*

George Orwell

(...) Early in life I have noticed that no event is ever correctly reported in a newspaper, but in Spain, for the first time, I saw newspaper reports which did not bear any relation to the facts, not even the relationship which is implied in an ordinary lie. I saw great battles reported where there had been no fighting, and complete silence where hundreds of men had been killed. I saw troops who had fought bravely denounced as cowards and traitors, and others who had never seen a shot fired hailed as the heroes of imaginary victories; and I saw newspapers in London retailing these lies and eager intellectuals building emotional superstructures over events that had never happened. (...)

(...) This kind of thing is frightening to me, because it often gives me the feeling that the very concept of objective truth is fading out of the world. After all, the chances are that those lies, or at any rate similar lies, will pass into history. (...)

(...) Yet, after all, some kind of history will be written, and after those who actually remember the war are dead, it will be universally accepted. So for all practical purposes the lie will have become truth. (...)

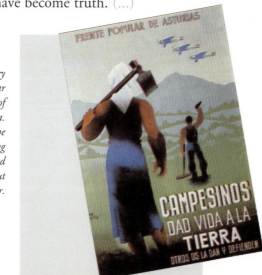

The poster making industry flourished during the war showing very early the power of political propaganda. Orwell was appalled by the ability of the press in creating official truth. Archie remained profoundly skeptical throughout the war and thereafter.

Brochure describing the Thaelmann Brigade (named after a German leader from the Communist Party) and edited in Barcelona by German refugees. Archie interacted with the Thaelmans Brigade in Grañen taking advantage of his mastery of the German language.

(...) After the fighting more particularly after the slanging-match in the newspapers it was difficult to think about this war in quite the same naively idealistic manner as before. I suppose there is no one who spent more than a few weeks in Spain without being in some degree disillusioned. My mind went back to the newspaper correspondent whom I had met my first day in Barcelona, and who said to me: *This war is a racket the same as any other.* The remark had shocked me deeply, and at that time (December) I did not believe it was true; it was not true even now, in May; but it was becoming truer. The fact is that every war suffers a kind of progressive degradation with every month that it continues, because such things as individual liberty and a truthful press are simply not compatible with military efficiency. (...)

Poster of the French section of the International Antifascist Solidarity (IAS) kept at the International Institute for Social History in Amsterdam.

Reproduced with permission of the International Institute of Social History

THE PARTY MILITIA AND THE POPULAR ARMY

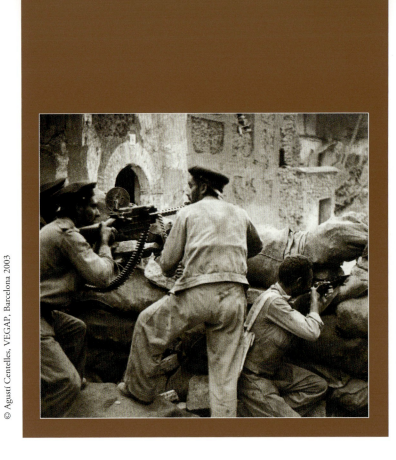

Street fighting in Belchite. September 1937. The militia was an informal and poorly equipped army. Most of the time the command was in the hands of political commissars of one or another affiliation. Anarchist columns were notorious for their lack of supplies.

© Agustí Centelles, VEGAP, Barcelona 2003

George Orwell

(...) When the Popular Army, which was a "non-political" army organized on more or less ordinary lines, was raised at the beginning of 1937, the party militias were theoretically incorporated in it. But for a long time the only changes that occurred were on paper; the new Popular Army troops did not reach the Aragon front in any numbers till June, and until that time the militia-system remained unchanged (...)

(...) The essential point of the system was social equality between officers and men. Everyone from general to private drew the same pay, ate the same food, wore the same clothes, and mingled on terms of complete equality. If you wanted to slap the general commanding the division on the back and ask him for a cigarette, you could do so, and no one thought it curious. In theory at any rate each militia was a democracy and not a hierarchy. It was understood that orders had to be obeyed, but it was also understood that when you gave an order you gave it as comrade to comrade and not as superior to inferior. There were officers and Non Commanding Officers (NCOs), but there was no military rank in the ordinary sense; no titles, no badges, no heel-clicking and saluting. They had attempted to produce within the militias a sort of temporary working model of the classless society. Of course there was no perfect equality, but there was a nearer approach to it than I had ever seen or than I would have thought conceivable in time of war. (...)

(...) Actually, a newly raised draft of militia was an undisciplined mob not because the officers called the private Comrade but because raw troops are always an undisciplined mob. In practice the democratic 'revolutionary' type of discipline is more reliable than might be expected. In a workers' army discipline is theoretically voluntary. It is based on class-loyalty, whereas the discipline of a bourgeois conscript

The Rakosi Battalion getting ready a machine gun. The Popular Army received better equipment, uniforms and weaponry.

army is based ultimately on fear. (The Popular Army that replaced the militias was midway between the two types.). In the militias the bullying and abuse that go on in an ordinary army would never have been tolerated for a moment. The normal military punishments existed, but they were only invoked for very serious offences. When a man refused to obey an order you did not immediately get him punished; you first appealed to him in the name of comradeship. Cynical people with no experience of handling men will say instantly that this would never 'work', but as a matter of fact it does 'work' in the long run (...)

(...) At the beginning the apparent chaos, the general lack of training, the fact that you often had to argue for five minutes before you could get an order obeyed, appalled and infuriated me. I had British Army ideas, and certainly the Spanish militias were very unlike the British Army. But considering the circumstances they were better troops than one had any right to expect. (...)

(...) In May for a short while I was acting-lieutenant in command of about thirty men, English and Spanish. We had all been under fire for months, and I never had the slightest difficulty in getting an order obeyed or in getting men to volunteer for a dangerous job. Revolutionary discipline depends on political consciousness - on an understanding of why orders must be obeyed; it takes time to diffuse this, but it also takes time to drill a man into an automaton on the barrack-square (...)*

* Orwell G. *Homage to Catalonia*. London: Penguin Books, 1968.

Copyright © George Orwell 1937. Extracts reproduced by permission of Bill Hamilton as the Literary Executor of the Estate of the Late Sonia Brownell Orwell and Secker & Warburg Ltd.

ARCHIE WAS AMONGST THE 2 000 VOLUNTEERS FROM BRITAIN THAT JOINED THE INTERNATIONAL BRIGADES, LARGELY ORGANIZED BY THE COMMUNIST PARTIES IN EUROPE. GEORGE ORWELL AND OTHER BRITISH NATIONALS WENT TO SPAIN BUT WERE ENROLLED IN THE POPULAR ARMY.
SCIENTISTS SUCH AS MADAME CURIE AND ALBERT EINSTEIN SHOWED SUPPORT AND SOLIDARITY.

F. XAVIER BOSCH, JUNE 2003

* *Credit & Legend, see page 326.*

THE INTERNATIONAL BRIGADES

Professor
Josep Maria Solé i Sabaté
Historian

Doctor of Contemporary History and Professor at the Autonomous University of Barcelona, Dr Solé Sabaté was appointed the first Director of the Museum of Catalan History. Specialising in the Spanish Civil War and its aftermath, he has authored fifteen widely recognized publications. In 1986, he received (jointly with Joan Vilaroya) the Research Award for his book Catalunya sota les bombes 1936-1939 *(Catalonia under the bombs 1936-1939). He has been a Visiting Professor in many universities in Europe and America.*

THE INTERNATIONAL BRIGADES

Few popular armed movements have produced such wide support throughout the international community, regardless of political or social allegiance, as the International Brigades.

Anti-fascist solidarity had already begun with the initiation of the Fascist revolt in July 1939. On the same Sunday, 19 July 1939, Barcelona was scheduled to host the opening of the alternative Popular Olympics in opposition to the Nazi propaganda surrounding the Berlin Olympics. Politically committed athletes joined with the people fighting the military rebels on the streets of Barcelona. Some joined the armed militants in the Catalonian capital and a few went as far as joining the Aragon front to fight fascists, who would later be identified as Franco supporters. Anti-fascist volunteers arrived in Spain shortly after the military revolt began. The Comintern of the Third International had prepared them for a double objective: to give hope worldwide to the idea of freedom under fascism and totalitarian power and to reinforce the prestige of the Soviet communism which was already being challenged by the parties that would resist Stalinist orthodoxy. The success of the response to stop the military up-rising was partly promoted as an international reaction to the direct military intervention by Mussolini's fascist government and Hitler's Nazi government.

Governments of the countries of Europe decided to sign a non-intervention agreement in August 1936. The policy was unpopular and because it was grossly violated, served to fuel the response to reinforce the International Brigades. The recruitment centre for the Brigades was located in Paris to facilitate the arrival of volunteers from around the world and their departure for Republican Spain.

Andre Malraux posing in front of one of the planes of the squadron "España". The fighting unit was made of French planes that were sent to Spain before the embargo in 1936. Photograph taken by Raymond Maréchal, who, later on in Barcelona. assisted Malraux in the making of the film "Sierra de Teruel".

From the very beginning, the Spanish conflict gave rise to a collective fascination. A shared panic at the idea of a defeated Republic united men and women, intellectuals and workers, employed and unemployed, whites and blacks, believers, non-believers, and agnostics. People from everywhere came to join the International Brigades. All had a firm purpose: to oppose fascism and fight against its crimes to the end. Paradoxically, Europeans ignored the crimes of Stalinism to join the Brigades, largely organized by Communists, to fight in Spain for the right of democracy and human rights. Voluntary participation was seen as a fight for the same principles that were upheld in their own countries. Indeed, fighting in Spain was perceived as fighting in their own countries.

Almost a quarter, of the 40 000 international brigadiers came from France; more than 3 000 from Italy; over 5 000 from Germany and Austria; 2 800, including the famous Lincoln Brigade, came from the USA; about 2 000 were from the United Kingdom, and the remainder from a variety of other countries. In total, there were 35-40 000, but, never more than 15 000 at the same time. Volunteers from 51 states were counted, and it is remarkable that their diverse backgrounds came together in a sort of universal brotherhood. The symbolism they created has prevailed in time and space. Amongst them there was not the bitter infighting that took place between Communists and Anarchists, militants from the POUM, Trotskyists and Socialists. For the most part, values of idealism prevailed.

The mythology of unselfish help from an international youth explains why the Spanish government with the support of all political parties in 1996, some 60 years after the start of the war, granted Spanish citizenship to all survivors of the International Brigades who had participated in the Civil War. The government

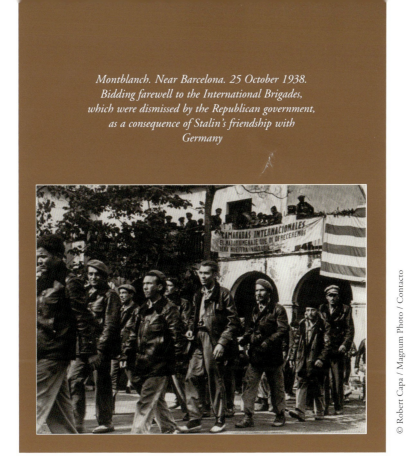

*Montblanch. Near Barcelona. 25 October 1938.
Bidding farewell to the International Brigades,
which were dismissed by the Republican government,
as a consequence of Stalin's friendship with
Germany*

The farewell to the Brigades in Barcelona was the last act of enthusiasm by the Republic and those who lived through the sufferings of the war. This sentiment was expressed in the words of the Communist leader, La Pasionaria:

Mothers... Women!... Talk to your children. Tell them about the men from the International Brigades. Tell them how they crossed seas and mountains, passing through armed frontiers, guarded by ferocious dogs who wanted to sink their fangs into them, reaching our land like freedom crusaders to fight and die for the liberty and independence of Spain. Tell them how they were threatened by German and Italian fascism. They left everything behind: Love, land, home, wealth, mother, wife, brothers, children and came to say to us: Here we are! Your cause, the cause of Spain, is our own cause. It is the common cause of every free human being.

The international brigadiers who fought in Spain were executed without trial when they were captured as prisoners. They were a symbol that the rebel Spanish military, and the political ideologies that gave them support, hated. It is not surprising then that, even after 60 years, the right-wing parties in Spain still fear the myth of the heroic Brigades. They still have not been able to acknowledge their role. The opposite has ben done by the democratic parties of the left and by the Catalan parliament, as soon as it was reconstructed after 40 years of dictatorship.

EXTRACT FROM
THE SPANISH CIVIL WAR
BY HUGH THOMAS

(...) The total number of foreigners who fought in the International Brigade was about 40 000, though the Brigades never exceeded 18 000 at any one time. Probably another 5 000 men fought at one time or another in other units of the Republican armies, chiefly in Catalonia. The largest national group of volunteers were the 10 000 French of whom 3 000 were killed. Germany and Austria together contributed about 5 000 of whom 2 000 died. Italy came the next with 3 350. The United States contributed about 2 800. Of these, about 900 were killed. There were about 2 000 British volunteers, of whom over 500 were killed and 1 200 wounded. There were about 1 000 Canadian volunteers, 1 200 Jugoslavs, 1 000 Hungarians, and 1 000 Scandinavians. The other 5 000 volunteers came from what was claimed to be 53 nations. Perhaps 3 000 members of the Brigades were Jewish in origin. The number of Russians in Spain was certainly under 2 000 and probably never exceeded 500 at one time. All served, however, in comparatively important positions, such as on the General Staff or as instructors at the Republican air fields. In the winter of 1936-7 most of the Russian aircraft in Spain were flown by Russian pilots, though later these were taken over by Spaniards. In addition, probably over 20 000 other foreigners served the Republic at one time or another, either in Medical Services or in other auxiliary units.

The Mexican Government sent about two million dollars' worth of military aid to the Republic. The State Department calculated that over two million dollars' worth of aid had been collected by 26 American organisations of whom they approved as bona fide relief bodies.

These figures do not give a full picture of the foreign aid to Spain, since both sides bought wherever they could from private firms abroad. Certain American war material was found among Republican arms captured by the Nationalists. The State Department, however, concluded that nearly all of this had been exported earlier than the arms embargo. No American arms were found with the Nationalist forces. Certain American war material did, however, find its way to Republican Spain via the Soviet Union and Mexico. (...)*

* Thomas H. The Spanish Civil War. London: Penguin, 2003
© Reproduced by permission of Penguin Books Ltd

ESTADO MAYOR		Terson, Lucien	
Walter, Carlos	General	Lazar, Franz	
Muñoz Lizcano, Julián	Coronel C. Pol.	Trifunoff, Stefan	
Putz	"	Etleny, Nicolás	
Petrovich Dusanz	Tte. Cor. C. Pol.	Vladie, Ivo	
Sabadosz Sandor	Comandante	Valentincic, Marx	
Morena Arenas, Luciano	Capitán	Bergfeld, Simón	
Biro, Oskar	"	Ksizanger, León	
Denis, Arturo	"	Lerat, Ferdinad	
Esinoski, André	"	Steffan, Antoine	
Kutin, José	"	Breugnot George	
Campiña Ontiveros, Antonio	"	**SERVICIO SANITARIO**	
Korcheevski, Alejandro	"	Dr. Dubois	
Martón Francisco, Pascual	"	Dr. Hart	
Raikovich, Stefan	Teniente	Dr. Asensio, Angel	
Malkmus, Teodor	"	Dr. Cohcrane	
Carrasco Serrano, Pablo	"	Abad, Román	
Perry, Raoul	"	Guerra, Guillermo	
Lazar, Franz	"	Dr. Grone	
Trifonoc, Estefan	"	Dr. Saxton	
Szurek, Alck	"	Dr. Frhmann	
Campos, Antonio	"	Sr. Steele	
Iraola, Alfredo	"	Dr. Hill	
Kersten Elsen, Herbert	"	Dr. Vinuesa	
COMPAÑIA DIVISORIA		Kupcicz, Wladimir	
Tzimbaluk, Vinceslab	Teniente	Dr. Ostry	
de la Faille, Gerard	"	Mlfred Rocklay	
Butrvski, Vladimir	"	Ramos, Chistoph	

Names of some of the members of the Health Services in the International Brigades. Archie's name is underlined as if it had been misplaced.

© Agustí Centelles, VEGAP, Barcelona 2003

*(...) One realized afterwards (...)
that one had been in a community
where hope was more normal
that apathy or cynicism,
where the word "comrade" stood
for comradeship (...)
One had breathed the air of equality (...)
for the Spanish militias,
while they lasted,
were a sort of microcosm
of a classless society. (...)**

* Orwell G. *Homage to Catalonia*. London: Penguin Books, 1968.

Copyright © George Orwell 1937.
Extracts reproduced by permission of Bill Hamilton as the Literary Executor of the Estate of the Late Sonia Brownell Orwell and Secker & Warburg Ltd.

ORGANIZING THE TRAFFIC OF WOUNDED AND SICK
WAS PART OF THE SUCCESS AND PRIDE
OF THE MEDICAL SERVICES ON THE REPUBLICAN SIDE.

MOISÈS BROGGI, JULY 2002.

* *Credit & Legend, see page 326.*

WAR MEDICINE: ARCHIE COCHRANE AND THE SURGICAL TRIAGE

Doctor Moisès Broggi

I met Archie around the first of March, 1937, on my way back to Torrelodones after the battle of Jarama. We were both heading for the XIV Brigade where I was named the head of the surgical unit. That unit was made up of English and French, where almost all of the higher-ranking medical personnel were English. The majority of the people were academics and well educated. Among them was lieutenant doctor Archibald Cochrane, who stood out due to his composure and distinguished looks. He was of average height, had red hair, was impeccably dressed and spoke French correctly. They say that, when he had come with one of the first English missions that had arrived around the end of 1936, the FAI had confiscated the car that he was driving!

THE ORGANIZATION OF THE HEALTH SERVICES AT THE BATTLE FRONT

Torrelodones was a summer village, close to the mountain range that separates the two Castillas, made up of isolated chalets and gardens. We entered a large house where they were waiting for us and showed us to a luxuriously furnished room with three beds already prepared for us. When we were ready to retire for the evening, the lights were turned on and a picturesque figure, resembling a ghost, appeared, carrying a tray with a bedtime meal welcoming us. He was a tall and trim, bowed frequently and wore a strange outfit, a sort of shirt that went down to his feet, and spoke French very well. It was Commandant Tudor Hart, the surgeon from London, who had arrived with the first of the British missions. He was now assigned as head of the surgical team from what remained of the XIV and XV Brigades that were reorganizing there.

A good portion of the medical personnel from the Brigades stayed in the villa where we were. The rest stayed in the nearby houses, joined by the gardens. Already on the first day, when we went down for breakfast, we were fully aware that the food ration was not the most critical issue and that the ham that I had bought in Albacete, in case of emergency, was left spoiling in the corner of a cabinet. It was to say that we lacked nothing and that we were treated with total respect. We grew to admire the order and the discipline that prevailed, especially due to the contrast, represented by the disorder, that was seen in the other troops. Hart introduced the personnel. Almost all were foreigners, mostly British and French. The Spanish were in the minority. Everyone talked about the recent battle of Jarama, where so many lives were lost, and about the heroic feat of Commandant Nathan. He had decided to try out his luck at the bridge of Arganda and the road from Valencia, without which Madrid would have been isolated and irretrievably lost.

At that time, Archie was with the group of Tudor Hart, a surgeon from London. In Torrelodones, three surgical teams were organized, the Hart team, the Quemada team, and ours. We were determined to be together to the end. What was just a single Brigade, converted, with time, into the 35th Division. This division was made up of four Brigades that formed an assault troop that took part in the principal battles of our war. In the battle of Guadarrama and, especially, that of Brunete, which was probably the bloodiest, Archie was right there by our side carrying out his important duty that was called the triage, or the sorting of the wounded that continuously poured into the hospital and sending them to the corresponding operating room. This was done in the order of priority, depending on the gravity of the wound. It was increasingly valuable at times when so many wounded were being rushed in. The task was alternated with another young doctor, Kenneth Sinclair Loutit, also English, and with whom I still keep close contact.

I can say that, during the time that Archie was with us, he made an important contribution to the Brigade. I remember, among other things, his receiving large quantities of tobacco; I don't know if it was delivered to him personally, or if he acted as an intermediary to some British benefactor.

After the defeat in Brunete, I lost sight of Cochrane, along with many other members of the surgical team that had been together up until this time. Everyone was left exhausted after that toil. Many of the British, at that time, returned to their country, and were substituted, for the most part, by Americans. I don't remember having seen Archie any more, neither in the battle of Belchite nor in the battle of Teruel. There we continued working along with Hart and Quemada, and possibly Archie. But, it's also possible that he withdrew along with Loutit, Thora, my scrub nurse, and other English comrades. Another possibility is that he had joined the Jolly team, a new surgeon that was a part of the same Division but worked separately from us. I knew nothing more of Archie until quite some time later.

On different trips that I made to England later on, I visited many of my old war friends. I was informed that Archie resided out of London, I think that it was Wales (I'm not quite certain of this). He was practising as an internist and had become well known in the field of public health. Afterwards, I don't remember the exact dates, I know he came for a brief stay in Barcelona, but I did not have the chance to see him. A friend, Acarín, who hosted him, told me that he had explained many stories about the Civil War. He had recounted about the time that he had been in the Brigade with us, that he had fought in the World War in which the Germans had held him as a prisoner of war in one of the eastern Mediterranean islands, and, finally, that he had returned to England where he went back to his important job in the field of public health.

Douglas Jolly, a colleague of Archie during the Ebro battle in 1938. Photograph from a journal named "Spain at War" published in London in 1938.

A surgical team in Torrelodones.
L to R: *Guardiola, Jordana, Broggi (author of this text) and Kiszely*

It's true that the Brigades had been left decimated, but they were soon replenished and re-enforced by the troops that were arriving from Albacete.

The other head of surgery was Luis Quemada, a native of Valladolid, who had been taken by surprise by the war while in Ciudad Real, where he practised surgery and was the director of the Provincial Hospital. He and Hart were both slightly older than me, I was not yet 30 and they were in their 40s.

Hart had been in Vienna with Böhler and knew his techniques well. We quickly agreed on important points, such as the best way to treat wounds of the extremities. Quemada was a good general surgeon, very responsible and who mastered abdominal surgery. He explained to me that he lived in Ciudad Real because he had passed the public competition exams from the hospital and that he was married to a Norwegian woman with whom he had a daughter. When the war broke out, he sent his family to Oslo, to his wife's parents. When the Brigades were starting to be formed, he offered to be a surgeon because he saw that it was the best organized part of the Republican army. He was accompanied by a helper by the name of Rojas, from Ciudad Real, and a farm worker from la Mancha named Timoteo Moreno who was illiterate but naturally bright, and had soon joined our team without any complaints from Quemada. Timoteo had become increasingly valuable to me because of his common sense, a great help in the hard times that came later on. The rebels of Valladolid had assassinated one of Quemada's brothers, also a doctor, because he held a political seat in the city government. He offered everything one needed and helped to orientate me in the middle of this new world that we found ourselves in. These three teams, Hart, Quemada, and mine, were the teams that had to work together in the unit that was being organized in Torrelodones.

There were numerous doctors, orderlies, nurses and all the other health care personnel required for an important centre. Of the doctors, other than those previously mentioned, I especially remember Kenneth Loutit, who had just graduated from Oxford; Johnny Kiszely, a Hungarian military doctor; Reggie Saxton, a haematologist and an analyst; Conrad Crome and Archibald Cochrane both British; Boulka, Polish; Ludwig, Viennese, José Vinuesa, a dentist from Segovia; and also Jordana and Guardiola, both of whom had come with me. All were assigned to assist in the tasks of the surgical unit except Boulka, Ludwig and Crome, who held administrative positions or were tied to the central government. While the latter declared that they were affiliated to the communist party, others had no concrete political commitment. They were there for different reasons, as was in our case, like Quemada and Vinuesa, who joined that side mainly because that's where they found themselves at the moment of the revolution. Among the heath care personnel, liberal attitudes predominated. They thought that they were acting on the side of reason, that they were fulfilling a humanitarian mission and, also, they were attracted to a certain spirit of adventure. I'm sure that Hart and Loutit were driven by family motives; and I suspect Loutit was attracted to Thora, a very intelligent and determined nurse, whom he followed all the way from England. Everyone had their own motives. I found it interesting to find out the motives that had driven each one to leave their country, home, and families, to be thrown into an adventure like this one. Some were from rich families who even made contributions to the Brigades, for example, sending packages of English cigarettes that were handed out in abundance and were well appreciated by everyone.

NOT ALL CHEESE THAT SMELLS BAD, IS BAD

148

1

Group of researchers who laid the ground for the widespread use of penicillin. Centre (sitting in dark suit) Professor Lord Florey (Nobel Laureate). Right (sitting) Professor Chain, chemist who stabilized penicillin (Nobel Laureate). Professor Trueta, standing behind Lord Florey, was among the first to give an injection of penicillin to one of his patients. (Dunn School of Pathology, Oxford 1940).

2

On 6 May 1943, Josep Trueta received an Honoris Causa doctoral degree from Oxford University. In the photograph with Professor Girdlestone.

3

Severo Ochoa and Josep Trueta, Oxford 1961.

4

Josep Trueta between Sir Hans Krebs (his right) and Sir Ernst Chain (his left), both Nobel Laureates in 1953 and 1945.
Photograph taken in Barcelona during an homage to Professor Severo Ochoa.

Josep Trueta with the Queen Mother of England.

JOSEP TRUETA I RASPALL
BARCELONA, 1897-1977

Surgery and orthopaedics flourish during war times and major advances usually follow the trail of war surgeons. Josep Trueta is probably the best known of the group of creative surgeons that took part in the Spanish Civil War. His method to cope with gangrene after war wounds, later known as the *Trueta method*,* was highly efficient in the prevention of amputations, septicaemia and death. In 1939, Dr Trueta went into exile, first to Perpignan and later to Oxford where he received the Honoris Causa doctorate in 1943. His experiences in the Spanish Civil War were then used extensively during World War II in Europe and at the African front. In 1941 he published *The Spirit of Catalonia* and in 1976 he received the Honoris Causa doctorate at the Autonomous University of Barcelona. At the reception in his honour on this occasion, he presented his last public address:

> *Having left Catalonia at a time when democracy was dying, it gives me great satisfaction to receive this honour at a time when democracy is returning... Liberty is essential to my life. Today's ceremony represents my true return home, to a country that I left because I did not want to see the death of its liberty.*

* The *Trueta method*, initially called *the Spanish method* or *the Catalan method* consisted of the immediate surgical cleaning of the wound, excision of the devitalized tissue and occlusion with a plaster cast. On removal of the cast, if the wound was correctly excised, there was a powerful and revolting smell and a clean, granulated scarring tissue. In 1939 Dr Trueta reported on 1073 cases with less than a 1% failure rate.

Josep Trueta in 1963 at a reception with the Baroness Rothschild and André Malraux. Trueta had just received the distinction "Officier de la Legion d'Honneur".

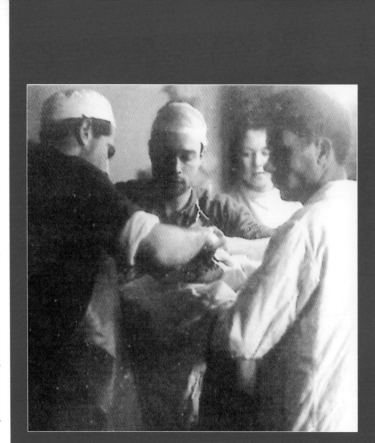

Dr Broggi during a surgical procedure in Teruel. In the photography is also Timoteo with a white coat.

As an example of one of the many motives, I note Kinszely, who was about my age. He was from a wealthy family from Budapest and after finishing his studies, he took a competition exam for a position as a military doctor. He received a degree as a lieutenant. His father, as a reward, paid for a trip to Italy where he went to visit various cities and the beautiful sites of that country. On his return to Hungary and the money spent, he found out that in Marsella they were recruiting people to go to Spain with the Brigade, so he joined up thinking that it was a good way to travel and visit another interesting country.

The majority of the people who formed the health care sector tended to have more humanitarian than political motives. The nurses were professionally well prepared. They had come almost as if they were on a religious mission. Some had arrived earlier, at the end of '36, with the group that came to Barcelona with Loutit and Hart, at the Aragon front. Dorothy Rutter had studied theology, and Patience had gone, after the war here, to China with an Evangelic Mission. Thora Silverstone was the surgical nurse assigned to our team; Ruth, the Irish nurse, was with Quemada's team; and Phyllis was with Hart's teams. Also, among the doctors, nurses, orderlies, and ambulance drivers, were young university students who were influenced by the communist propaganda, a very notable trend at that time in all of democratic Europe, contrary to the doctrines and the methods of the Italian Fascists and of the German Nazis. I remember that one of them was named Clive, a direct descendent from the famous Clive of India, the creator of the Company of the Indies and a principal founder of the English colonial empire.

Archie having his uniform repaired by a nurse in a quiet moment during the Spanish Civil War.

Of the administration, I must mention an Australian named Eileen Palmer and a very polite young Spanish woman named Aurora Fernandez, who had studied at the Instituto Escuela of Madrid, one of the few places in the city where the people could move out with a certain amount of freedom. She reminded me of a very efficient teacher from Sarinyena, who had treated the Nogueras with a great deal of humanity. I'm sure that this kind of people would do good with anything and any kind of political ideas.

Apart from the medical personnel, the entire group of brigadiers, in general, were very heterogeneous. There was a little of everything. Besides idealists, poets, journalists, and university students, there were people who were running from their countries, following their left-wing ideas, others, because they were liberals, communists, Jewish, and others who were driven by the spirit of adventure. This was the case with Kiszely. All together, it was a very diverse group, united for a common cause, to fight for a better society, and to oppose fascist despotism.

My interest in biographies and history has allowed me to keep alive my memories of our war. With respect to the military, it is worth mentioning the publication by Manuel Tagueña Lacoste "Testimonio de dos Guerras" (Witness of Two Wars). The author is a professor in physics and mathematics, a communist at the time, who became successively the chief officer of a Company, a Batalion, a Brigade and finally of the XV Corps of the Republican Army. The latter was one of the key players of the limited winning intervals, for our side, of the Ebro battle in the summer of 1938. With respect to health care in our Army, reading the biography of Dr Trueta is a matter of pride and comfort.

But the sad reality was rather different. At the time I was a student aged 19 enrolled as an infantry trooper in the anarchist-ruled 14th Division under the command of Cipriano Mera. While operating on the front lines of Guadalajara and Teruel, I witnessed a political commissar who recognised that, because we were anarchists, we would not receive the support of planes, artillery or armoured cars and had to rely merely on our courage, our rifles and a few machine guns. That was all the encouragement we received to push forward to consolidate the line between Escandon and Gandesa.

Our health services were honoured to have a medical Captain who offered his good will and, I suppose, his science as well. However, we were dramatically deprived of any medical equipment or medicines. At some point in time our doctor had only two options to relieve suffering: if conditions were traumatic, he would recommend iodine and if they were medical, he would prescribe aspirin.

Jaume Bosch i Pardo
14th Division

FOUR WORDS TO WIN A WAR

IODINE / ASPIRIN BOLYE / BOLI

While acting as a medical officer caring for a contingent of Jugoslav prisoners of war, Archie learned some Serbo-Croatian. For some time his medical rounds included and were limited to two magic words:

Bolye (better) and *Boli* (pain)

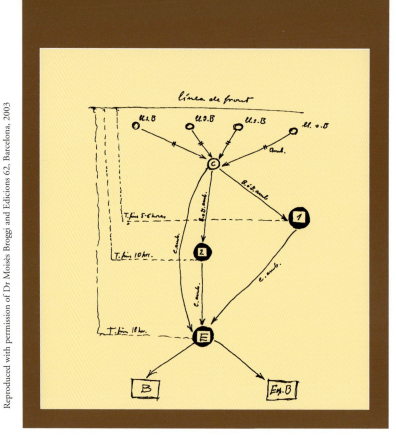

The transfer of the wounded from the front line was organised in stations: to the ambulance waiting posts (C), mobile hospitals (1) where patients stayed up to 5/6 hours, the rearguard hospitals (2 and E) where hospitalisation lasted for up to 18 hours and the Base Hospital (B).

When I became re-incorporated again, I found my unit stationed in tents on the outskirts of Tembleque, a village in the province of Toledo. Our team incorporated two new lieutenant doctors, Drs Dénia and Fausto González, both from Madrid. We were notified that our medical team was no longer limited to the XIV Brigade, but formed a part of the 35 Division, which also included the XV, XI and the XII Brigades, which were previously assigned with the name Thaelmann and Garibaldi, respectively. Initially, they had been formed by central Europeans mainly Germans in the former, and Italians in the latter. In fact, this 35 Division held the bulk of the International Brigades. Later on, our countrymen would replace the casualties. They also announced that another team, headed by a surgeon from New Zealand, Douglas W Jolly, would be added.

As was promised, at the end of June, the first mobile surgical unit was delivered. The first Auto-Chir (Mobile Surgery) included every detail and condition that we could have imagined. It was financed by a popular Swiss union. It was an enclosed truck, with a door at the rear and a self-sufficient operating theatre. In no time one could set up an operating room anywhere and start working without missing a single detail.

The driver, Joe Coomes, was responsible, not just for the truck, but also for having everything sterilized as specified by the surgical nurses. He was helped by Andrews, a member of the medical group from Britain, who was a good mechanic and electrician, adept at fixing all sorts of problems.

At the door of the Auto-chir Dorothy and Andrews.

A few days after the delivery of the Auto-Chir and after receiving the news of the fall of Bilbao (18th of June), we were notified that we should have everything prepared to re-locate. We did not know where we were headed, but we saw that we were leaving Madrid behind us and that we were heading north, in the direction of Las Rozas and the area near the mountain range that was so well known to us until we arrived at San Lorenzo of Escorial, where a huge monastery with the graves of the Spanish kings was located. We arrived at night, close to the Sanctuary, and away from the village. There we installed the hospital in just a few hours and had the operating rooms almost ready to go, as in Navacerrada. The only difference was that now the hospital was much larger and the number of beds had increased as well.

Thora still supervised the operating room, assisted by Timoteo and Andrews, who acted as the link between the operating room and the Auto-Chir. With the addition of Fausto and of Dénia, we had two more helpers and two more anesthetists available, which facilitated the job. The three teams agreed that Kiszely be in charge of the sorting of the wounded along with Loutit and Cochrane. A little while later, Jolly and his team arrived, with another Auto-Chir just like ours that they had just received. In due time, the Brigades would be outfitted with seven Auto-Chirs like these that would be distributed amongst the different units. A day later, the battle of Brunete started.

Professor
Max Blythe
Epidemiologist

Professor Max Blythe, co-author of Archie Cochrane's acclaimed biography One Man's Medicine, *combines interest in disease prevention and the recollections of leading contributors to clinical science. He is the founder of* Oxford's Medical Sciences Video-Archive, *based on his interviews with hundreds of leading 20th century doctors and medical scientists, including Archie. He is less well known for his role in establishing nursing and midwifery degree courses in Oxford where, until recently, he was Reader in Clinical Sciences at Oxford Brookes University. Now he writes and lectures on his research and prevention interests. His latest scientific publication,* Muscle Sounds[1], *is the first monograph on the application of muscle acoustics in clinical research and rehabilitation medicine. Two further medical biographies are in preparation. He looks forward to a film of Archie's life "in black and white, reflecting the greynesses tough-forging him". He is a member of Green College and the Faculty of Clinical Medicine, Oxford University. Times with Archie at Rhoose Farm plotting the text of* One Man's Medicine *rank high in indelible memories.*

1. Stokes, Maria & Blythe, Max. Muscle sounds in physiology, sports science and clinical investigation: applications and history of mechanomyography. Oxford: Medintel (Medical Intelligence), 2001.

ARCHIE COCHRANE IN THE SPANISH CIVIL WAR:

(*)

SPAIN, 1936-37

EXTRACT FROM *ONE MAN'S MEDICINE, AN AUTOBIOGRAPHY OF PROFESSOR ARCHIE COCHRANE* BY ARCHIBALD L COCHRANE WITH MAX BLYTHE. COPYRIGHT ©: MAX BLYTHE

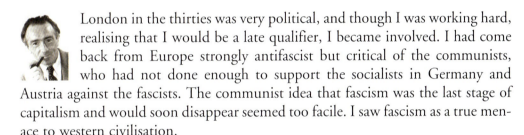London in the thirties was very political, and though I was working hard, realising that I would be a late qualifier, I became involved. I had come back from Europe strongly antifascist but critical of the communists, who had not done enough to support the socialists in Germany and Austria against the fascists. The communist idea that fascism was the last stage of capitalism and would soon disappear seemed too facile. I saw fascism as a true menace to western civilisation.

It was the time of the Hunger March, Mosley's Blackshirts, and a round of antifascist meetings. Then came the Popular Fronts in France and Spain, and a stream of refugees. Finally, in the summer of 1936, Franco and his Moors invaded Spain[1] and the pot boiled over. My friends and I feared that if Spain went fascist and joined with Hitler and Mussolini, France and the UK were doomed; but we were admittedly ignorant of the complexities of Spanish politics. We were incensed by the UK's commitment to a non-intervention pact,[2] especially when it became clear that Germany, Italy, and Portugal were openly flouting such a policy.

Behind the scenes in the UK an important Spanish Medical Aid Committee was set up. The president was Dr Christopher Addison MP,[3] and the main committee contained a galaxy of important names, with peers, MPs, professors, and leading communists appearing united. There was also a working committee, which I gather was left wing. Ostensibly, the intention was to organise and fund a field ambulance unit to serve the Spanish Republican cause. When an advertisement appeared asking for *offers* from doctors and medical students who were prepared to serve in Spain I began to think of joining them.

---

* *Copy of the military pass issued by the government of Catalonia for Archie to reach Albacete where the headquarters of the International Brigades were located.* Reproduced by permission of Max Blythe.

Source unknown

I thought I knew more about fascism and its probable effect on Western European civilization than most other British medical students. I was unmarried and had no one dependent on me. My friends and family would miss me if I were killed, but they would believe that I had died in a worthwhile cause. Those were my conscious thoughts, but I suspect there were other factors. I do not remember how conscious they were underneath my political excitement, but there were the elements of a real depression. I still sincerely wanted to do some worthwhile medical research, but the prospects seemed to get worse and worse. I had developed grave doubts about psychoanalysis and also knew that I was no good at laboratory research. On top of this, I now realised that I would never be a first rate clinician, which would bar my way to clinical research and any chance of following in the footsteps of the likes of Sir Thomas Lewis. All roads seemed barred. I think I discussed the idea of volunteering for the Spanish Medical Aid Ambulance Unit with Philip D'Arcy Hart and George (later Sir George) Pickering, and I think both of these tutors approved. There was, however, one unexpected difficulty. My great friend George Rink had been seriously ill, and although he was now off the danger list I still felt that the shock of telling him of my decision to go to Spain might cause a setback. Therefore I left a note with Richard Cohen's wife, Margaret, asking her to break the new when the time seemed right. She had become very fond of George during his illness and I knew that she would choose the right moment. It was also at this time that I told my sister of my decision. Although she seemed to thing little of the idea I still went ahead and volunteered, and dropped out of medical training for the second time. It was a very serious drop out, which indefinitely postponed my date of qualifying. I also ran the risk of being seriously wounded or even killed; but as an enthusiastic antifascist I volunteered.

Before recounting my subsequent experiences it seems only fair to admit how little I knew about the Spanish Civil War until I read Hugh Thomas's excellent book[4] many years afterwards. For a year, however, I did experience sectors of this war very clearly.

Although I have little recollection of the occasion, I understand that the small medical aid ambulance unit I joined attracted large crowds and tumultuous applause when it set out from London's New Oxford Street on its journey to Spain.[5] Those travelling by train were conveyed to the station in Daimlers supplied by the London Cooperative Society Funeral Department. The ambulances, trucks, and those travelling by road were led down to the ferry by my Triumph Gloria, with Lord Peter Churchill the front seat passenger. It was all well organised, but I hated such occasions and, being tired, slept throughout the ferry crossing. This meant that my meeting with other members of the party was delayed. Our arrival in Paris was marked by a tumultuous reception organised by Leon Jouhard, Secretary General of the Trade Union Federation, CGT. There were other receptions too. At one I was told that I had shaken hands with Tito, who then had a quite different name. I do not suppose it was true. With all this entertaining and sleeping late to recover from driving so far I still had little chance to get to know the other members of the unit well, although I did obtain insight into one member's mentality very clearly during a big political rally in Paris's Stade Bufalo, where the overwhelming cry was for more planes for Spain. He made a stupid speech and spoke for far too long. On the way down to Port Bou the next day I asked Churchill who the speaker was and discovered that he was the unit's chief political administrator. I was horrified and dubbed him my much-to-be-avoided political commissar of the future.

We probably attempted to complete the next stretch of the journey too quickly, hoping to catch up with those travelling by train. As a result we experienced our first casualty when one of the drivers crashed during a night-time leg of the operation and had to return to the UK injured. Another rapturous welcome awaited us in Port Bou, but I had already had enough of such demonstrations. My main objective was to avoid drink and get as much sleep as possible, ready for the journey to Barcelona; but one still had to make concessions to the public relations demands of the venture. After another massive reception in Barcelona I finally got to bed and had a long sleep.

I awoke to a very unexpected world: a city relaxing after a "great victory". The explanation was that the anarchist dominated public militias in Barcelona had in a few days dealt with the rebellious regular army units there and then used this success as a platform from which to launch an anarchistic class war over the whole of Catalonia, in which they seemed to have been completely successful. This presented the leaders of the field ambulance unit with something of a problem. I had already diagnosed several of the leading lights as secret party members who clearly wanted to link up with the International Brigade[6] in the Madrid area. Now they found themselves in a city dominated by the anarchists (FAI),[7] who wanted us to help on the northern Catalan front[8] to support, inter alia, the siege of Huesca.[9] I kept quiet, sunbathed, tried to learn Spanish and Catalan, and observe an anarchist city. I was young and immature and the idea of anarchism was mainly, for me, associated with Tolstoy. On the whole the city seemed to be doing rather well. It was clear that a revolution had taken place. Industry seamed to be run by

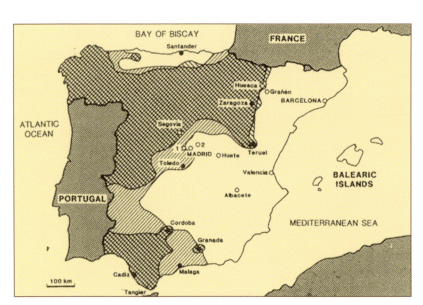

Figure 1
Places visited by the author (O) during the time he spent with the Spanish Medical Aid Committee's field ambulance unit, August 1936-August 1937.

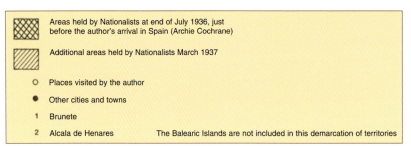

workers, the clergy had more or less disappeared, and there was no tipping; but life seemed to continue with a few shortages and a general feeling of good will. The only freedom that had been lost was religious freedom. Here, I also learnt something about the Trotskyites (POUM).[10] In England "Trotskyite" was a term of abuse - usually applied to me. In Barcelona they seemed an organised, serious political party which I ought to respect, not least because they had run the PSUC,[11] a combination of socialists and communists, into third place in the political power structure. Our unit was clearly going to be associated with the weakest political party. I had, at one time, an awful picture of myself helping to run a communist-dominated, front-line hospital in an anarchist revolution in Spain.

If there was further cause for disquiet it came from getting to know more about the team I had joined. I remember making a miserable, exaggerated summary of their credentials to myself after a few days in their company. There were two homosexuals, one alcoholic, one schizophrenic, eight open party members and about 10 secret party members.[12] Time showed that I was wrong, but not by much. (I was assisted in my diagnosis of secret party members by experience recently gained in London. There I knew two secret party members very well and had the chance to discern various characteristic phrases they used in discussing politics. Such conversational clues proved a great help in spotting other secret party members. My greatest triumph was to introduce two secret party members to each other, saying I was sure they would find they had a lot in common. Later they were both very angry).

On the other hand I found several members of the team I liked and admired.

Everyone liked and admired Aileen Palmer, an Australian, for her friendliness, devotion, and hard work. Everyone trusted her, although she was a self-confessed party member. Another self-confessed party member was Thora Silverthorne, a highly skilled surgical theatre sister. Despite a hard streak, she was friendly and amusing. I also liked Ruth Prothero, a charming, migrant doctor from Vienna. I talked fluent German and she introduced me to some of her Swiss and German friends. Margot Miller, another Australian, was a journalist and party member. She was a robust, efficient hard worker and later became a well known writer of detective stories. I enjoyed her company. A fifth female member of the original party I never did get to know. She was a complete loner and soon separated from us.

The males were worse than the females. Lord Feter was a good public relations figure, a fair administrator, and a friendly person; but I was worried that his fairly obvious homosexuality or bisexuality might run the unit into legal trouble, although I knew little of the laws in Spain. Kenneth Sinclair-Loutit, the official leader of the unit, was a likeable medical student and an obvious secret party member, but I did not think that he would be a good leader. He had a weak streak. O'Donnell, the chief administrator, who had made the bad speech in Paris, was even worse when I met him. I thought him stupid, conceited, and erratic. I certainly did not like the idea of his being in charge. The quartermaster, Emmanuel Julius, also seemed second rate and rather schizoid. The only surgeon, A Khan, who was studying in the UK for the FRCS, was reserved, non-political, and rather worried. Of the other two male doctors, one was an American, Sollenberger, and the other, Martin, a former member of the Royal Army Medical Corps. I took a poor view of them both. In addition there were two other medical students.

I did not have very close contact with the drivers. Harry Forster, a cheerful London taxi driver, proved a great success as an electrician on one occasion, but he moved on all too quickly. Alec Wainman, a Quaker photographer, was a charming, if neurotic, character, whom I liked but never got to know. Leslie Preger, an open communist, was rather a shocker. He admitted that he had only got into the unit because he had claimed that he spoke Spanish and knew about first aid. Both claims were false, but no one seems to have checked. The remaining drivers were the two Charlies, Hunt and Hurling. They were two young, extrovert, working class volunteers who wanted adventure and women. I enjoyed their presence at first, but they quite definitely disliked me, particularly my Cambridge accent. Fortunately they were not permanent. They motored backwards and forwards between London and Spain, so that I saw them only infrequently.

Inevitably some of these views are influenced by what happened later, but I have tried hard to recount my first impressions. Even if I have been only modestly accurate it is easy to understand how depressed I became in Barcelona in those early days. I found the anarchistic political picture confusing. I thought the Spanish Medical Aid Committee should have briefed us better, and I considered the choice of people it had made for the team unsatisfactory and possibly dangerous. I had expected at least one experienced casualty surgeon, one or two experienced male nurses, and some ambulance drivers who had military experience. It was difficult to believe, when I recalled the enthusiasm I had experienced in London, that there were not enough volunteers of the right kind. On the other hand, there was a suspicion that some undesirables got the job 'on the nod' if they had a party card, in order to ensure communist control of the unit. (Much later I tried to solve the problem by tracing the committee papers of the Spanish Medical Aid Committee. I was surprised that this was not possible. I was told that all the papers had been

Rural Spain in the 40's. Chariots under an olive tree.

bombed. As both committees had large memberships and all must have received papers, the bombing must have been very accurate and selective!) I wondered what to do and came to the conclusion that as I had volunteered I must stay on and see if something anti-fascist could emerge from the mess.

Another issue added to my early unhappiness in Spain. When it became clear that we had little alternative than to establish the field hospital in support of republican forces besieging Huesca, Peter Churchill, using a Michelin map, suggested Grañén as a suitable place because of its rail and road communications. It turned out to be a good choice geographically. He and Sinclair-Loutit asked me to lend them my car to go ahead and locate a suitable building. Most people would have asked me to drive them up, but I suppose they wanted to talk politics and I was not a party member. The result was unfortunate. They allowed the anarchists to steal the car. It was rumoured that it was due to Sinclair Loutit's carelessness. I was fond of this, my first car, which had already proved useful to the unit, and I was angry despite deciding not to make a fuss.[13] It was an incident that certainly increased my depression.

Our move to the windswept anarchist village of Grañén was on 3 September. The house of a fascist doctor who had fled the district was chosen as the best available for a field hospital. It was well situated as regards Huesca, where the main fighting was, and reasonably near the railway line. We worked hard at converting the house into a hospital, with two operating theatres, wards, and rooms for staff. The fighting at Huesca was always spasmodic, with increasingly long inter-vals between offensives. One such outburst of activity occurred shortly after we were ready and we coped surprisingly well. We had established a first aid post, with an ambulance,

Archie in uniform, in Spain in 1937, while serving with the Spanish Medical Aid Committee's Field Ambulance Unit in support of the International Brigades.

as close as possible to Huesca. There we came upon the Thaelman battalion of German volunteers,[14] who were pleased to hear of the existence of the hospital and with whom I communicated regularly as my German was better than anyone else's in the unit. They were stationed in a series of shallow trenches in front of Huesca; a remarkable group of men and one woman which included Hans Beimler,[15] former communist deputy to the Reichstag, and Ludwig Renn, author of the pacifist novel Der Krieg. I got to know them well. They were highly critical of the anarchists, who had run out of steam after Catalonia had been liberated. The Germans believed that with reasonable anarchistic support they could have taken Huesca and Zaragoza and linked up with the Basques to consolidate the northern front. Now they wanted to move to the Madrid front, where they thought the most important fighting would be.

A good deal of my time needed to be spent at the first aid post, giving me the opportunity to spend much of it with the Thaelmans. This was preferable to confining myself to the post and the companionship of Preger, with whom I often shared duties there. Even at the hospital life was dreary, although the regular staff seemed to be doing a job with the walking wounded, giving anti-tetanus injections, cleaning and dressing wounds, feeding the hungry, and setting them on trains for Barcelona. I saw far less of how the more serious cases fared, although I did transport many of them to the hospital from the field, including some with serious head wounds. It was in this first period that the unit experienced the loss of one of its own members. Our quartermaster, who had already appeared erratic, disappeared and was later reported killed at the front some distance away. We gave him a full, rather embarrassing, military funeral. He was the one I thought to be schizoid.

Then came a lull. This provided an opportunity for us all to meet and a flood of complaints to be vented. The main one was about food, which consisted of hard meat, beans, olive oil, and garlic, resulting in a painful type of diarrhoea we dubbed the "Grañén gripes." There was little we could do about it, except write to the committee in London. Similar action was taken as regards our lack of news. We felt cut off. We even lost our radio. I cannot remember whether it was broken, stolen, or confiscated, but its loss increased our sense of isolation. The most political subject discussed was the problem of secret communist meetings and separate reports to the committee and the British Communist party. I was by this time on friendly terms with Sinclair-Loutit, Thora Silverthorne, and Aileen Palmer, and I think I raised the subject with them, pointing out that although we accepted that the communists and secret communists made up most of the unit, we did not think it reasonable for them to hold secret meetings. These were undoubtedly disruptive. I pointed out that three people had already left the unit, possibly because of this. For a time a compromise was reached, in which I was allowed a seat on their committees. I was unable to speak but not to vote. Later O'Donnell came up and denounced this, but I think finally the secret meetings were given up. There was also a lot of criticism of Dr Sollenberger as a disruptive element, bur he did not leave until much later.

The periods of activity became shorter and the lulls longer, until there was nothing but lull towards the end of October 1936. The weather became worse. It was often very cold. The food was no better. The food sent from England got held up, first in Port Bou, then in Barcelona. In a recent book I am credited with its recovery.[16] I hope it was true. I cannot remember. More volunteers arrived; some also left. Morale slowly fell. It was to be expected. We were divided by age, sex; class, intelligence, political allegiance, and mental stability and had not enough to do.

A few events are worth recording. Margot Miller was wounded and had to return to the UK. She was a loss as she was one of the more sensible communists. Amongst the newcomers Dr Reggie Saxton[17] proved most useful. He began a general practitioner service for the village of Grañén and later helped to start blood transfusion on the Madrid front. Another valuable acquisition was the RAMC orderly Keith Anderson, who impressed us all by his dependability and skill. He was immensely likeable. There were also several good nurses, although they were not really needed in this period of inactivity. There were two incidents which I shall mention. The first I considered horrific. During a sunny afternoon I came out of the building to find a heated discussion going on on the back door steps of the hospital. I quickly realised that our Indian surgeon was under attack. A patient had died. I cannot remember whether he had or had not operated to remove a bullet which had lodged near an important artery or nerve. The whole scene of harsh judgment seemed incredible. No one had the knowledge or experience to criticise a surgical decision. I believe and hope that I defended the surgeon. I suspected the communists of organising the attack. The result was disastrous. Our one surgeon, furious at unwarranted criticism, left and returned to the UK. I was glad to discover later that he had got his FRCS.

The next incident was different. It originated in the failure of Churchill and Sinclair-Loutit to consult the Mayor of Grañén at the outset and persuade him to accept a predominantly communist hospital in his anarchist village. The Mayor and leading anarchist, who was actually called Pancho Villa, clearly found this

Edward Barsky from New York, headed a medical team and a mobile hospital that was operational in the Jarama Front.

irritating and in November took his revenge by cutting off food and petrol supplies. Fortunately the food from the UK had recently arrived and there was little need for petrol as the front was now dead. In fact the situation quickly resolved itself, due to an accident to Pancho Villa who tended to smoke while allocating petrol rations. He was admitted to our hospital with semi-serious burns and we were able to put on a rather good act. I think we turned one operating theatre into his private room, where English nurses in starched uniforms waited on him and gave him English food. He also had a good deal of skilled medical attention from our new and excellent surgeon Dr Aquilo, who had arrived to replace Khan. Pancho Villa's wounds healed quickly and as a reward he gave us a feast. A special pan was made and into it, according o rumour, were put a sheep and a goat, chickens and masses of rice, tomatoes, and pimientos. We were truly well fed for once. The scene itself was memorable, lit by an enormous fire. Goya would have relished it. In fact the whole party, with its remarkable paella and what Villa described as 'the biggest frying pan in the world,' has been well described in *The Distant Drum*.[18]

Our troubles - lack of work, political and other quarrels, a sense of isolation and low morale - were becoming well known and various people were sent up to sort us out. There were four or five of them. I shall comment only en the worst and the best of a bad lot. The worst was a communist English novelist domiciled in Barcelona, who had been a good friend to the unit by giving a home in Barcelona to a number of our convalescent cases. His lecture was a flop. Assuming that a good deal of the discord and unhappiness within the unit must result from sexual frustrations, he took the line that for the duration of the war we should all give up sex. He ended the lecture by saying that until the end of the war he and his wife were going to share something of the deprivation by sleeping in different rooms. We were not

© Agustí Centelles, VEGAP, Barcelona 2003

In a great part the Spanish civil was a war of trenches. The photograph corresponds to the battle of Belchite in September 1937

impressed, especially when we heard that he was sleeping with his secretary. Also, without outside advice, we had already managed to organise, on a very sensible basis, 'married quarters' for those wanting to sleep together. It is an interesting fact that most of the couples for whom we supplied these quarters later married.

The most sensible visitor was Tom Wintringham,[19] a communist then, who took the hard line. The hospital, he pointed out, had great propaganda value in the UK, which enabled the committee to collect a lot of money. He agreed that we might do better en the Madrid front, but explained the political difficulties of transferring from an anarchistic front to a PSUC front. So, we had to put up with it. (Tom was later taken ill - I think it was typhoid - and I visited him in hospital in Valencia. I met both his claimant wives, one communist, one non-communist. I understood why he resigned from the Communist party and was later a great success as a journalist on *Picture Post*.)

The debate as to what to do continued inside the unit. I became, inevitably, the main speaker for the non-communists. The line I developed was that by staying in Grañén, eating Spanish food, using Spanish petrol and electricity, and doing nothing to help we represented little more than an economic burden. (I like to think that this foreshadows some of the 'cost effective' arguments I produced later in my career.) I argued that we should either go home or be moved to the Madrid front. Against me the communists argued the established propaganda benefits of the hospital at Grañén, as well as the uncertainties of military control if we did join up with the International Brigade (IBM) on the Madrid front.

The committee in London was almost certainly having similar discussions and Sinclair-Loutit was recalled to report. It was just a little while later that I was sent

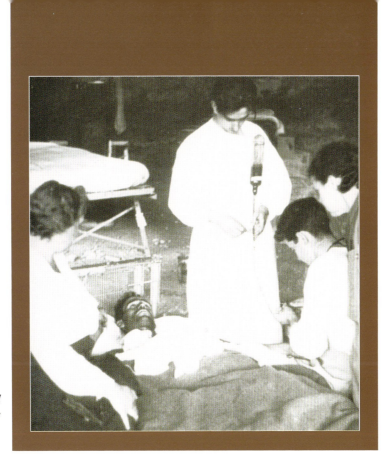

Supervising a blood transfusion during the Ebro Battle in 1938.

to meet André Marty, the leader of the International Brigade.[20] I was, however, under no illusion that I was going to conduct important negotiations. I was almost sure everything had been arranged by the Communist party in the UK and that I, a non-communist, had been chosen to put a Popular Front flavour on the deal.

I was glad to leave Grañén. I had never been happy there and looked forward to the trip, although I was rather worried when I got my travel document from O'Donnell. With his usual inefficiency it was undated, did not say where I was going, and merely stated that I could negotiate on behalf of the Spanish Medical Aid Committee. This was the one thing I was sure I was not entitled to do. In the event the trip to Albacete went off smoothly. I had one interesting meeting in a bar in Barcelona with a tall Englishman with big feet, who had been fighting with the POUM militia. In the course of the conversation I criticised the anarchist and POUM militia for not capturing Huesca and Zaragoza and linking up with the Basques. He argued fiercely that the anarchists and the POUM had been perfectly correct to consolidate their revolution before thinking of assistance for the communists in Madrid. I later asked him why he had joined the POUM. As far as I remember he admitted it was by chance. They were the first people he met and he liked them. He said his name was Blair.[21] I often wonder what would have happened to his literary output if he had joined the International Brigade. I later enjoyed his books more than I had that conversation.

The train journey to Valencia was uneventful, but it was interesting how the atmosphere changed from one of happy victory to that of a depressing war zone. I think I briefly met Peter Churchill and Lady Hastings (a real charmer) in Valencia before moving on in some haste to Albacete, where I was apparently

Near The Escorial. The building hosted the hospital where Archie worked (the roof is also shown on the cover page). In the region, or at this very building Julian Bell's death occurred.

expected. After being allocated board and lodging I received the news that I could see Marty that evening. I was nervous. He was already well known as an intolerant leader who was prepared to shoot those he did not like. My only hope seemed my flourishing red beard, although I did take care to prepare a short, cautiously worded speech in French. The meeting went off well. Someone introduced me, while I had a look at Marty. He was an impressive figure - tall, with a bushy heard and small dark hard eyes. I then made my speech offering the services of the Spanish Medical Aid Committee field hospital unit. He replied briefly in French, thanked me, and embraced me. We then sat down and had a drink and I was introduced to the chief medical officer of the International Brigade, a Dr Neumann, who was Austrian, and to Dr Dubois of the XIV Brigade, to which it was though our mobile unit would be attached. We talked in French and German for a time and then, with a broad grin, Marty turned and asked, 'Do tell me, what are you, an English gentleman, doing in Spain?' I replied that I was a Scots anti-fascist who had experienced fascism in Germany and Austria and feared its spread. I also made it clear that I was not a member of the Communist party, but that I was a strong supporter of the Popular Front. He laughed, embraced me for a second time, and handed me over to Dr Neumann and Dr Dubois. The latter, a dashing Pole educated in France, although a communist was much more interested in practical than doctrinal matters. The former, a charming, intelligent Viennese doctor, seemed pleased to have the opportunity to tell me, in German, about the difficulties of building up a medical service for the brigades.

As I left the meeting I suspected that I had been part of a prearranged scenario in which the communists had arranged that a non-communist should hand over a

Nurses were a most important component of the Health Services. The editors apologize for not having been able to contact any of them or their families for a direct contribution to this book.

field ambulance, financed in the UK by a supposedly humanitarian committee, to an organisation which was becoming increasingly accepted as communist controlled. By then I did not care. I had decided that despite evils on both sides, the republican side was the lesser evil, and I believed the ambulance unit would be more effective in its support on the Madrid front - and so it worked out.

> Here I would like to interpolate a short note on a return visit to Grañén in 1978.[22] I had decided not to return until the doctors eventually allowed Franco to die, although at one time I thought he was going to outlive me. Eventually I did return, through the kindness and arrangements of Dr Xavier Bosch, a young Spanish epidemiologist I met on a visit to the USA in the 1970s. My great embarrassment on arriving in Grañén was that I could not recognise the house of the fascist doctor where we had based our hospital. I later discovered that this was not surprising as it had been bombed and rebuilt as a café and cinema, but enough remained to bring back a flood of memories. Grañén is really rather a distinguished place. It is the site of the first international hospital in the Spanish Civil War in 1936. Tito of Jugoslavia lived there in 1937, as did General Walter, later Polish Minister of Defence in 1938. Orwell certainly visited in 1937, and John Cornford, probably wrote his well known poem "The Last Mile to Huesca" there.

When the mobile team finally arrived in Albacete only four of its original members remained - Kenneth (Sinclair-Loutit), Thora (Silverthorne), Aileen (Palmer), and myself – a situation which I feel reflected the inadequacy of the original selection process. There were, of course, others from subsequent waves of volunteers. I was

Dr Bethune was a Canadian surgeon and a socialist who came to Spain with the project of creating and running a blood bank that was operational on the front lines in Malaga, Madrid and Guadalajara.

glad that Reggie Saxton and Keith Anderson were there. Recent arrivals included Dr Tudor Hart,[23] who had some surgical experience, Joan Purser, a nurse, and Max Colin,[24] a mechanic. Reorganisation and membership changes led to a new leadership contest. To non-communists this proved an amusing open battle for power between two communists. Usually they settled things in secret. Tudor Hart won and Kenneth became his chief administrator.

The unit soon left for the Madrid front to support the XIV Brigade.[25] We had some difficulty in discovering the position of the brigade and even more in locating *Sol-y-Cine*, a hotel near the Corunna road where we were to establish our field hospital. We lost our way and arrived, inconveniently, after dark. It was on this journey that I first met Joseph Edenhoffer, a Czech driver and mechanic. In those days he spoke only Czech and German and as I was the sole German speaker we saw a lot of each other and got on well.

Even when we reached the hotel there was further trouble. Three Poles appeared from Dubois's staff intending to take charge of the unit This was strongly resisted and eventually a truce was agreed until after the battle. We then set out, after midnight, to make the hotel's unsuitable accommodation into a functional field hospital. We even got some sleep before the first wounded arrived at around 9.00 a.m.

My job was to do the triage, as the brigade had its own first aid post. This consisted initially of dividing the wounded, on arrival, into three categories: those with superficial injuries who could be quickly assisted, those more seriously wounded but eminently treatable, and the hopeless. The first decision was whether they were well enough to be evacuated after their wounds had been cleaned and dressed and

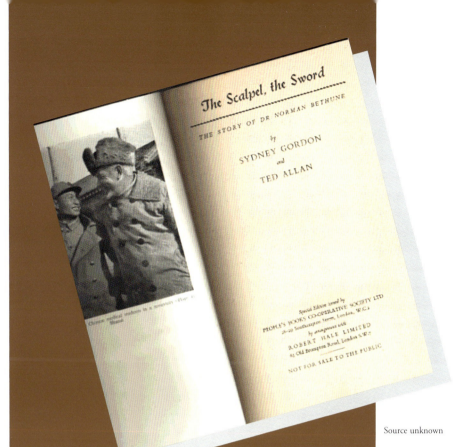

After March 1937 Dr Bethune was placed under the supervision of some political and medical commissars, became too supervised and left with his colleagues Sorensen and Hazen. After Spain Dr Bethune went to China and helped in the organization of the medical services under Mao Zedong. Archie worked with Bethune during the Jarama battle.

Source unknown

they had been given anti-tetanus injections (if available). We had to evacuate these people quickly as triage space was limited. The remainder were classified as "flesh", "orthopaedic", "abdominal", and "other", and I added a severity scale. There were inevitable some who were beyond our help. I hated playing God, but I had to. I sought medical advice as far as it was available, but the doctors were far too busy. Therefore it largely fell to me to get on as best I could, preparing the wounded for the theatre and making the dying as comfortable as possible. I do not remember having any morphine. Then came the problem of priority for operation. At first Hart came out and chose his cases, but he soon got tired. Reggie Saxton took the flesh wounds, using local anaesthetic, and Kenneth Sinclair-Loutit gave anaesthetics for Hart. With some cases I noticed that Hart took a long time. A nurse told me, as he did later, that he was not a very experienced abdominal surgeon. I then decided to give priority on his list to orthopaedic cases and accept that some abdominal cases would consequently die. I think I was right.

Fortunately the attack did not last long, but we were all desperately tired. Opinion, thank God, thought that I had run triage rather well. I was pleased that I had discovered an activity in which I appeared to be effective and which also offered some intriguing problems as to how to save the most lives, given a certain mixture of wounded and limited resources with which to treat them. I was also fortunate to have been spared the most harrowing experience of the triage process. That came later.

After the attack Dubois gave us light jobs. I think Kenneth went as medical officer to the brigade to cover for Dubois, whose duties had expanded. The rest of us were sent to organise a medical hospital and a surgical hospital at El Goloso. It was light

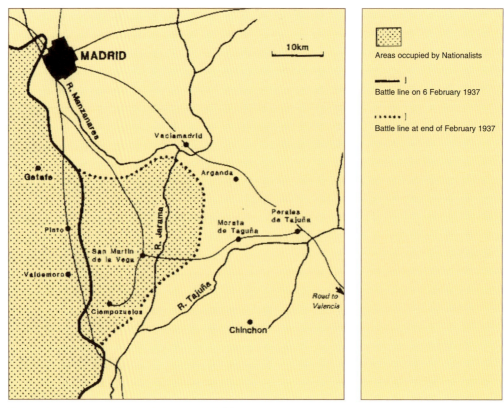

Figure 2. The Battle of Jarama, February 1937. Nationalist troops advance over the Jarama River in an attempt to cut the Madrid-Valencia highroad.

work for a short time, but the comfortable relief was soon shattered by Dubois's promotion of one of the Poles he had attached to the unit. The rather insignificant looking Dr Boulka, who spoke good English, became the unit's political commissar. He claimed to have a medical qualification from Edinburgh and to be the Scottish representative of Communist International. The medics disputed the first claim and the communists the second. He was conceited, stupid, and loved interfering - a general nuisance - and his compulsory educational lectures were puerile.

It was during this brief break, in January 1937, that I managed to visit Madrid, just a month or so after the battle of Madrid.[26] There were still many stories of the hand-to-hand fighting in the University City and occasional outbursts of shelling and bombing to reinforce continuing fears for Madrid. On the social side of this visit to the capital I met Ernest Hemingway, who seemed an alcoholic bore, and J B S Haldane, who had failed to teach me chemistry at Cambridge. I spoke at length with Haldane and somehow we got on to the subject of what motivated people to come to Spain. He was almost childlike in his belief that most of them came for purely political reasons. I argued that motivation was a far more complicated issue and that I should arrange a football match between escapists and masochists. He was shocked!

The short break did not last long. We were soon called upon to set up a field hospital at Villarecho,[27] near to where fascist troops were attempting to cross the Jarama River to cut the Madrid-Valencia highroad (see figure 2).[28] I believe Hart chose the house, a beautiful old hotel. It was an easy choice. It was the biggest building available and the only one with running water, although sanitary facilities were primitive. It was of course no longer a British hospital but an international one, although the hard core was still there: Hart, surgeon; Kenneth, anaesthetist; Thora, chief operating sister; Aileen, principal secretary; and myself, still running triage.

We started with only one surgeon and too few nurses, but additional staff were quickly drafted in to increase our potential once the scale of the offensive had registered. With more surgeons, more nurses, and more drivers we achieved a reasonably efficient hospital. It was also a reasonably happy one. I do not remember many quarrels. Certainly this situation was helped by Boulka keeping a low profile in the early days. There was also the fact that no one worked too long at a stretch, though we did work long hours. My own work benefited greatly from the collaborative spirit of the new surgeons, who liked my way of organising triage and helped me to improve it through various useful discussions. Both new surgeons were Spanish, and one of them, Broggi,[29] was of high calibre. Another improvement in circumstances was the provision of a separate area for the dying, removing them from the tensions of triage space and reducing some of the stress of the overcrowding there. I also found myself with helpers to assist with the cleaning of patients awaiting surgery. Perhaps the most significant advance, however, was the arrival of blood for transfusion from the transfusion service Dr Norman Bethune had established in Madrid. Bethune brought supplies of stored blood and a refrigerator from the capital to inaugurate this facility, which was steadily expanded by Reggie Saxton, who soon had local donors involved. Although blood transfusion initially generated some disagreement as to who should receive blood – the most critical or those for whom there was greater hope – such questions were amicably resolved and there were far more benefits than difficulties.

It was at Villarecho that I started making "aeroplane splints" for upper arm and shoulder injuries, devices so named because of the way in which they elevated the arm up and out from the shoulder, rather like a wing.[30] It was fascinating to find how, by working at various opportune moments to maintain a ready supply, I managed to reduce throughput problems in the operating theatre. For the first time I was also called upon to give some anaesthetics (God forgive me!). In addition I did a vast amount of dirty work, as orderly, nurse, and grave digger. I certainly worked hard and became exhausted as well as deeply shocked by the carnage.[31] My only comfort was the thought that I was being of use.

In addition to enormous casualties - many on both sides -the most difficult aspect of the battle of Jarama was its duration. It lasted far longer than anything we had previously experienced, taking up most of February 1937, a month which at times seemed as though it would never end.

> When I revisited Spain in 1978 I went to Villarecho and parked in the village square for Xavier to make inquiries. To my embarrassment the parking officer claimed that he recognised me as the doctor who, by surgery, had saved his life in 1937. I did not believe it, but if it was true it was my only surgical success in a long medical life, with the possible exception of a child at Wittenberg-am-Elbe much later. We discovered that the house in which we had based the hospital had at one time belonged to Don Juan of Austria, who had saved western civilisation from Islam centuries before. I wondered which side he would have been on in this later conflict of values. Sadly, I concluded that he would have supported Franco, as the defender of the Faith.

Archie revisiting the battle fields in 1978.

I shall always remember the Jarama valley by McDade's sad dirge:[32]

There's a valley in Spain called Jarama.
It's a place that we all know too well,
For 'tis there that we wasted our manhood.
And most of our old age as well

After Villarecho the 35th Division we had been supporting was rested at Alcala de Henares, and we went with it. For me, however, the rest ended all too prematurely. First Boulka took me with him on a fool's errand, trying to trace the whereabouts of a Canadian driver who had disappeared from the unit. He even insisted that I should be the one to accompany him on a visit to the Canadian Consulate in Valencia. I think he chose me because of my being non-communist and my Cambridge accent. (I am reminded now of how some committee makers search for black lesbians. Although they dislike both characteristics, they think they will look well on a committee.) Then came orders for me to organise a convalescence hospital at Valdegrango, which I did fairly successfully. It was not a difficult assignment. I was pleased to find two of the patients arriving there comfortable in the aeroplane splints I had made. My next assignment was a much bigger job - the conversion of a lovely old nunnery at Huete into a base hospital. I started out with only a German sergeant to help, but I soon devised a plan and recruited others locally, including an exceptional find - an English plumber. Certainly considerable enterprise was involved in preparations for an efficient hospital centre there and I surprised myself by my own courage in undertaking such a task.

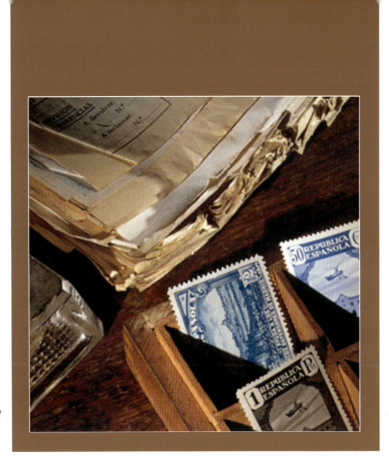

Republican stamps and documentation.

I did not, however, have time to carry all my plans through to completion, although the hospital had started to function. Dubois arrived in a car chauffeured by Joseph Edenhoffer to take me on a tour of convalescent camps on the south coast to attempt to locate volunteers lost but not accounted for. He had already made arrangements for my replacement at Huete. The tour proved interesting and an enjoyable break. Dubois was in jubilant mood because of the war news. The Italian fascists who had attacked at Guadalajara had been satisfactorily repulsed by the Italian International Brigade. We visited several pleasant convalescent homes, including one at Benicasim, named after the young English communist poet, Ralph Fox, who was killed on the Andújar front. We received only minor complaints, but the main subject of discussion inevitably became the seriously wounded who could not fight again. Dubois had considerable power and I think it was during this tour that he set in progress arrangements for many of the badly disabled to go home, if their return home was possible. Repatriation to France, Belgium, and the UK was not too difficult. Getting people back to the USA was more of a problem. And of course there was no chance of returning volunteers to Germany and Italy. For such unfortunates Dubois thought Mexico might be the solution, and so it proved for some cases.

I returned to Huete and was warned on arrival to expect a difficult situation. It was thought that I would object to finding myself with little authority in a hospital I had brought into commission, and especially to the appointment of Mildred,[33] an American, to my former position of hospital administrator. They little knew that I had come to the conclusion that there was no point in a non-communist wanting a senior post. There would always be a communist plot to get rid of him or her. It was not difficult, therefore, to take a back seat. I also retired to bed with dysentery, an indisposition made memorable only by an unlikely visitor, Harry

Pollitt, the leading communist in the UK, who was spending a day at the hospital. He had a perfect bedside manner and would have made an excellent general practitioner. On my recovery I took satisfaction from discovering how well the hospital was functioning on the lines that I had planned.

Towards the end of May 1937 an attack was to be launched towards Segovia, and a team of staff from Huete, which included a number of us from the old group, was summoned to man a new front line[34] hospital at Club Alpino, a skiing resort on the road from Madrid to Segovia. (It is generally recognised that this was the site of the attack round which Hemingway built his novel For Whom the Bell Tolls. The site chosen for the hospital seemed good, with adequate space for triage. I can remember taking a good supply of aeroplane splints with me. Again, Reggie Saxton was there with blood supplies and I think we had two or three good surgeons on the team.

The Republican offensive – one of two mounted in the last week of May 1937 to draw the Nationalist fire from the heavily pressurised Basque front around Bilbao – began on the morning of 31 May.[35] It was heralded by some spasmodic shelling and then we heard the sound of Republican aeroplanes attacking. The casualties arriving at the hospital were high for two days and then fell on the third, when it became clear that the attack had failed. Sadly, in the closing hours of the action a bomb fell close to the hospital and killed a delightful young Canadian driver, Issie Kupchick, and wounded another colleague. Soon afterwards a retreat was ordered and the hospital staff were despatched in various directions to work in base hospitals at Huete, El Goloso, and Alcala de Henares.

There was about a month between the Club Alpino attack and the next offensive. I think I spent this period at Huete, although I find I have only vague recollections of the place. What I do remember clearly is that it was a depressing time. There were rumours of disagreements in the Madrid government; there were rumours about the suppression of the POUM in Barcelona; there were rumours of volunteers from the UK being discouraged from joining the International Brigade by our representatives in Barcelona and Valencia. In addition, the problem of whether or not the communists should hold their secret meetings surfaced again. It had been simmering since Grañén. But there were also newcomers to cheer us up. I remember Julian Bell,[36] Sir Richard Rees, John Boulting, Chris Thorneycroft, Portia Holman, and Larry Collier. I was particularly glad to meet Julian Bell, who had been a good friend of mine at King's College, Cambridge, in what seemed another world. Julian was a striking, almost old world figure in his topee, but everyone soon recognised his courageous driving.

The lull was eventually jolted by growing rumours of plans for a massive Republican attack to relieve the pressure on the west of Madrid. We could only wait, but morale rose. I think I slightly increased my rate of splint making. The call soon came to go to El Escorial, 30-40 kilometres north-west of Madrid and some 10 kilometres north of the battle lines,[37] to set up a large, front line hospital. I was involved only in the organisation of triage. The building chosen was a modern monastery, down the hill from El Escorial. It was large enough and gave good facilities for the arrival of ambulances and enough space for triage, but the stairs up to the wards were steep and difficult for stretcher bearers. The wards themselves were reasonable, although water supplies were inadequate and the sanitation deplorable.

Rural Spain in the 40's. Mother and child.

However we made vas advances in triage. As we had three theatres to serve I was given a nurse and an orderly to help me; Reggie Saxton was there with his blood transfusion service and there was even a small ⁻ ray unit, which did occasionally locate odd bullets.

There were three chief surgeons, Jolly, Broggi, and Hart. I had worked for Broggi and Hart before, but no Jolly, who turned out to be a man of the highest competence for whom I developed a great admiration. He was a New Zealander and was, in my opinion, the most important volunteer to Spain from the British Commonwealth. (Much later when I read his obituary I could not understand how he never got his FRCS.) The hospital was well prepared when the attack started. We hoped the attack was equally well prepared.

The battle of Brunete was quite different from that of Jarama. Jarama had been essentially a defensive measure. Brunete started with the great hope that it was going to end the encirclement of Madrid. The plan was to advance on the small village of Brunete and break through enemy lines to cut off troops besieging Madrid from their supplies and reinforcements from the west. At first alt went well. There was a rapid advance and casualties were slight, with the hospital functioning well and within its capacity. But soon the atmosphere changed. The casualties mounted rapidly and we were all put under real strain. What I particularly remember of this exhausting period are the valiant efforts of the ambulance drivers, who were always under pressure and often under fire. I also think that we in triage coped rather well and that Jolly ran a remarkably efficient ward for abdominal cases. There was so much activity that inevitably much of it is hazy in retrospect. Towards the end of the battle[38] there was a small incident which upset me,

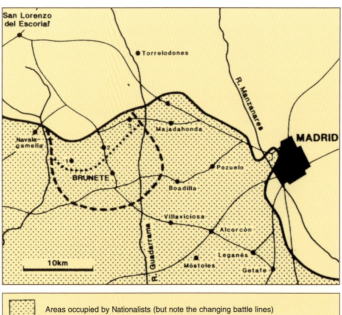

Figure 3
The Battle of Brunete, June 1937. A massive Republican offensive intended to end the encirclement of Madrid. Early successes were soon reversed and the Spanish Medical Aid Committee's field ambulance unit found itself under intense pressure in the second half of June.

possibly unreasonably, but I was tired and emotionally overexcited after two or more weeks of triage. An ambulance arrived. The stretchers were brought in and I hurried to classify the wounded. The first case was lying on his right side with his face partially hidden. His left thorax was completely shattered. I could see a heart faintly beating. I signaled to the nurse, by dropping my thumb, that the case was hopeless (language was dangerous). I moved left to see the next case and, by chance glanced back. To my horror I recognised the face of Julian Bell. (I suppose one must accept the probability of putting a good friend amongst the hopeless category. I have never met anyone who had run a triage in any war, but I am sure the effect is always devastating. A still small voice from your unconscious mutters, 'You have condemned your friend to death!' I rushed off, telling my nurse to carry on, to find a surgeon or physician to confirm or refute my diagnosis. Fortunately I found Philip D'Arcy Hart, who was visiting the unit. I showed him the wound. He agreed with my opinion. I did not know whether to be pleased or sorry. We moved Julian to a ward, where he died some time afterwards,[39] and I went back to triage, a changed man.

The battle ended towards the end of July. There had been little to lighten my depression. Julian had died. Another colleague was missing and others, including Dubois,[40] were wounded. I was further depressed by the poor results of the Spanish Republic's efforts to build an army; The pathetic young Spaniards whom I tried to comfort in triage were not trained soldiers. I began to doubt that the Republic could win. But I kept this doubt to myself.

Back at Alcala de Henares, to where many of us were returned, there were dramatic changes. Nearly all the old gang of British volunteers had been given leave in the

Near Fraga, the Aragon front. 7 November 1938. Loyalist troops during an offensive along the Rio Segre.

UK. Rather more surprisingly, all medical students were ordered to return home to qualify. This was just what my unconscious wanted, but my conscious, as a volunteer, had been too proud to suggest it. I was delighted.

On my flight back to the UK I tried to sum things up. I was glad I had gone to Spain; glad that I had not given up in despair at Grañén. Given my limited abilities, I had made a reasonable contribution to the anti-fascist cause, rather than merely talking about it. I had also learned a lot. Although I had come to hate war, I now knew that fascism would have to be fought and that pacifism was impossible. I had, too, become increasingly suspicious of the communists. There had been valuable opportunities to discuss political theories with knowledgeable people of different persuasions – anarchists and Trotskyites; Russian, German, French, and American communists; British socialists and communists; and a few British liberals. I realised that no one knew how to run a country or a revolution. There were also a number of friendships I valued, some of which were to endure. As I write, I am still in touch with Joseph Edenhoffer, who was treated abominably when he returned to Czechoslovakia in 1946. Overall I had a general feeling of satisfaction that I had risked my life for a cause I believed in; but I was relieved that I had not lost it in the process. (…)*

NOTES:

1. Between 29 July and the 5th of August 1936 German and Italian planes conveyed the first airborne contingent of Franco's Moorish troops from Morocco to Seville, where Franco arrived on 6 August. The first major military airlift in history had begun. When the operation ended in September 1936, a total of 12000 men of the Army of Africa had been transported to the mainland.
2. In August 1936 a number of European powers, including France, Britain, Germany, Russia, and Italy, agreed upon a policy of non-intervention in the affairs of Spain.
3. Later Viscount Addison.
4. Thomas H. The Spanish Civil War. 3rd ed. London, 1977. See also Firth D. The Signal Was Spain. London, 1976. It includes reference to the Medical Aid Committee's field ambulance Unit.
5. The Spanish Medical Aid Committee's field ambulance unit set out for Spain on 23 August 1936.
6. The author is here anticipating interests which were to develop in later months. The International Brigades were not inaugurated until 12 October 1936, the result of an international collaboration of Communist parties. The brigades have been described as 'legions of anti-fascist volunteers,' many of them exiles from fascist or other extreme right wing regimes.
7. FAI: Federación Anarquista Ibérica.
8. More commonly referred to as the Aragon front.
9. Huesca: the only remaining point of hostilities on an otherwise quiet Aragon front.
10. POUM: Partido Obrero de Unificación Marxista.
11. PSUC: Partido socialista Unificado de Cataluña.
12. Of a party of 28.
13. The Spanish Medical Aid Committee in London duly reimbursed the author for this loss.
14. The Thaelman Centuria: named after Ernst Thaelman, German communist leader in late 1920s, who at this time was held in a concentration camp.
15. Beimler had also been imprisoned in Germany but had made a remarkable escape from Dachau.
16. Cochrane's recovery of the food supplies is also acknowledged in a report from the unit's quartermaster to Spanish Medical Aid committee headquartes, 15 November 1936.
17. Reginald Somes Saxton.
18. Toynbee P, ed. The distand drum. London, 1976.
19. Tom Wintringham, an editor of the Left Review and a military correspondent of the Daily Worker, commanded the British Battalion of the 15th International Brigade at the battle of Jarama, February 1937.
20. André Marty: French communist leader.
21. Eric Arthur Blair: George Orwell.
22. See Cochrane AL. Forty years back, a retrospective survey. BMJ 1979; ii: 1662-3.
23. Alexander Ethan Tudor Hart.
24. Then Max Cohen.
25. At the battle for Las Rosas.
26. November 1936.
27. Villarejo de Salvanes.
28. The attack in the Jarama Valley, which took Republican forces by surprise, began on 6 February 1937. On II February fascist troops crossed the Jarama River (see fig 1).
29. Dr Broggi-Valles.
30. Injuries to the upper arm, including the shoulder, often required the elevation of the upper arm to a right angle with the trunk. Light metal splints could be bent to the appropriate angle, with one arm of the splint bound to the trunk and the other to the damaged limb. Dr Tudor Hart had learnt this method in Vienna and introduced its extensive use in Spain. Held by such a splint, the arm gives the impression of imitating an aeroplane; hence the name "aeroplane spling.".
31. On the Republican side there were more than 10000 casualties, including around 1000 deaths. On the other side the Nationalists suffered over 6000 casualties.
32. A McDade, to the tune of 'Red River Valley.'
33. Mildred Rackley.
34. 36 The Segovia front.
35. Three Republican divisions broke through opposition lines at San Ildefonso.
36. Julian Heward Bell (1908-37): son of Clive and Vanessa Bell, grandson of Leslie Stephen, nephew of Virginia Woolf, and first cousin once removed of HAL Fisher.
37. See figure 3.
38. 18 July 1937.
39. Julian Bell was struck by a fragment of bomb while sheltering beside or under his ambulance at the battle of Brunete. He was brought into the 35th Division hospital. Dr Reginald Somes Saxton has pointed out that he did receive greater attention than the author suggests. Despite the hopelessness of his condition, Bell received a blood transfusion and careful dressing of his chest wound.
40. The author's friend Noel Carritt was later found to have died in this battle. The Battle of Brunete also claimed the life of Dr Sollenberger.

* Cochrane AL, Blythe M. One Man's Medicine. An Autobiography of Professor Archie Cochrane. London: BMJ (Memoir Club), 1989. Reproduced by permission of Max Blythe.

RIGHT: *Barcelona. January, 1939. At a refugee transit center during the evacuation of the city, which was being heavily bombed by fascist planes, as General Franco's fascist troops rapidly approached.*

Doctor
Reginald Somes Saxton
Haematologist

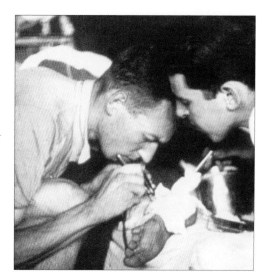

*Thank you for your card and attached document dated July 17th 2001.
Archie Cochrane was a good scientist and had personal experience of fascism. With good reason, like most of us, he hated fascism. He was senior medical student who worked hard and efficiently. The only episode that might interest you and that I know of first hand was in the Gandesa Battle. I mention his work in the Jarama battle to illustrate his skill and versatility. Yours sincerely,
R S Saxton*

THE DEATH OF JULIEN BELL

Archie was one of those who formed a British Unit, which gradually merged with the Servicio Sanitario of the Republican Army of Spain while still keeping useful contact with England.

I was with Archie during some of the major early battles of 1937 until he returned to continue his medical studies at the University Hospital in London. At Jarama, February to April 1937, where the International Brigades helped defend the Madrid-Valencia road, finally dashing the fascist hopes of a victory march into Madrid. Archie became an anaesthetist for major surgery, owing to our shortage of qualified staff and the large number of wounded.

In the summer of 1937 the battle for Brunete was desperate and terrible. The object was to divert the enemy troops attacking the Basque country. It was a costly failure. Our hospital was in a monastery near the Royal Palace of El Escorial. Here Archie had the job of triage, which essentially meant selecting from the many severely wounded, those to pass on to the surgeon, from those who were beyond hope of survival with the facilities available. I recollect the time when he had to decide the immediate fate of Julian Bell whom we all knew, who was brought in with a severe penetrating chest wound. He had been bombed beside the ambulance he had been driving.

Archie was checking the wounds and condition of the new admissions and signaling his decision to the stretcher bearers: the hopeless mortally wounded to one side and those who might survive with surgery to the other. Before he had recognized his patient, Archie had concluded that the wound was fatal and inoperable; then he recognized Julian and felt the responsibility of denying him surgical treatment was too great. He decided to get Dr Broggi, one of our best surgeons, to see him and make the decision. Meanwhile I was asked to give Julian a blood transfusion.

Julian was still conscious: he knew me and welcomed my involvement. Dr Broggi then examined the wound lender anesthesia, removing the dressings while a number of British medical and nursing staff, including, I think, Archie, looked on. The terrible wound had carried clothing and the contents of a breast pocket with it into the chest. Open chest surgery was not then technically possible. Dr Broggi retrieved a few documents near the surface, redressed the wound, and confirmed Archie's original prognosis. (The account is confirmed by Dr M Broggi).

I saw Archie again after the Civil War in London, where he generously allowed some of us poorer colleagues the use of his service flat; and much later in Wales, where he was researching pneumoconiosis in coal miners.

(...) NO ONE IN HIS SENSES SUPPOSED THAT THERE WAS ANY HOPE OF DEMOCRACY (...) IN A COUNTRY SO DIVIDED AND EXHAUSTED AS SPAIN WOULD BE WHEN THE WAR WAS OVER. IT WOULD HAVE TO BE A DICTATORSHIP, AND IT WAS CLEAR THAT THE CHANCE OF A WORKING-CLASS DICTATORSHIP HAD PASSED. THAT MEANT THAT THE GENERAL MOVEMENT WOULD BE IN THE DIRECTION OF SOME KIND OF FASCISM... THE ONLY ALTERNATIVES WERE AN INFINITELY WORSE DICTATORSHIP BY FRANCO, OR (ALWAYS A POSSIBILITY) THAT THE WAR WOULD END WITH SPAIN DIVIDED UP, EITHER BY ACTUAL FRONTIERS OR INTO ECONOMIC ZONES. (...)

GEORGE ORWELL, 1969.*

Credit & Legend, see page 326.

FAREWELL TO THE BRIGADES, FAREWELL TO SPAIN

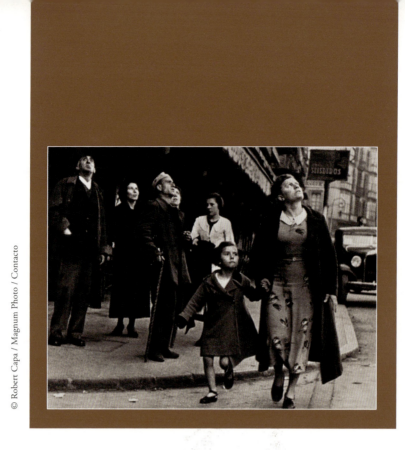

Bilbao. Basque region. May, 1937. Running for shelter during an air raid.

EXTRACT FROM *HOMAGE TO CATALONIA* BY GEORGE ORWELL

George Orwell (...) I suppose I have failed to convey more than a little of what those months in Spain meant to me. I have recorded some of the outward events, but I cannot record the feeling they have left me with. It is all mixed up with sights, smells, and sounds that cannot be conveyed in writing: the smell of the trenches, the mountain dawns stretching away into inconceivable distances, the frosty crackle of bullets, the roar and glare of bombs; the clear cold light of the Barcelona mornings, and the stamp of boots in the barrack yard, back in December when people still believed in the revolution; and the food-queues and the red and black flags and the faces of Spanish militiamen; above all, the faces of militiamen - men whom I knew in the line and who are now scattered Lord knows where, some killed in battle, some maimed, some in prison - most of them, I hope, still safe and sound. Good luck to them all; I hope they win their war and drive all the foreigners out of Spain, Germans, Russians and Italians alike. (...)

(...) This war, in which I played so ineffectual a part, has left me with memories that are mostly evil, and yet I do not wish that I had missed it. When you have had a glimpse of such a disaster as this - and however it ends, the Spanish war will turn out to have been an appalling disaster, quite apart from the slaughter and physical suffering - the result is not necessarily disillusionment and cynicism. Curiously enough, the whole experience has left me with not less but more belief in the decency of human beings. And I hope the account I have given is not too misleading. I believe that on such an issue as this no one is or can be completely truthful. It is difficult to be certain about anything except what you have seen with your own eyes, and consciously or unconsciously everyone writes as a partisan. In case I have not said this somewhere earlier in the book I will say it now: beware of my partisanship, my mistakes of fact, and the distortion inevitably caused by my having seen only one corner of events. And beware of exactly the same things when you read any other book on this period of the Spanish war. (...)

The battle of London started in June 1940

Note from the editors: George Orwell left Spain in 1938 while his political comrades in the POUM (assimilated to a Trotskyist movement) were actively condemned, incarcerated and tortured by the communists and the police. On his arrival to London, Orwell published *Homage to Catalonia*, whose last words were tragically premonitory of the disasters of World War II.

(...) and then the huge peaceful wilderness of outer London, the barges on the miry river, the familiar streets, the posters telling of cricket matches and Royal weddings, the men in bowler hats, the pigeons in Trafalgar Square, the red buses, the blue policemen - all sleeping the deep, deep sleep of England, from which I sometimes fear that we shall never wake till we are jerked out of it by the roar of bombs.*

* Orwell G. *Homage to Catalonia*. London: Penguin Books, 1968.

Copyright © George Orwell 1937. Extracts reproduced by permission of Bill Hamilton as the Literary Executor of the Estate of the Late Sonia Brownell Orwell and Secker & Warburg Ltd.

(...) HIS FOUR YEARS AS A PRISONER OF WAR WERE AN ORDEAL OF THE SEVEREST KIND, CALLING ON RESERVES OF MORAL COURAGE AND PHYSICAL ENDURANCE TO A DEGREE THAT CAN FAIRLY BE TERMED HEROIC. AT SOME CRITICAL PERIODS HE WAS THE ONLY OFFICER AND THE ONLY DOCTOR IN THE CAMP AND MORE OFTEN THAN NOT HE WAS IN THE EXPOSED POSITION OF BEING THE ONLY FLUENT GERMAN SPEAKER AMONG THE PRISONERS AND THUS, INEVITABLY, THE NATURAL NEGOTIATOR ON THEIR BEHALF. IT WAS THESE YEARS WHICH WERE THE FOUNDATION OF HIS ABIDING BELIEFS ON PATIENT CARE AND MEDICAL TREATMENT AND HE NEVER FORGOT THE LESSONS THEY TAUGHT HIM. (...)

RICHARD COHEN, 1989.*

Credit & Legend, see page 326.

WORLD WAR II: MEDICAL CARE AND TRIALS AT THE CONCENTRATION CAMP

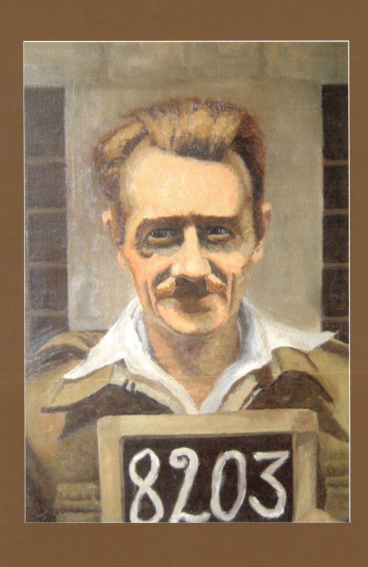

23 October 1937. Hitler greets the Dukes of Windsor. Edward VII, after resignation, spent some time travelling trough Germany.

Source unknown

EXTRACT FROM *CIVILIZATION AND BARBARITY IN 20TH CENTURY EUROPE* BY GABRIEL JACKSON

Gabriel Jackson

(...) By the end of March 1939, Hitler had completed the destruction of Czechoslovakia, and his junior ally, General Franco, had completed his victory over the Spanish Republic with the occupation of Madrid. The Italian and German troops could now be repatriated for use in other fascist adventures. Thus on April 7th, Mussolini invaded Albania without informing Hitler (who had occupied Prague on 15 March without notifying Mussolini).

One week earlier England had formally offered guarantees to Poland. Moreover, in the following weeks the Chamberlain government introduced peacetime conscription for the first time in British history and offered guarantees to Greece and Romania as well. On May 3rd, Stalin replaced Maxim Litvinov, the foreign minister who had been the spokesman of cooperation with the League of Nations and then of collective security. His successor was one of the few really able 'Old Bolsheviks' whom the dictator had spared in the 1936-38 purges, Vyachislav Molotov. In the course of the summer, France and Germany both increased the garrisons manning their lines of defensive forts, the so-called Maginot and Siegfried lines.

Thus it was clear that, while they had not been openly disavowed, both appeasement and collective security were no longer the guiding policies of the Westerns powers and Russia, respectively. Hitler in turn was quite ready to provoke war with his next aggression, but he wanted to be sure not to provoke a two-front war - the strategic error which had been fatal to Germany's ambitions in 1914. Thus, while he fulminated against the Poles, he welcomed the secret feelers being extended by his long-proclaimed principal enemy, the Soviet Union.

The British and French governments could not conceive of the possibility of an alliance between the world's two greatest ideological enemies. Unhurriedly, they

London May 1939. Sir Oswald Mosley (left) leader of the English fascists in a meeting of the Union of British Fascists.

Chamberlain at London airport in 30 September 1938. On return from Germany he is waiving an agreement with Hitler claiming to have achieved "peace in our time".

sent a low-level diplomatic mission to Moscow to discuss defensive military arrangements against Hitler. This mission could not seriously consider the Soviet demands for a military protectorate over the Baltic republics and was not disposed to press the Polish government to allow the passage of Russian troops in case of war. Meanwhile, by late July, Herr Hitler - prepared as always, to make promises and sign agreements which he had no intention of fulfilling - decided to conclude a treaty with Russia in order to free his hands in the rest of Europe.

Thus on 23 August 1939, the pipe-smoking, benign-looking Soviet dictator, the broadly smiling and very Aryan-looking German Foreign Minister Joachim von Ribbentrop, and the dour-faced Molotov announced the completion of a traty of non-aggression between their two peace-loving governments. Hitler had the guarantee needed before launching the invasion of Poland, the appeasement governments were now left to face Germany alone, and the world communist parties needed between a week and a month (depending on the flexibility of the personalities involved) to discover that the coming war was purely a war between 'imperialists'.

World War II thus began with the diplomatic humiliation of the democratic powers, a new masterpiece of calculated hypocrisy by Hitler, the renunciation of collective security by the Soviets, and the confusion and demoralization of the world communist parties, as well as that substantial portion of the democratic Left which had admired the soviet stances during the Spanish Civil War and the Czechoslovak crisis. (...)*

---

* Jackson G. Civilization and barbarity in 20th century Europe. Amherst, NY: Humanity Books. Copyright © 1999 by Gabriel Jackson. Reprinted with permission.

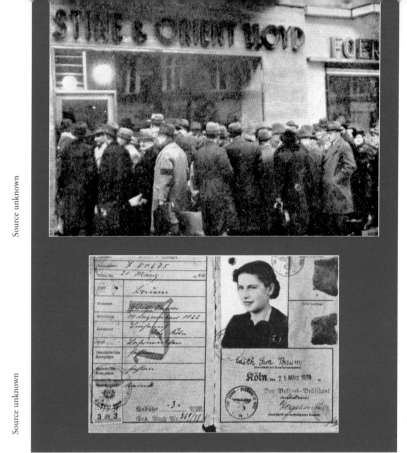

Jewish citizens in Berlin queuing to get transport to escape from Germany.

A passport from a young woman marked with the J

(...) On the outbreak of war, our paths separated but they met again in January 1941 when we found ourselves members of a 50 strong body of medical reinforcements aboard a troopship bound for Egypt. We sailed in a convoy from Greenock and it took us six weeks to reach Port Said via the Cape of Good Hope with only one day ashore at Durban. Time hung heavily on board and after all our money had been lost to Australian troops, the men playing two up and the officers chemin de fer, there was little left to do, except to organise concert parties and play bridge. As far as I could make out, Archie and I were the only officers who spent any time trying to learn Arabic - Archie from a large tome that began with the Arabic script and me from the Berlitz paperback Teach yourself Arabic in three months.

On arrival in Egypt our paths separated again. I went to a small hospital in Cyprus and he went to a general hospital between Cairo and the Suez Canal. He had not been there long, however, before he was asked to volunteer for a post with a commando regiment, which included 70 Spanish refugees from the civil was who had eventually, after my vicissitudes enlisted in the British Army, and he always thought he was asked to join them because he was the only medical officer in the Middle East who spoke Spanish. The regiment was sent to Crete where he was captured by the invading Germans and he spent the last four years of the war as medical officer, and sometimes officer in charge, of large prisoner of war camps in Greece and Germany. I wrote to him periodically during his captivity, but had little contact with him after our return to the United Kingdom until he was appointed to the staff of Medical Research Council's Pneumoconiosis Research Unit near Cardiff in 1948. (...)*

---

* Doll R. A reminiscence of Archie Cochrane. In: Maynard A, Chalmers I. Non-Random Reflections on Health Services Research. On the 25th Anniversary of Archie Cochrane's Effectiveness and Efficiency. London: BMJ Publishing Group, 1997. p.p. 7-10.
Reproduced with permission from the BMJ Publishing Group.

Notre Dame de Cenilly, southwest of St Lô. July 28th, 1944. A French farmer offers cider to American soldiers.

*Archie was liberated from the camp at Wittenberg-Am-Elbe in Germany on 26 April 1945.
Most of his writings and notes were lost in the turmoil, the testimony of his time as a POW is dramatically described in his autobiography.*

After Spain, Archie spent a period of his life in London with a permanent sense of immediate danger stimulated by the passage of Jews trough London and the signing of the treaty between Germany and The Soviet Union. Archie joined the Army, took some courses at the London School of Hygiene and Tropical Medicine and was sent to the battle front in Crete, briefly sharing the trip with Richard Doll.

On arrival he was destined to a battalion named Layforce which included some Spanish Republican soldiers who, as many in Europe, spent the war time wondering countries and armies with no place to rest.

Soon after landing in Crete, the battalion was under severe attack. The evacuation of the island by the British forces was already under way and Archie's fighting unit was ordered to stay behind to delay the German troops. The Layforce Battalion was hold prisoner and Archie found himself as a doctor, often as the only doctor, in charge of very large number of prisoners of war. The following four years was a transit from camp to camp, from Salonica to Germany until liberation on April 1945.

Anglican priest on the edge of a grave, saying - as noted by the German photographer - the last mass for a prisoner from Australia. Provisional camp in Kalamata, 1941.

(...) The first experience was in the Gulag at Salonica where I spent six months. I was usually the senior medical officer and for a considerable time the only officer and the only doctor. (It was bat enough being a POW, but having me as your doctor was a bit too much). There were about 20 000 POW's in the camp, of whom a quarter were British. The diet was about 600 calories a day and we all had diarrhoea. In addition we had severe epidemics of typhoid, diphtheria, infections, jaundice, and sandfly fever, with more than 300 cases of "pitting oedema above the knee." To cope with this we had a ramshackle hospital, some aspirin, some antacid, and some skin antiseptic. The only real asset were some devoted orderlies, mainly from the Friends' Field Ambulance Unit. Under the best conditions one would have expected an appreciable mortality; there in the Dulag I expected hundreds to die of diphtheria alone in the absence of specific therapy. In point of fact there were only four deaths, of which three were due to gunshot wounds inflicted by the Germans. This excellent result had, of course, nothing to do with the therapy they received or my clinical skill. It demonstrated, on the other hand, very clearly the relative unimportance of therapy in comparison with the recuperative power of the human body.

The second experience in POW life was very different. It was at Elsterhost where all the POW's with tuberculosis (most of whom were far advanced) of all nationalities were herded together behind the wire. Conditions were in many ways not too bad. Through Red Cross parcels we had sufficient food; we were able to "screen" patients and do sputum "smears" but radiographs were very limited. We could give our patients bed rest, pneumothorax, and pneumoperitoneum. There was a French physiologist who was expert in "adhesion-section," and thoracoplasty was a possibility. We knew our patients almost too intimately. We spent most of the day with them and at night were locked in the same building. We had to attend their funer-

Salonica camp.

als and I usually acted as a priest (I got quite expert in the Hindu, Moslem, and Greek Orthodox rites). I remember at that time reading one of those propaganda pamphlets considered suitable for POW medical officers about *clinical freedom and democracy*. I found it impossible to understand. I had considerable freedom of clinical choice of therapy; my trouble was that I did not know which to use and when. I would gladly have sacrificed my freedom for a little knowledge. I had never heard then of *randomissed controlled trials*, but I knew there was no real evidence that anything we has to offer had any effect on tuberculosis, and I was afraid that I shortened the lives of some of my friends by unnecessary intervention. (...)*

---

* Cochrane AL. Effectiveness and Efficiency. Random Reflections on Health Services. London: Nuffield Provincial Hospitals Trust, 1972. (Reprinted in 1989 in association with the BMJ, reprinted in 1999 for Nuffield Trust by the Royal Society of Medicine Press, London).

Reproduced with permission from the BMJ Publishing Group and the Royal Society of Medicine Press.

Provisional concentration camp for British prisoners of war. Photos taken on 30 April 1941. In the next days began the transportation of the prisoners to concentration camps in central Germany.

EXTRACT FROM *ONE MAN'S MEDICINE, AN AUTOBIOGRAPHY OF PROFESSOR ARCHIE COCHRANE* BY ARCHIBALD L COCHRANE WITH MAX BLYTHE. COPYRIGHT ©: MAX BLYTHE

SALONICA

(...) The old cavalry barracks were in an appalling state of repair and grossly overcrowded with about 10 000 prisoners,[1] including Jugoslavs, Greeks, Cretans, Cypriots, Palestinians, Arabs, Indians, Australians, New Zealanders, English, Scots, Irish, and Welsh, and of course the Spaniards from Layforce. My first impressions were lack of food and lack of sleep. The diet consisted of one cupful of unsweetened coffee for breakfast, one plate of vegetable soup with a vestige of meat at midday, and two slices of bread (or a large biscuit) at night. Sleep was wrecked in two ways: by bed bugs, and by having, at first, to sleep on long sheets of wire netting, stretched in three tiers over wooden struts. There was an unmusical twang when anyone moved, and in the night there was a hideous cacophony.

There was a large hospital with about 200 beds. Surgeon Lieutenant Singer, a charming doctor from New Zealand, was in charge. He appeared to be doing a good job under difficult conditions. I joined the hospital to help out, and quite soon, to my surprise and embarrassment, was appointed chief doctor by the Germans as Singer had had an inevitable row with them. He was, fortunately very good about it and my knowledge of German helped communications, not only with our hosts but also with the Jugoslavs. I soon realized what a thankless job I had.

The one great asset I had were the orderlies, a mixture partly from a section of the Friends Ambulance Unit (Quakers) and others from Australia, New Zealand, the UK, and Jugoslavia. They were all devoted workers but chief praise must go to the Quakers, who were magnificent. Amongst them was Bill Miall, who later worked with me in Cardiff, became director of the MRC Epidemiological Unit in Jamaica, and is now at the MRC unit at Northwick Park. Another was Duncan Catterall, now director of the Venereology Unit at the Middlesex Hospital.

Life at the beginning of July was jus tolerable. A typical day was as follows: reveille 5.30 am; parade 6 a.m. (this often lasted an hour, for the Germans seemed incapable of counting correctly); then there was time for the 'acorn' coffee and any bread one had managed not to eat the night before; then sick parade for other ranks (there were often 200, of which I did half); then another sick parade for the officers (we were lucky to finish by 10.30 am); then a ward round (I often had 100 medical cases); then I did a short sanitary round to try and keep the latrines working. At midday we had our soup, which did not take long to swallow. I rested until 1 p.m. when I either went to make complaints to the Germans – a rather profitless task as they always claimed that Salonica was a transit camp and that all prisoners of war would soon be sent to Germany(it is true that all officers, except two or three medical officers, were soon despatched to Germany, to be followed later by the Jugoslavs) or tried some crude psychotherapy on those suffering from severe battle neuroses. I saw them in my room alone and encouraged them to tell me about their experiences and fears. They soon started crying, which I encouraged. The sessions often lasted some time and the men often fell asleep afterwards. It seemed effective in most cases. At 4.30 p.m. we ran a skin sepsis clinic. After that I did another medical round, then got my two slices of bread and went on parade at 7 p.m. Next followed an 'outpatients' for those who had been working in the town. Then there was curfew, after which it was dangerous to go out. You could get shot. In the evenings I was tired but had difficulty in sleeping because of the bed bugs. I sometimes talked to the Jugoslavs, but more often to the Quakers. Sometimes to comfort myself I wrote verse.[2] There is one poem I still like. It combines my generation's guilt at not preventing the war and my personal guilt I felt when travelling to Edinburgh too late to see my mother before she died in 1937.

> SIMILARITY
>
> The track was hard as fate,
> The train was singing:
> "She must not die"
> (I'd loved but not enough)
> The wheels were ringing
> "She cannot die"
> (I'd tried but not enough)
> and then I came too late.
>
> Now prisoner, down in Greece,
> The news is stinging.
> We're down and out
> (I'd loved but not enough)
> The 'goons' are grinning[3]
> of Russian rout.[4]
> (I'd tried but not enough)
> and there is no more peace.

There were some other curious incidents in those early days. The first was my only success. I still felt responsible for the Spaniards who had been in Layforce and were worried about what would happen to them when they had to register as prisoners of war and give personal details. I promised to be there with them and argue that they were in the British Army and must be treated as British prisoners of war. As we began to march up to get registered I was suddenly inspired. I decided that all the Spaniards had been born in Gibraltar! I held a hurried discussion with them and the whole registration went off without the Germans raising one eyebrow. The Spaniards were delighted and I felt a mild glow, but I had another problem on my

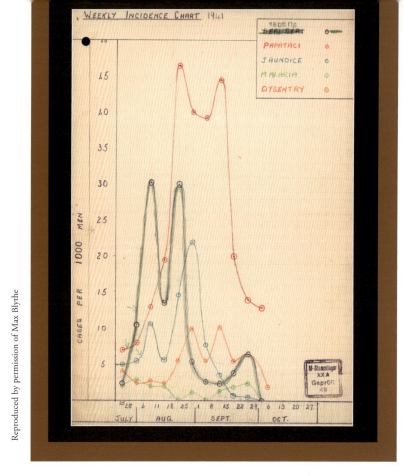

Copy of a graph of sickness in a German POW camp, compiled by Archie, July-October, 1941.

hands - a really unpleasant one - a traitor. He was an English regular sergeant major, about twice my size and very muscular. He had a German wife, and on capture expressed his willingness to join the German Army. He lived with the Germans but moved freely in the camp and had a devastating effect on morale. It fell to my lot to see him, read a quote from King's Regulations, and promise that I would try and see that he was court martialled after the war. He roared with laughter throughout and I felt rather foolish. I checked up after the war. He was killed on the Eastern Front.

Another incident showed the effect of chronic hunger. During my sanitary round I found a prisoner, whom I had met earlier in Alexandria, taking food out of clothes stupidly left in the barracks while the owner was out working in Salonica. I went up to him and said, 'You must not do this. It's stealing.' He answered without any show of embarrassment, 'Why? I'm hungry.' I know no better example of the awful effect of hunger. There was another level at which hunger showed its ill effects - the language and dreams of the British Army. The language of the British Army must have bored others as well as myself by its compulsive sex orientation. This disappeared completely in three weeks on the German diet of 600 calories per day.[5] The talk was only of beef steak and milk chocolate. I remember a tough sergeant major telling me all about a dream he had had about a Cadbury's bar.

After this early period (I remember saying I could only last out four weeks) the situation deteriorated in two different ways - disease and shooting. Both climaxed at about the same time. I know how near to breakdown I was driven.

Dealing with the shooting first. There had always been some intermittent shooting at night, but it slowly increased. Whenever I complained the Germans said that

(...) For some time I was the only POW medical officer to a 'punishment area' near Wittenburg. Everyone was supposed to work particularly hard and discipline was very strict indeed, both for us and the Germans. The German MO knew that if he were caught allowing any malingering he would be sent to the Eastern Front. In spite of this I found it perfectly possible to quadruple the umber of people 'off sick' at the sick parade. The POWs were carefully trained, and I specialized in the headache-migraine syndrome and back-ache. I used the French rather that the British as they were better actors. I also stage-managed small epidemics of mumps and acute nephritis. No one was ever shot or punished as a malingerer. (...)*

if no one left the barracks at night there would be no shooting. I wanted permission for prisoners to go to the outside latrines when necessary as the inside ones were often insufficient, with results that can only be imagined. They refused.

In August the bad month when everything happened, night shooting increased and then day shooting started, and for some reason it was concentrated on the hospital. The first shot put a bullet into the roof of the dental clinic and brought down plaster on the head of the New Zealand dentist when he was extracting a tooth. A few days later a bullet whizzed through my hair when I was doing my inpatient round. I remember that my right hand had just felt the outline of the spleen in a case of malaria. I have never felt the same about spleens since! On each occasion, of course, I made my routine complaints. The Germans apologised and said it was all a mistake and that it would not happen again, but of course it did.

Then came a day I shall never forget. It was in August. I had nearly finished my inpatient round when a terrified orderly told me that another orderly, a New Zealander, had been shot in the arm at the door of the hospital. I rushed to the Germans to organise his transport to the local hospital for surgical emergencies. They wounded orderly later lost his arm. I was on my way back when news came that two more orderlies had been shot, a Jugoslav and another New Zealander. They both had serious abdominal wounds. Again I was successful in arranging ambulance transport, but the German doctors refused to speak to me. I was in a rage. The Germans refused to see me at 1.30 p.m., the usual time, so I had a while to cool down a little. I could not understand why they were shooting at us.

* Cochrane AL. Effectiveness and Efficiency. Random Reflections on Health Services. London: Nuffield Provincial Hospitals Trust, 1972. (Reprinted in 1989 in association with the BMJ, reprinted in 1999 for Nuffield Trust by the Royal Society of Medicine Press, London).

Reproduced with permission from the BMJ Publishing Group and the Royal Society of Medicine Press.

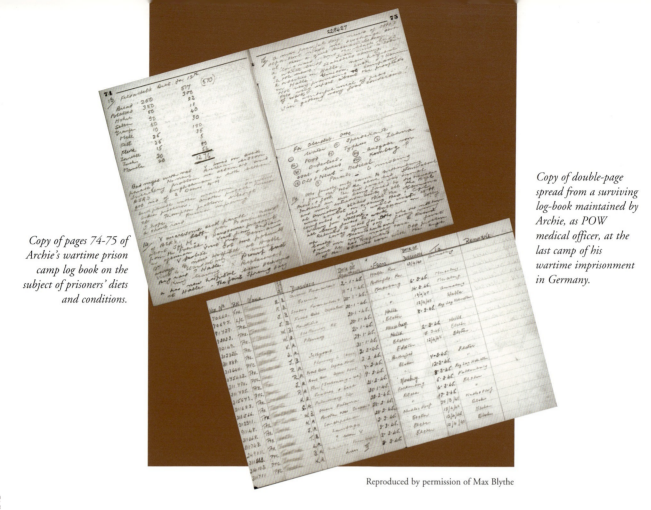

Copy of pages 74-75 of Archie's wartime prison camp log book on the subject of prisoners' diets and conditions.

Copy of double-page spread from a surviving log-book maintained by Archie, as POW medical officer, at the last camp of his wartime imprisonment in Germany.

Reproduced by permission of Max Blythe

Still worse was to come. One of the orderlies died - though the other made a more or less complete recovery. That night there was a lot of noise. A German sentry called me out and led me to a lavatory in one of the barracks. There I saw blood, faeces, and naked human flesh, illuminated by flash light. I vomited. I remember hearing the German sentry telling his sergeant that he had thrown a hand grenade into the latrine because of verdächtiges Lachen (suspicious laughter). I collected some devoted orderlies and together we treated the wounded and cleaned up the mess. Fortunately the wounds were not serious, but I spent a sleepless night. The final insult came the next morning when I was ordered to attend a German parade during which the Kommandant congratulated the sentries on their vigilance. I took the rest of the morning off.

Surprisingly, at 1.30 p.m. I received an order to appear before the Germans. Usually it was hard work persuading them to see me. It was curious that both the Kommandant and his deputy were present. I also sensed some disagreement between them, for I noticed that they were sitting fairly far apart. They asked me if I had anything to say. I had recovered from my wild rage and decided to try another line. I said in fluent German - and in German I have rather an upper class accent - how much I had admired German culture in the past. I mentioned the usual names - Goethe, Heine, Beethoven, and Mozart - and how much had been contributed to medicine through Robert Koch and, more recently, the discovery of the sulphonamides. How shocked I was therefore to find Germans, in breach of the Geneva Convention, trying to starve prisoners of war to death, murdering medical orderlies, and attempting to shoot dentists and doctors. There was a short silence, after which the Kommandant said the past might have been unpleasant though necessary, but the future would be much better. And this time he was right.

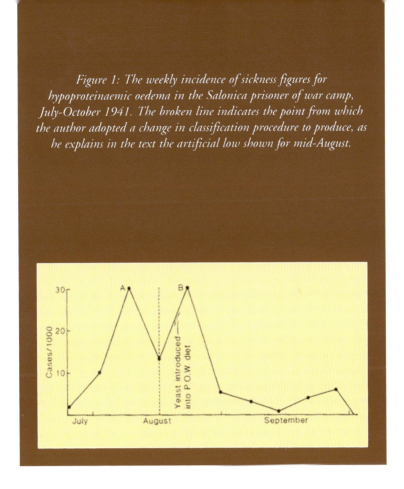

Figure 1: The weekly incidence of sickness figures for hypoproteinaemic oedema in the Salonica prisoner of war camp, July-October 1941. The broken line indicates the point from which the author adopted a change in classification procedure to produce, as he explains in the text the artificial low shown for mid-August.

The medical troubles started slowly, with skin sepsis, dysentery, and sandfly fever. The Germans gave us an old pink solution for skin sepsis and some curious pills for dysentery; both medications were ineffective. They gave us aspirin for sandfly fever, which is, fortunately, a self-limiting disease. There was a little malaria for which we got a small quantity of quinine. I thought we could survive, but then came the deluge: epidemics of diphtheria, typhoid and hepatitis. I was not too bad at diagnosing the cases. To my credit I diagnosed the early diphtheria cases and even got the first typhoid case right. The 'rose' spots were unmistakable. But what could I do about them? The Germans would give me no help, either in treatment or prevention. I had to watch the epidemics go through the camp. I was terrified and sleepless night after night; but in the event very little happened. Those with diphtheria developed frightening neurological complications but no one died. The only intervention I could think of was the forceful removal of the membranes twice a day to be sure no one suffocated. I told those with typhoid to lie still on their own faeces and I would see they were well hydrated and given as much glucose as I could get out of the Germans, and in fact only one died. Hepatitis was a different story. Everyone wanted it because it stopped hunger although it made one itch. I had it myself and it gave me my first good night's sleep for a long time, but it did not stop me worrying about the long term consequences.

Then came the final blow. Towards the end of July I noticed an increasing number of prisoners complaining of heavily swollen ankles – ankle oedema. This seemed to affect the British most seriously. The few remaining Indians, Jugoslavs, and other non-British prisoners were less affected. I also noticed that cooks were not affected, and assumed, I hope reasonably, that the cause was nutritional. I diagnosed hypoproteinamic oedema (famine oedema) and asked the Germans to measure the protein level of the blood. They refused, saying it was all due to the sun. I asked for senior physicians, who had been captured and whom I knew were in Athens, to be brought in to advise me. I was conscious of my own ignorance. They refused, saying 'Ärzte sind überflüssig' ("doctors are superfluous"). In retrospect, I think they were probably right, but it made me angry at the time and I was driven to write some verse:

> ### SUPERFLUOUS DOCTORS
>
> "Superfluous doctors- what a phrase to rouse
> Dulled prison fires to flicker with the muse
> And build a brave new world. There, there would be
> No famines, wars, or other acts of God
> To break the Peace on Earth. No! Man would turn
> From wanton killing of his cousin's kin
> To face his very foes, and Science and Art,
> With Labour an ally, would fight and kill
> Want and its very fears, disease, its very roots,
> Squalor and filth and loneliness and pain,
> And then let doctors quit the centre stage
> To usher in the prophylactic age.
> But death was near and hunger, and prisoners'
> Dreams were rare.
> The doctor in Salonica sat down and tore his hair.

We were soon seeing more than 20 new cases of severe oedema every day, and the figures were rising. As soon as the pressures of the diphtheria outbreak had subsided we had established a simple procedure for assessing disease incidence levels. This was based upon the efforts of a disabled Quaker colleague (he had been at King's College Cambridge), who sat through all sick parades and to whom doctors reported their findings. In the case of all the main diseases diagnostic checks were then carried out in the hospital and incidence levels calculated. This we did using the prisoner of war population figures supplied to the cookhouse by the Germans.

It was thorough this crude epidemiological procedure that my fears and problems grew rapidly. In fact, the rate of incidence rose so dramatically that I felt obliged to change the diagnostic criteria to disguise the fact. To qualify for inclusion in the incidence figures oedema now had to be 'pitting' oedema above the knee. Many people saw the figures and did not want a panic to add to the troubles we already had. Even then the number kept rising, and I became desperate. I knew I must do something, despite the Germans' lack of concern, and I examined the problem from a number of directions. Then I remembered having read somewhere of 'wet beriberi,' caused by vitamin B deficiency, which resulted in severe oedema. For a time I must have convinced myself that I was witnessing an epidemic of 'wet beriberi,' for I decided to do an experiment modelled on that of James Lind, one of my medical heroes.[6] I chose 20 men, all in their early twenties, all emaciated and with oedema above the knee. I put 10 in each of two small wards. They all received the standard rations, but those in one ward were given a supplement of yeast three times a day (I had to use my own reserve of Greek money to get it on the black market). In the other ward they got one vitamin C tablet each day (I had kept a small reserve for an emergency). I had meant to measure the volume of urine passed, but that provided impossible. I could obtain no buckets, so I had to fall back on 'frequency' measurements. Each man counted the number of times he passed water in 24 hours. I kept the whole thing secret. I expected, and feared, failure. I noted the numbers each morning. There was no difference between rooms for the first two days; on the third day there was a slight difference; and on the fourth it was definite. In addition, eight out of the ten men in the 'yeast room' felt better, while no one felt better in the 'vitamin C room.' I wrote it up carefully and took it to the Germans at 1.30 p.m. I must have presented an odd figure, in tattered khaki shirt and shorts. My face was emaciated and deeply jaundiced, but it was surrounded by a mass of red hair and an impressive red bear. The oedema round my knees was all too obvious.

I told them what had been done and what the results were. I claimed that it was a proof of a serious deficiency disease, 'wet beriberi', in the camp. I suggested some of the dire consequences that would result if nothing was done and became very emotional. I suddenly realised that I had truly shaken the Germans. One reason for this was the fact that the younger German doctor had heard of the trial of lemon juice in the discovery of the cure of scurvy. He even asked what I wanted in a very civilised way. I said, 'A lot of yeast at one, an increased diet as soon as possible, and the rapid evacuation of the camp.' And the Germans promised to do their best. I felt elated as I left them, but I was as depressed as ever by the time I reached the hospital. I did not think the promises would be kept. I did not really believe in 'wet beriberi' and was horrified that I had, for a time, deceived myself and the Germans. I was, deep down, sure it was famine oedema. I was also aware that it was a pretty awful trial, so I did not talk about it further. I merely closed it won by giving all those in the 'vitamin C room' a good helping of yeast. Afterwards I returned to my room and wept. The outlook seemed hopeless.

But the miracle happened. The next morning a large amount of yeast arrived; in a few days the rations were increased to provide 800 calories a day; and the evacuation of the camp was speeded up. The results of my trial were even more miraculous. They are shown in figure 1, which illustrates something of the speed with which the incidence of famine oedema declined after supplies of yeast arrived, an improvement which preceded the slight upgrading of the diet. Unfortunately I cannot pinpoint the date from which yeast was added to the diet. My notes were taken away from me when I left Salonica – but not the original graph, from which figure 1 has been prepared. Nevertheless, it is possible for me to be accurate to within a day or so, because the climax of the shootings, which I can date, coincided with the trial period. On this basis I have placed the arrival of yeast supplies three to four days before the main peak (point B) in the oedema curve.[7]

In retrospect it is impossible not to accept the causal relationship between, on the one hand, the rapid fall in incidence and rapid clinical improvement of the cases and, on the other, the consumption of yeast and the slight improvement in diet. Although I am almost certain now that the condition was hypoproteinaemic oedema and not 'wet beriberi,' the mystery still remains as to why it appeared and disappeared so quickly. The simplest explanation is that it was the protein in the yeast that did the trick, but there could well have been something else.

As regards the trial, I have always felt rather emotional about it and ashamed of it. I have seldom referred to it since. It was a poor attempt. I was testing the wrong hypothesis, the numbers were too small, and they were not randomized. The outcome measure was pitiful and the trial did not go on long enough. On the other hand, it could be described as my first, worst, and most successful trial.

Prisoners of war at the concentration camp in Salonica, Greece. Archie stayed in the camp as did many of his comrades from the Layforce Battalion.

Courtesy Theo Agorastos, Greece 2002.

Whatever the cause, a vast change came over the camp in September and October. The shooting stopped; the oedema disappeared; we were less hungry; and the evacuation of the camp started. (The Germans did not tell me that the delay in evacuation was due to the Germans' rapid advance into the Soviet Union.) We all began to relax a little. I started playing bridge and even once played for bread - winner takes all. I have never played so well.

After a time we were even able to discuss the 'bad old days.' One subject which always came up was which nationality had behaved best during the bad period? There was a curious unanimity that the New Zealanders were the best and the Australians the worst.

The next big event was the evacuation to Salonica of the prisoner of war hospital in Athens. The doctors, orderlies, and patients arrived, in the charge of Lieutenant Colonel Le Soeuf, an Australian surgeon whom I liked and respected. With him was my old friend, Bill Foreman, who I was to see so much of in the future. I have never handed over responsibility more willingly.

The camp was not completely evacuated until 30 November, but I had a much happier life. I was able to write a letter home, and to add a PS, 'Love to Sonia. ALC' (an anagram of Salonica), which amused my sister. Later we even got British Red Cross parcels, and the effect was amazing. A lot of people seemed to be drunk on tea, while wondering what to eat first. We felt, for the first time, that we were not altogether forgotten. There was a charming Scots doctor called Johnny (I have forgotten his other name), who improved my bridge enormously. I noticed that I had had no attacks of migraine since arriving in Salonica, but if this was a cure I preferred the disease.

August in Salonica was perhaps the grimmest month in my life - so bad that I almost gave up. I managed to survive, chiefly, I think, because I had responsibility and was able to write (bad) verse. The following poem, 'Duet for Two Voices,' was written in the depths of despair.

My Body

A- My eyes and ears, back, arms and leaden feet
send to the brain their neutral neural waves;
They cross the synapse, surge and meet
To etch in blood, and weariness and graves,
A martial chaos, gluttonous in defeat.

B- Oh, Christ, make memory blank.
Give cloud in clear!
What fool or blackguard gave me eyes to see
Or ears to hear.

My Heart

A- My heart is tired of war and all its
Lonely boredom under redcapped fools,
Comma'ed by steel of blitz,
With pity for the men, the patient tools,

And fear for them - for me - in sudden fits.

B- And yet this heart would gladly die for England.
Oh, Christ, you fool, you're still that fat and filthy fag,
On the touch line
Shouting 'Up, up School.'

My Mind

A- My mind can pierce the cause of war today
And see the moneyed marrow of its ills,
The way the Marxists say - can see much good can grind from
martial mills,
And can approve the end, but not the way.

B- And so the intellectual picks his doubts,
But never clean.
Oh, Christ! Decide! Come left or right!
There's no room in between.

The 'I'

A- And then the "I" - the body, heart and mind.
What can it do to make a perfect whole
Of doubt, divided, blind.
How can it case the tumult of a soul
By treating sick? By trying to be kind?

B- "Christ that my love were in my arms
and I in my bed again!" (...)*

NOTES:

1. Possibly an underestimate.
2. For another example of verse written at Salonica see page 198 ("Superfluous doctors").
3. Goons: Germans.
4. Written after the German invasion of the Soviet Union.
5. Kilocalories. Such a diet supplied only a quarter of the calories generally required.
6. James Lind's mid-eighteenth century investigations of scurvy demonstrated the link between the disease and a deficiency in diet, made good by an intake of citrous fruit, resulting in the subsequent widespread use of fruit supplements to shipboard diets.
7. See also Cochrane AL. Sickness in Salonica, my first, worst and most successful clinical trial. BMJ 1984; 289: 1726-7. The author has also discussed this trial in a video interview recorded for the Royal College of Physicians / Oxford Polytechnic Video-Archive. (Royal college of Physicians Library VTR RCP / OP12).

* Cochrane AL, Blythe M. One Man's Medicine. An Autobiography of Professor Archie Cochrane. London: BMJ (Memoir Club), 1989. Reproduced by permission of Max Blythe.

(...) RETURNING TO MY EARLY ENTHUSIASM FOR THE IDEA OF AN NHS, I SOON DISCOVERED WHAT I WANTED: EQUALITY. THE DIFFERENCE IN THE MEDICAL CARE OF THE RICH AND THE POOR WAS SUFFICIENT TO TOUCH THE HARDEST-HEARTED STUDENT IN THE 1930S. THE WORD "EQUALITY" IN MEDICAL CIRCLES HAS BEEN CORNERED TOO MUCH BY THE MEDICAL POLITICIANS, BUT I HOPE TO SHOW THAT IT HAS WIDER USES. (...)

ARCHIE COCHRANE, 1972.*

Credit & Legend, see page 326.

A RESEARCH LIFE IN WALES

Switzerland, ski party.

A RESEARCH LIFE IN WALES

"Archie was, towards the end of his life, a little disappointed that he was just regarded as someone interested in controlled trials, and not as a general epidemiologist. He liked to think that much of his best work was straightforward epidemiology. The most original and most potentially important study that he ever did was the one to find out whether tuberculosis was necessary for the production of the disabling pneumoconiosis of miners. The study which he designed for the Pneumoconiosis Research Unit sought to eliminate tuberculosis in the usual way from one of the Welsh industrial valleys, while intensive efforts were made to detect and treat all case of tuberculosis in another Welsh valley. He might have had an interesting result if streptomycin hand not just been introduced, which successfully treated tuberculosis in both valleys. That design was typical of Archie's way of thinking on a large scale and dealing with whole populations. Later, of course, he carried out many surveys of the frequency of conditions in whole populations."*

Sir Richard Doll
5 May, 2003

* Fragment of the interview with Sir Richard Doll by Susana Sans.

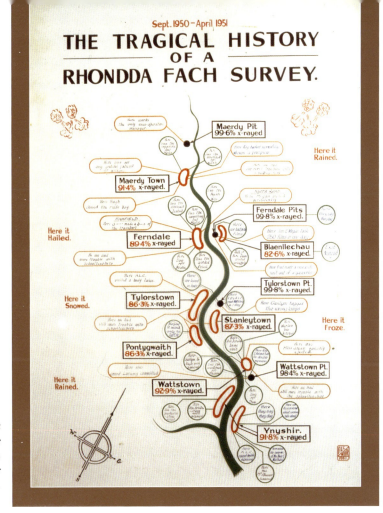

Chart of the Rhondda Fach Valley where populations surveys were conducted for over 30 years.

COHORT STUDIES AMONG MINERS

EXTRACTS FROM THE VIDEO INTERVIEW: *PROFESSOR ARCHIE COCRANE CBE (1909-1988) IN INTERVIEW WITH MAX BLYTHE. CARDIFF, SEPTEMBER 1987.* THE MEDICAL SCIENCES VIDEO ARCHIVE©

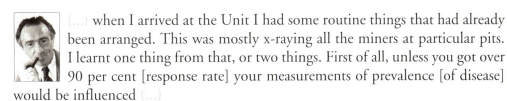 (...) when I arrived at the Unit I had some routine things that had already been arranged. This was mostly x-raying all the miners at particular pits. I learnt one thing from that, or two things. First of all, unless you got over 90 per cent [response rate] your measurements of prevalence [of disease] would be influenced (...)

(...) The second was that it was no good just x-raying people working at a pit. You must x-ray all the ex-miners from that pit to get an estimate. Those were the first two things I learnt. And then Charles [Fletcher] asked me to put forward a big epidemiological scheme and to do that I obviously wanted to test the main hypothesis about the aetiology of progressive massive fibrosis, which was much the most serious form of coal miners' pneumoconiosis. At that time, chiefly influenced by Professor Gough in Cardiff, the main hypothesis was that it was due to a mixture of tuberculosis and dust. This hypothesis I thought could be investigated by taking two [comparable mining] valleys. In one valley I would x-ray everybody, man and woman over the age of five, and get all the people with a positive sputum for tuberculosis put into hospital, thus reducing the amount of tuberculosis floating about, which we call exogenous tuberculosis infection. In the other valley I would only x-ray the working miners. Then we could measure after a time the rate of appearance of progressive massive fibrosis of simple pneumoconiosis background in the two valleys, and the amount of exogenous tuberculosis should be very different in the two valleys, and it was a rough test. (...)

X-rying of one of the civilians contributing to the study.

(...). We then, after three years, went back and did the whole thing over again. This enabled us to ... measure the attack rate of tuberculosis by age and sex and the attack rate of progressive massive fibrosis. There was a slight difference in the two valleys, but it wasn't significant and we decided to do it again in eight years and in eight years there was absolutely no difference. So we could give no support to the main hypothesis ...and all the work after that has confirmed this, that tuberculosis is not important in the aetiology of progressive massive fibrosis. (...)

(...) I have, just now, completed a thirty year follow up of those 8 400 men over the ages of twenty-one and each follow-up has produced results. The only trouble was waiting for an experimental technique....You remember in Salonika I had done a little experiment there.... I wanted something to be invented like that, and that's why I was so delighted when the randomized controlled trial was introduced into British medicine by Sir Austin Bradford Hill, who'd actually taught me when I got my DPH before going to America. I was absolutely fascinated by this ... and we applied it to some extent to pneumoconiosis. (...)*

---

* Professor Archie Cochrane CBE (1909-1988) in interview with Max Blythe. Cardiff, September 1987. London: The Medical Sciences Video Archive, Oxford Brookes University, 1987 (video interview MSVA 024).

Reproduced with permission from the Medical Sciences Video Archive Oxford Brookes University and Prof Max Blythe.

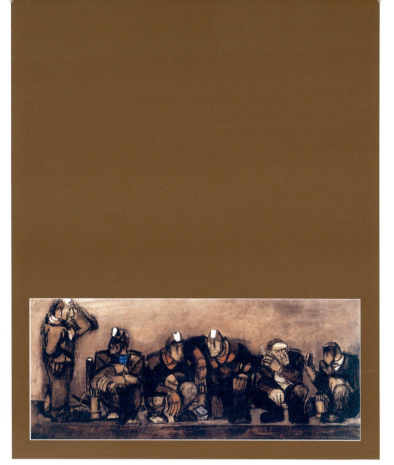

Miners crouching by Josef Herman. The picture was probably presented to Archie by the Miners' Union as a recognition of the research efforts on lung disease among miners.

ABSTRACT

COCHRANE, A L, HALEY T J L, MOORE F, HOLE D. THE MORTALITY OF MEN IN THE RHONDDA FACH, 1950-1970. BR J IND MED 1979; 36:15-22.

A more detailed analysis of material from the 20-year follow-up of men in the Rhondda Fach confirms the similarity between the Standardised Mortality Ratios (SMRs) of miners and ex-miners with radiological categories 0, 1, 2, 3 and A (120.3, 116.5, 119.0, 115.7, and 120.1 respectively) as well as the difference between these SMRs and that of the non-miners (98.7). The specific death rates show a raised SMR for bronchitis and other respiratory diseases excluding pneumoconiosis for all categories including category 0, but little difference between those for category 0 and those for simple pneumoconiosis. The SMRs for ischaemic heart disease and other circulatory diseases for categories A, B and C combined are lower than those for simple pneumoconiosis and category 0 (84.2 and 85.0, compared with 109.8 and 121.8 for simple pneumoconiosis, and 117.5 and 114.6 for category 0). Fortunately the SMR for leukaemia is low. A comparison between the survival rates of men aged 55-64 in Leigh, Lancashire and those in the Rhondda Fach suggests that non-miners in the two areas have similar survival rates while the survival rates for category 0 and simple pneumoconiosis are lower in the Rhondda Fach.

Professor Anthony J. Newman Taylor
Epidemiologist and Inmunogeneticist

Professor Newman is the Medical Director and the Director of Research at the Royal Brompton Hospital in London. He is also Chairman of the Industrial Injuries Advisory Council. He has worked in the epidemiology of asthma in relation to occupational and other environmental exposures. In September 2001 he presented The Colt Lecture with the title: Asthma and Work, delivered at the Ninth International Symposium on Inhaled Particles held in Cambridge, UK. (Ann Occup Hyg 2002: 46; 563-574). Professor Newman knew Archie and has continued working on the topic of respiratory conditions related to workplace exposures.

CURRENT EVIDENCE ON THE AETIOLOGY OF PROGRESSIVE MASSIVE FIBROSIS

COCHRANE AND COAL

Archie Cochrane joined the UK Medical Research Council (MRC) pneumoconiosis unit in the late 1940's as an epidemiologist and x-ray film reader. According to his (self written) obituary[1]:

> *"There the next 10 years were probably the most productive of his life. With an almost obsessional interest in reproducibility, low rates of refusal and validation, he showed that measurements could be made on populations defined geographically with about the same known inaccuracy as measurements made in laboratories. This helped to make epidemiology a quantitative science, but had many other results, notably in pneumoconiosis among coal miners...."*

He later regretted that the success of "Effectiveness and Efficiency" had overshadowed these achievements. In an afterword he said that *"after the publication of the book, the medical world forgot my work on pneumoconiosis and common diseases in Rhonda Fach. I believe I did my best work there and I'm sorry to see it forgotten"*.[2]

Cochrane's studies of pneumoconiosis in South Wales miners occurred at a propitious time. An MRC study, which reported in 1942, had found that the greatly increased dust levels which had followed large scale mechanisation of coal mining in the 1930's had caused an epidemic of progressive massive fibrosis (PMF).[3] Understanding the cause of PMF and the means of preventing it was an important public health priority. Three major aetiological hypotheses had been advanced: 1. PMF was caused by an interaction of coal dust and tuberculosis; 2. PMF is a reaction to the silica content of coal dust; 3. PMF is due to retained coal dust and is a progression from simple pneumoconiosis.

To test the tuberculosis hypothesis, Cochrane aimed to eliminate sources of infectious TB in Rhonda Fach by identifying sputum positive cases, having them admitted to hospital, and compare the incidence of PMF in Rhonda Fach with the neighbouring Aberdare valley, where no unusual measures had been taken to identify and isolate infectious TB cases. Cochrane's 1952 report of the prevalence of pulmonary TB in the Rhonda Fach is remarkable for the response rate he had achieved.[4] Earlier estimates of the prevalence of pulmonary TB, based on open access to mass screening units, had at best included 30% of the population. This study included 92% of men and 86% of women among a population of 19218. The response for miners was 98% and for ex-miners 95%.

In a series of subsequent papers during the next decade, Cochrane continued his investigation of the aetiology of PMF in this population. In 1962 he reported an 8 year follow up of the miners and ex-miners of the Rhonda Fach and Aberdare valleys.[5] The only important determinant of PMF identified was category of simple pneumoconiosis: rising from nil at category 1 to 30% at category 3, with an intermediate rate at category 2; although tuberculosis infectivity fell in both valleys, there was no evidence of any reduction in the attack rate of PMF. He concluded that *"the logical way to control the appearance of progressive massive fibrosis is to concentrate on preventing miners reaching category 2 of simple pneumoconiosis"*. This conclusion formed the basis in UK of the control levels of coal dust in coal miners, associated surveillance of miners by regular chest radiograph and complementary statutory compensation arrangements.

Cochrane also investigated the loss of life and lung function associated with the development of coal workers pneumoconiosis. In a paper published in 1976 he emphasised the importance of including ex-miners and miners, of "within area comparisons" and of comparing "like with like".[6] Mortality among miners and ex-miners with simple pneumoconiosis and Category A PMF was not importantly different from non miners; cases of PMF categories B and C had markedly increased death rates (SMR 232). Similarly, lung function among cases of simple pneumoconiosis was not lower than those with Category 0; only in those with PMF was lung function significantly lower. From this he argued it was unlikely that coal dust caused chronic bronchitis and airway narrowing. However, he had long recognised that the measures of coal dust exposure available to him – length of time underground, and x-ray category of pneumoconiosis, were imperfect surrogates for inhaled dust dosage, which might provide a different answer.[6] The results of the Edinburgh studies, which he awaited, demonstrated a clear correlation between FEV_1 reduction and cumulative coal dust exposure in both smokers and non-smokers.[7] This also explains a previously un-addressed observation of Cochrane's: unlike mortality rates which did not differ between non miners and simple pneumoconiosis, lung function although not different across categories 0 to 3 simple pneumoconiosis, was markedly reduced in miners as compares to non miners.[8]

Cochrane's meticulous study of the Rhonda Fach population demonstrated the importance of PMF in life and causing respiratory disability in coal miners, and showed the means to prevent it by not allowing miners to develop Category 2 pneumoconiosis. Of even greater importance he demonstrated the remarkable strength of the inferences, and the confidence in the benefit of associated interventions, which can be based on rigorously conducted population studies.

Miner being interviewed by one of Archie's team.

REFERENCES:

1. Cochrane AL. A L Cochrane [obituary]. BMJ 1988;297:63.
2. Cochrane AL. Effectiveness and Efficiency. Random Reflections on Health Services. London: Nuffield Provincial Hospitals Trust, 1972. (Reprinted in 1989 in association with the BMJ, reprinted in 1999 for Nuffield Trust by the Royal Society of Medicine Press, London).
3. Hart Pd'A, Aslett EA. Chronic pulmonary disease in South Wales coalminers. 1. Medical studies. MRC Report Seies No 243. London: HMSO, 1942.
4. Cochrane A L, Cox J G, Jarman T F. Pulmonary tuberculosis in the Rhondda Fach. BMJ 1952; 843-853.
5. Cochrane A L. The attack rate of progressive massive fibrosis. Br J Ind Med 1962;19:52-64.
6. Cochrane A L. An epidemiologist's view of the simple relationship between pneumoconiosis and morbidity and mortality. Proc R Soc Med 1976;69:12-14.
7. Marine WM, Gurr D, Jacobson M. Clinically important respiratory effects of dust exposure and smoking in British coal miners. Am Rev. Respir Dis. 1988;13:106-112.
8. Cochrane AL. Chronic bronchitis and occupation. BMJ 1966;1:858-859.

THE ASPIRIN TRIAL

(...) The method in this first trial was that male patients were identified immediately after discharge from one of a number of local hospitals, having been diagnosed as having had a myocardial infarct. The general practitioner (GP) of the patient was contacted, and the suitability of the man for the trial agreed. The patient was then visited in his own home, the trial explained, and his cooperation sought. A copy of the randomisation code was kept by Peter Sweetnam, the statistician in the Unit, and the code was broken only if a physician or GP required to know what his or her patient was receiving.

The dose of aspirin which was used in this trial had been long debated. Inhibition of platelet aggregation was judged to be the effect of aspirin of relevance to infarction and laboratory evidence from the studies by O'Brien and others, strongly indicated that a single tablet (then 5 grains or 330 mg) daily would be more than adequate.

Moreover a small dose was attractive because undesirable side effects would be less likely to occur. On the other hand, colleagues other than clotologists considered a single tablet inadequate. They recommended multiple daily doses, and all the trials which were set up later reflected the persuasiveness of clinical opinion, rather than evidence, and larger doses were generally used.

Amongst colleagues the trial received general support – and not a little amusement. In the field, however, the reception was rather different. Several aspects came under attack, not least the dose of aspirin, which some physicians dismissed as 'homeopathic'. On the other hand, aspirin was under a cloud because of its irritant effect on the gastric mucosa at high doses. For these and other reasons not a few physicians were reluctant to allow the inclusion of their patients in the trial, though only one physician refused to collaborate. Many patients were also reluctant to become involved. The idea that aspirin might actually be beneficial was quite novel to them, and seemed even bizarre, or contrived, to some. At the end of the explanation about the trial an occasional patient would ask: "Come off it, Doc, what do these capsules really contain?" (...)*

---

* Elwood P. Cochrane and the benefits of aspirin. In: Maynard A, Chalmers I. Non-Random Reflections on Health Services Research. On the 25th Anniversary of Archie Cochrane's Effectiveness and Efficiency. London: BMJ Publishing Group, 1997. p.p. 107-121.

Reproduced with permission from the BMJ Publishing Group.

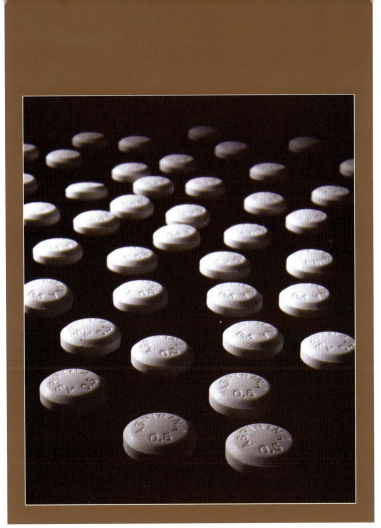

© Albert Fortuny

SUMMARY

ELWOOD PC, COCHRANE AL, BURR ML, SWEETNAM PM, WILLIAMS G, WELSBY E, HUGHES SJ, RENTON R. *A RANDOMIZED CONTROLLED TRIAL OF ACETYL SALICYLIC ACID IN THE SECONDARY PREVENTION OF MORTALITY FROM MYOCARDIAL INFARCTION.*
BR MED J 1974 MAR 1:436-440.

The results of a randomized controlled trial of a single daily dose of acetylsalicylic acid (aspirin) in the prevention of re-infarction in 1 239 men who had had a recent myocardial infarct were statistically inconclusive. Nevertheless, they showed a reduction in total mortality of 12% at six months and 25% at twelve months after admission to the trial. Further trials are urgently required to establish whether or not this effect is real.

CURRENT EVIDENCE ON THE ROLE OF ASPIRIN (AND OTHER ANTIPLATELET THERAPY) IN CARDIOVASCULAR MEDICINE

ABSTRACT

ANONYMOUS. COLLABORATIVE OVERVIEW OF RANDOMISED TRIALS OF ANTIPLATELET THERAPY--I: PREVENTION OF DEATH, MYOCARDIAL INFARCTION, AND STROKE BY PROLONGED ANTIPLATELET THERAPY IN VARIOUS CATEGORIES OF PATIENTS. ANTIPLATELET TRIALISTS' COLLABORATION. BMJ 1994 JAN 8 308:6921 81-106

OBJECTIVE– To determine the effects of "prolonged" antiplatelet therapy (that is, given for one month or more) on "vascular events" (non-fatal myocardial infarctions, non-fatal strokes, or vascular deaths) in various categories of patients.

DESIGN– Overviews of 145 randomized trials of "prolonged" antiplatelet therapy versus control and 29 randomized comparisons between such antiplatelet regimens.

SETTING– Randomized trials that could have been available by March 1990.

SUBJECTS– Trials of antiplatelet therapy versus control included about 70,000 "high risk" patients (that is, with some vascular disease or other condition implying an increased risk of occlusive vascular disease) and 30 000 "low risk" subjects from the general population. Direct comparisons of different antiplatelet regimens involved about 10 000 high risk patients.

(...) It is surely a great criticism of our profession that we have not organised a critical summary, by speciality or subspeciality, adapted periodically, of all relevant randomized controlled trials (...)*

Archie Cochrane

RESULTS– In each of four main high risk categories of patients antiplatelet therapy was definitely protective. The percentages of patients suffering a vascular event among those allocated antiplatelet therapy versus appropriately adjusted control percentages (and mean scheduled treatment durations and net absolute benefits) were: (a) among about 20 000 patients with acute myocardial infarction, 10% antiplatelet therapy v 14% control (one month benefit about 40 vascular events avoided per 1 000 patients treated (2P < 0.00001)); (b) among about 20 000 patients with a past history of myocardial infarction, 13% antiplatelet therapy v 17% control (two year benefit about 40/1000 (2P < 0.00001)); (c) among about 10 000 patients with a past history of stroke or transient ischaemic attack, 18% antiplatelet therapy v 22% control (three year benefit about 40/1 000 (2P < 0.00001)); (d) among about 20 000 patients with some other relevant medical history (unstable angina, stable angina, vascular surgery, angioplasty, atrial fibrillation, valvular disease, peripheral vascular disease, etc), 9% v 14% in 4 000 patients with unstable angina (six month benefit about 50/1 000 (2P < 0.00001)) and 6% v 8% in 16 000 other high risk patients (one year benefit about 20/1 000 (2P < 0.00001)).

* Cochrane AL 1931-1971: a critical review, with particular reference to the medical profession. In: Medicines for the year 2000. London: Office of Health Economics, 1979: 1-11

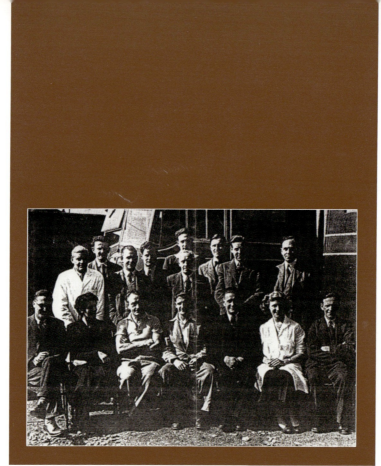

The research team in Wales.

Reductions in vascular events were about one quarter in each of these four main categories and were separately statistically significant in middle age and old age, in men and women, in hypertensive and normotensive patients, and in diabetic and nondiabetic patients. Taking all high risk patients together showed reductions of about one third in non-fatal myocardial infarction, about one third in non-fatal stroke, and about one third in vascular death (each 2P < 0.00001). There was no evidence that non-vascular deaths were increased, so in each of the four main high risk categories overall mortality was significantly reduced. The most widely tested antiplatelet regimen was "medium dose" (75-325 mg/day) aspirin. Doses throughout this range seemed similarly effective (although in an acute emergency it might be prudent to use an initial dose of 160-325 mg rather than about 75 mg). There was no appreciable evidence that either a higher aspirin dose or any other antiplatelet regimen was more effective than medium dose aspirin in preventing vascular events. The optimal duration of treatment for patients with a past history of myocardial infarction, stroke, or transient ischaemic attack could not be determined directly because most trials lasted only one, two, or three years (average about two years). Nevertheless, there was significant (2P < 0.0001) further benefit between the end of year 1 and the end of year 3, suggesting that longer treatment might well be more effective.

Among low risk recipients of "primary prevention" a significant reduction of one third in non-fatal myocardial infarction was, however, accompanied by a

[...] Archie believed that the most important single development in medical research had been the introduction of the randomized controlled trial. I believe that had he lived to see more recent developments, he would have judged that the development of the 'overview' or 'meta-analysis' is a development of equal importance. The aspirin trials played a significant part in this further development. [...] *

non-significant increase in stroke. Furthermore, the absolute reduction in vascular events was much smaller than for high risk patients despite a much longer treatment period (4.4% antiplatelet therapy v 4.8% control; five year benefit only about four per 1000 patients treated) and was not significant (2p = 0.09).

CONCLUSIONS– Among a much wider range of patients at high risk of occlusive vascular disease than is currently treated routinely, some years of antiplatelet therapy – with aspirin 75-325 mg/day) or some other antiplatelet regimen (provided there are no contraindications) – offers worthwhile protection against myocardial infarction, stroke, and death. Significant benefit is evident not only among patients with unstable angina, suspected acute myocardial infarction, or a past history of myocardial infarction, stroke, or transient ischaemic attack, but also among many other categories of high risk patients (such as those having vascular procedures and those with stable angina or peripheral vascular disease). There is as yet, however, no clear evidence on the balance of risks and benefits of antiplatelet therapy in primary prevention among low risk subjects.

* Elwood P. Cochrane and the benefits of aspirin. In: Maynard A, Chalmers I. Non-Random Reflections on Health Services Research. On the 25th Anniversary of Archie Cochrane's Effectiveness and Efficiency. London: BMJ Publishing Group, 1997. p.p. 107-121.

Reproduced with permission from the BMJ Publishing Group.

Reproduced by permission of the Royal College of Physicians

Archie conducted a number of epidemiological studies correlating mortality rates to age 65 in 18 developed countries with a number of indices of socioeconomic status, nutrition and health services. The finding of a positive association between the prevalence of doctors and mortality in the younger age groups intrigued him.[1] He also found a negative correlation with the consumption of alcohol, almost entirely described by the consumption of wine.

1. Cochrane AL, St Leger AS, Moore F. Health service 'input' and mortality 'output' in developed countries. J Epidemiol Community Health 1978;32:200-205.

WINE CONSUMPTION: THE CORRELATION THAT WOULD NOT GO AWAY.

ABSTRACT

ST LEGER AS, COCHRANE AL, MOORE F. FACTORS ASSOCIATED WITH CARDIAC MORTALITY IN DEVELOPED COUNTRIES WITH PARTICULAR REFERENCE TO THE CONSUMPTION OF WINE. LANCET 19/9 MAY 1:1017-1020.

Deaths from ischaemic heart-disease in 18 developed countries are not strongly associated with health-service factors such as doctor and nurse density. There is a negative association with gross national product per capita and a positive but inconsistent association with saturated and monounsaturated fat intake. The principal finding is a strong and specific negative association between ischaemic heart-disease deaths and alcohol consumption. This is shown to be wholly attributable to wine consumption.

CURRENT EVIDENCE ON THE ROLE OF WINE CONSUMPTION

 (...) When I chose the benefits of wine as the title of this lecture[1], I did not expect to conclude that wine was specifically more beneficial than other alcoholic beverages. I chose it, because I wanted to draw attention to Cochrane's work as an epidemiologist and because I thought that Cochrane would have wanted me to discuss some subject of present interest relevant to the practical prevention of disease. Cochrane's observation that wine consumption was negatively correlated in national vital statistics with the mortality from ischaemic heart disease and that wine consumption alone could account for the negative correlation with the consumption of alcohol led to a revival of interest in the possible beneficial effects of alcohol. It has not been possible to prove that alcohol does have such effects by means of a randomized controlled trial, nor do I think that any such trials are likely to be carried out in the future, because of the practical and ethical difficulties to which Cochrane drew attention.[2] The beneficial effect is, however, sufficiently well established for the purpose of prevention without randomized trials, as a result of case-control and cohort studies backed up by the results of the sort of physiological experiments that Cochrane proposed. (...)

(...) That the drinking of wine may be more effective that that of beer or spirits in at least some cultures seems likely; but if it is, its special benefit might well be explained by the customary patterns of drinking, with small amounts of wine being characteristically drunk every day rather than large amounts being drunk on one or two days of the week, and so ensuring that the constituents of the blood that contribute to thrombosis, are continually modified, as is achieved by small doses of aspirin taken on alternate days. We can agree with Cochrane, that the medicine is already in a highly palatable form and no-one should be called on to commit 'almost a sacrilege' by trying to isolate a specific prophylactic constituent from wine other than ethanol. We can, however now give with some confidence the information to our friends that he regretted not being able to give in 1979[2] – namely, that the relative effects of red, white, and rosè wine would all seem to be about equal. (...)*

1. Sir Richard Doll. Fourth Archie Cochrane delivered at Green College, Oxford, on 21 March 1996.
2. St Leger AS, Cochrane AL, Moore F. Factors associated with cardiac mortality in developed countries with particular reference to the consumption of wine. Lancet 1979; i: 1017-1020.

*. Doll R. Cochrane and the benefits of wine. In: Maynard A, Chalmers I. Non-Random Reflections on Health Services Research. On the 25th Anniversary of Archie Cochrane's Effectiveness and Efficiency. London: BMJ Publishing Group, 1997. p.p. 58-74.
Reproduced with permission from the BMJ Publishing Group.

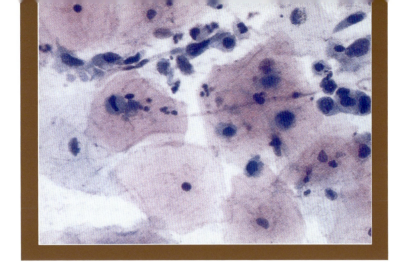

STUDIES ON SCREENING

(...) Apart from the immunization programme the record of the NHS is patchy. There are sins of omission and commission. Of the later the introduction of the programme of cervical smears in the hope of preventing carcinoma of the cervix is the saddest. It illustrates so clearly the consequences of assuming a hypothesis is correct, and translating the consequences into routine clinical practice before testing it by an RCT. Scientifically the story is relatively simple. The original idea was undoubtedly a good one. It was taken up by enthusiasts and became rapidly almost a routine clinical practice in the USA. It soon spread to this country. When suggestions were earlier made of doing an RCT it was considered unethical and the same decision has been taken in all countries ever since. It is very difficult to test the hypothesis by observational evidence. The death-rate from carcinoma of the cervix was falling before smears were introduced and has continued to fall at roughly the same rate in most areas. No convincing evidence has been published of a greater fall of this death-rate in areas where there has been a high coverage of the female population when compared with similar areas where little such work has been done. The difficulty in interpreting any difference in rates of fall of death-rates from carcinoma of the cervix (if it ever occurs) will be considerable. Areas in which there is a high coverage with smears nearly always have a much increased incidence of hysterectomy and as would be expected) a higher percentage of invasive carcinoma diagnosed at an earlier stage. If this later alters the natural history of disease it will be almost impossible to decide which of these three factors is causing the difference.

It appears to me still possible that smears may have some preventive effect, but we may never know, and the health services of the world may well expend thousands of millions of pounds in the hope of preventing a relatively rare though severe condition whose mortality rate is decreasing fairly rapidly. (...)*

---

* Cochrane AL. Effectiveness and Efficiency. Random Reflections on Health Services. London: Nuffield Provincial Hospitals Trust, 1972. (Reprinted in 1989 in association with the BMJ, reprinted in 1999 for Nuffield Trust by the Royal Society of Medicine Press, London).

Reproduced with permission from the BMJ Publishing Group and the Royal Society of Medicine Press.

Several decades later, the evidence on screening still retains some of the intellectual issues of the discussion described by Archie and his colleagues. Because of the rapidity of introduction, no randomized controlled trial was ever organized to evaluate the presence of repeated cervical cytology for the prevention of mortality due to cervical cancer. The evidence of its effectiveness eventually relied on time-trend monitoring and case control estimates but the quantification of the protective efficacy remains elusive. Ethical discussions arise endlessly on the frequency and length of intervals between screens. Cost-benefit evaluations have clearly indicated that less frequent screening (that is, every three years) offers the same level of protection against death from cervical cancer as do yearly screens. Yet a limited number of countries over-screen and most grossly under-do it. Issues of the viral origin of cervical cancer suspected at the time proved to be true, although herpes was not the culprit but the Human Papillomavirus (HPV).

On going randomized controlled trials are providing consistent evidence on the value of screening for the presence of HPV DNA. Trials are able to compare DNA tests to the standard cytology test developed in the 50s and evaluated by Archie and his colleagues. It is now largely accepted that HPV testing has greater sensitivity at a similar level of specificity in middle age women for the prevention of cervical cancer.

THE ROCK CARLING FELLOWSHIP

1971

RANDOM REFLECTIONS ON THE HEALTH SERVICE

A. L. Cochrane

CBE, FRCP
Honorary Director
M.R.C. Epidemiological Research Unit
Cardiff

THE NUFFIELD
PROVINCIAL HOSPITALS TRUST
1972

Archie's original title for "Effectiveness and Efficiency" was "Random Reflections on Health Services"; a title changed at the last hour. Here is a copy of the original proof title page, before his change of mind.

Reproduced by permission of Max Blythe

HEALTH SERVICES RESEARCH

(...) The MRC inevitably was biased towards the pure and opposed to applied research. I do not mean by this that it encouraged 'useless research' in the sense of my Cambridge days, but that it encouraged research that might in time illuminate a large field. It could at times be very liberal on the applied side, for example, the setting up of the Pneumoconiosis Research Unit, but there was an ill-defined line beyond which the MRC would not go. It is summed up for me by the phrase "The protocol's all right, but this isn't quite the sort of thing the MRC does." (...)*

---

* Cochrane AL. Effectiveness and Efficiency. Random Reflections on Health Services. London: Nuffield Provincial Hospitals Trust, 1972. (Reprinted in 1989 in association with the BMJ, reprinted in 1999 for Nuffield Trust by the Royal Society of Medicine Press, London).

Reproduced with permission from the BMJ Publishing Group and the Royal Society of Medicine Press.

HEALTH SERVICES RESEARCH

228

© Albert Fortuny

SUMMARY

COCHRANE AL. ACUTE MYOCARDIAL INFARCTION: PLACE OF TREATMENT AND LENGTH OF STAY. HERZ 1981 APR 6:112-115.

To assess whether all patients with acute myocardial infarction benefit from admission to a coronary care unit and prolonged hospitalization in relation to their substantial costs, a limited number of randomized controlled trials have been carried out under strict ethical constraints. The results indicate that a certain percentage of patients, especially those over 60 years with no complications less than three hours after onset of symptoms or late first medical contact face equally whether treated at home or in the hospital. Patients seen less than three hours after onset of symptoms, with complications such as hypotension, heart failure or arrhythmias and those who cannot adequately be cared for at home require hospitalization. An alternative combining the best features of both hospital and home care appears feasible through patient monitoring for two hours in the home by a team of technicians dispatched with a specially equipped ambulance. The outcome of patients admitted to the hospital with uncomplicated acute myocardial infarction, with respect to short and long-term mortality and morbidity, has not been adversely affected by progressively early mobilization and discharge indicating that a length of stay of more than seven to nine days would no longer seem necessary.

Field survey on nutritional deficiencies in rural China.

(...) He (Archie Cochrane) even turned his attention to dental treatment, arranging for two dental surgeons to examine the same group of patients and prescribe treatment. He claimed that the only agreement between them was over the number of teeth in each patient's mouth (...) *

MEASUREMENT ERROR

(...) As regards laboratory tests I have always found it surprising how uninterested clinicians are in the 'between, and within, laboratory variation' in test results. Epidemiologists, making measurements on defined communities, often use the same laboratory facilities as the clinician and the preliminary investigations of the reproducibility of laboratory work made by the epidemiologists often alarm them so much that they go elsewhere or do the work themselves. One particular facet which worried me personally about laboratory biochemical work is the almost complete lack of interest in whether the blood was taken fasting, the time interval and temperature of the blood between taking and spinning, and spinning and analysis. It is, I suppose, reasonable for clinicians not to be as obsessional as epidemiologists, and that they should not be so interested in 'between laboratory' variation, but I am surprised they have not insisted much more on the reduction of 'within laboratory' variation. One can only conclude that the results are not particularly important in the clinical decision-making. (...)**

---

* Archie Cochrane. Obituary. King's College Annual Report. October 1989.
   Reproduced by kind permission of the Provost and Scholars of King's College, Cambridge.

** Cochrane AL. Effectiveness and Efficiency. Random Reflections on Health Services. London: Nuffield Provincial Hospitals Trust, 1972. (Reprinted in 1989 in association with the BMJ, reprinted in 1999 for Nuffield Trust by the Royal Society of Medicine Press, London).
   Reproduced with permission from the BMJ Publishing Group and the Royal Society of Medicine Press.

OVER TIME, MANY OF THE PARTICIPANTS IN THE SPANISH CIVIL WAR
WENT BACK TO THE FRONT IN AN EMOTIONAL EXERCISE OF SELF-DISCOVERY.
AS A RESULT, SEVERAL WRITTEN TESTIMONIES ARE AVAILABLE SUCH AS THE ONE
PUBLISHED BY ARCHIE SOON AFTER HIS VISIT.
TO BE PART OF SUCH A MENTAL AND EMOTIONAL EFFORT, EVEN AS A TRAVEL
COMPANION, WAS A MOST ENRICHING EXPERIENCE AS WELL AS
A LIFE LONG STORY TO TELL OTHERS.

F. XAVIER BOSCH, 1978

* *Credit & Legend, see page 326.*

BACK TO THE FRONT

FORTY YEARS BACK: A RETROSPECTIVE SURVEY

British Medical Journal 22-29 December 1979.

COCHRANE AL
PERSONAL PAPERS
FORTY YEARS BACK: A RETROSPECTIVE SURVEY
BMJ 1979; II: 1662-3.

When Franco was finally allowed to die I felt vaguely that I should return and visit the hospitals where I had worked as a medical student during the Spanish Civil War in 1936-7. But my Spanish is now negligible and it all seemed too difficult, until by chance, at a party given by Professor Lester Breslow in Los Angeles, I met a young Spanish epidemiologist, Dr Xavier Bosch, a Catalan from Barcelona. I was fascinated by the fact that he knew the village of Grañén, where I had first worked as a student in 1936. I thought I amused him by my sudden memory of a song about Catalans in Hemingway's *For Whom the Bell Tolls*:

Reproduction of the poem by Hemingway handwritten by Archie Cochrane in a postcard sent to author.

Near el Escorial, 1978.

But the main reason, as I learned later, for his agreeing to take me to Grañén was the kindness of his Catalan heart.

Later we lost contact and a telegram went stray, but we finally met at Barcelona airport, both rather nervous that we wouldn't recognise each other; but all went well. Xavier had organised everything. After a quiet and amusing dinner on Thursday night I slept in the new Hotel Colon. The old one in 1936 was the headquarters of the anarchists. On the Friday I gave a lecture on applied epidemiology (I think, for the first time in my life, my audience was more interested in me as a member of the International Brigades than as an epidemiologist). This was followed by a most amusing lunch with some young Catalan clinicians. Xavier then drove us, very carefully, the long, rather weary way up to Huesca through Lerida and Barbastro, where we spent the night.

The next day was to be the high point of the trip when we drove the few miles to Grañén, but there was an unfortunate anticlimax. I had been certain that I would recognise the old, large house of the fascist doctor, who had run away in 1936, but after monitoring and walking round the small village I couldn't find it. My morale sank low. Xavier, as always, came to the rescue. He talked to the old men, who were gossiping in the sun in the small village square. Suddenly it became clear that everyone over 55 knew all about the "English" hospital. I was escorted there in style but, even when in front of it, I could not recognise it. There was some excuse.

Grañén, 1978.

It had been bombed in 1938 and reconstructed partly as a cinema and partly as a bar.

I was enthusiastically welcomed by Antonio, the owner of the bar, and his family, who showed me around. The bar was unrecognisable, as was the restaurant behind. Permission to go upstairs was quickly granted, but the next storey had been subdivided to house many families after the bombing. I could recognise nothing. I moved towards a window and suddenly found myself in our old so-called "operating suite". It was now a sitting room and two bedrooms, but it was unmistakable, and from this stable point I was able to recognise much else. Memories flooded back. The shock of the difference between University College Hospital and Grañén's windswept plain; the satisfactory feeling of doing something anti-fascist, instead of talking about it; the feeling of playing a small part in something historically important is there something missing here?. On the other hand, there were minor memories of the breakdown in morale when we hadn't enough to do , the awful enteritis (Grañén "gripes"), and the everlasting beans we had to eat.

I talked to many people in the following hours. I was clear that the hospital had had a much better reputation than my memories suggested. (Perhaps it improved after I left for Madrid in December 1936.) Nobody was remembered by name, but there was one English doctor whom everyone remembered. He bathed everyday in the Rio Flumen, even when he had to break the ice- such is fame. Let this doctor stand up and be counted and join those distinguished people whose names are associated with Grañén. It really is distinguished for a village that had a population under 2000 in 1936. In the first place, it housed the first international hospital to be established in

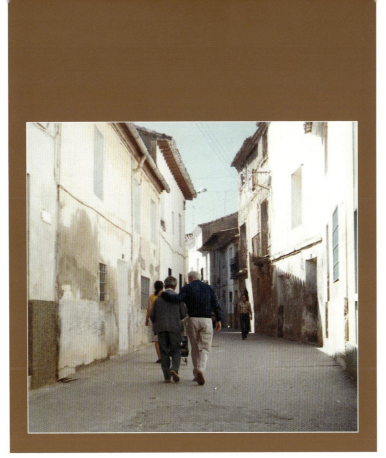

Grañén, 1978.

the Spanish Civil War. It was, indirectly, made immortal by John Cornford's poem "The Last Mile to Huesca", which must have been written at or near Grañén. Tito of Jugoslavia had a house there in 1937, and General Walter – later Minister of Defence in Poland – lived in another house there in 1938. It was certainly visited in 1936 by Ludwig Renn, who wrote the famous novel Der Krieg after the First World War. Orwell too was probably there, and, at a lower level, Sefton Delmer of the Daily Express and Lord Churchill (of All My Sins Remembered) also visited.

The one depressing feature of the visit was evidence that the division among the political left, which was so fatal during the civil war, had continued. One man excused himself from arranging an introduction because of political differences (presumably socialist-communist). In a discussion I asked one of the elders if he thought the idea of the International Brigades a good one. After thought he answered (through Xavier as interpreter) that it was, but that it wasn't enough. I found how right he was when I checked the figures in Hugh Thomas's book The Spanish Civil War. On Franco's side, in addition to the 75 000 Moors, there were 75 000 Italians and 17 000 Germans, while on the Republican side the International Brigades numbered only 2 000 Russians and 10 000 others. This was certainly not enough.

There was also the farce of the "non-intervention committee." Hugh Thomas has some apt comments: "From the start the British and French Governments were occupied less with the end of intervention on all sides than with the appearance of such an end ... When it was clear that the intervention pact was being disregarded, it was cynical to insist on its maintenance. The cynicism brought the British Government as little credit as it did advantage."

Near Brunete, 1978.

The comparison with the Rhodesian oil sanction is, I think, immediately obvious. How is it that we have so often elected the stupid and insincere to rule over us?

It was for me a most memorable weekend, and my thanks to Dr Xavier Bosch are great: but the word weekend reminds me of my welcome at University College Hospital after a year in the Spanish Civil War. I had left the hospital without permission. I came back a year later, very bronzed with a red beard. I did not know what would happen. To discover, I went on a ward round with the most conservative physician. He spotted me and said "Ah, Cochrane, back again. Had an interesting weekend?".*

---

* Cochrane AL. Forty years back: a retrospective survey BMJ 1979; ii: 1662-1663.
  Reproduced with permission from the BMJ Publishing Group.

Archie and Xavier. Dinner in Grañén in 1978.

A TRIAGE OF TRAVEL ANECDOTES

In one of the villages, an old fellow volunteered to show us the house where the English hospital was located. He could not speak English, neither could Archie speak Spanish. They were roughly the same age. On our way he explained that his son was among the wounded who were helped at the English hospital. He remembered the names of several young women from the village who had served as nursing Sisters in the surgical ward and he was deeply grateful because his son had kept his leg following an operation. Archie was sceptical about the medical success and could not remember the women but went along without speaking. The villa was a ruin, with the remaining walls still showing past splendour. Archie felt that it was the right place and climbed inside. On his way out the old man offered him some wild flowers that he had picked from the garden. They hugged each other in a moment of intense emotion. I could not see a tear in Archie's or the old man's eyes.

In El Escorial, home of one of the treasures of Spanish history, the International Brigades were supporting the front at Madrid. At seven in the morning we were wandering the streets and decided to start our quest with two characters that seemed to be enjoying an early Sunday walk. One was a priest. Soon after our ritual introduction the conversation became tense. I never knew if Archie noticed. It so happened that our counterpart was the son and heir of a wealthy family whose properties, in particular the mansion, was used by the Brigades as their camp and the hospital was installed in its spacious grounds. The furniture was used as firewood and the place was somehow damaged. After the war, the family could not cope with the cost of buying the place again and after years of decay the building was transformed into an elegant hotel and vacation resort. While the frustrated heir

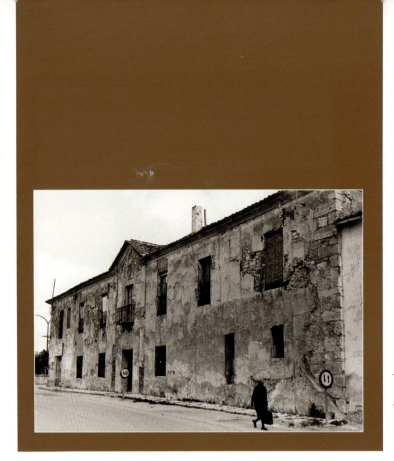

Old palace near the Jarama Valley where the English hospital that provided medical services to the International Brigades was installed.

was telling us the story and showing us the way to his ancestor's mansion, the priest, still using the traditional cassock kept blaming us in whispers for all the evil that had happened to his friend's family. He labelled us as "rojos" (reds) mimicking astonishment at our nerve to come back to the scene of the crime. At the new and flamboyant hotel the owner received us politely, offered us breakfast and listened to our story with professional non-emotion.

After El Escorial, we were guided to the top of a hill where we found a huge building that seemed untouched since the war. Archie recognized the place, burned and broken as a skeleton abandoned in nature. He described the convenience of the place because of the battle line position and the escape routes. He recognized the triage area and the surgical room. He wandered, lost in thoughts, for some time. We climbed the roof and stared at the impressive scenery. His mind always dominated and he never indulged in an emotional spell (cover page).

Near Madrid, the Valle de los Caidos (Valley of the fallen), was conceived as the war memorial for the leaders and the troops of the nationalist side. Franco is buried there as well as Jose Antonio Primo de Rivera, considered one of the intellectual leaders of the fascist party "Falange Española". Archie believed that some English soldiers were buried in the basilica and we, naively, went inside and requested to look over the archives. The monk who listened to us showed us a master book and we immediately understood that the valley was not green enough for us.

In the summer of 2001 a British nuclear submarine, The Tireless, was harbored in Gibraltar for repair. That created yet another national debate on the presence of the British flag in Southern Spain.

A recurrent topic in our conversation as we drove along was the conflict of interest around Gibraltar. On several occasions the claim of the Spanish government over the custody of the Rock was jokingly discussed by Archie who could not see any reason to give it back to the Spanish government. Archie liked to explain an anecdote about his time in Salonica. At a point in time the prisoners were selected in groups and the implication was that some would be treated better than others. Archie was fond of his Spanish friends and feared that they would be placed in the wrong group. He reacted rapidly and claimed that they were English nationals who, unfortunatelly, could not speak English because they were originally from Gibraltar, which was indeed English territory.

Occasionally Archie used to see other veteran members of the Brigades in London. Some ceramic plates were made to keep the memory alive.

The Cochrane Collaboration logo illustrates a systematic review of data from seven randomized controlled trials (RCTs), comparing one health-care treatment with a placebo. Each horizontal line represents the results of one trial (the shorter the line, the more certain the result); and the diamond represents their combined results. The vertical line indicates the position around which the horizontal lines would cluster if the two treatments compared in the trials had similar effects; if a horizontal line touches the vertical line, it means that that particular trial found no clear difference between the treatments. The position of the diamond to the left of the vertical line indicates that the treatment studied is beneficial. Horizontal lines or a diamond to the right of the line would show that the treatment did more harm than good.

This diagram shows the results of a systematic review of RCTs of a short, inexpensive course of a corticosteroid given to women about to give birth too early. The first of these RCTs was reported in 1972. The diagram summarises the evidence that would have been revealed had the available RCTs been reviewed systematically a decade later: it indicates strongly that corticosteroids reduce the risk of babies dying from the complications of immaturity. By 1991, seven more trials had been reported, and the picture had become still stronger. This treatment reduces the odds of the babies of these women dying from the complications of immaturity by 30 to 50 per cent.

Because no systematic review of these trials had been published until 1989, most obstetricians had not realised that the treatment was so effective. As a result, tens of thousands of premature babies have probably suffered and died unnecessarily (and needed more expensive treatment than was necessary). This is just one of many examples of the human costs resulting from failure to perform systematic, up-to-date reviews of RCTs of health-care.

THE LEGACY

THE
COCHRANE
COLLABORATION

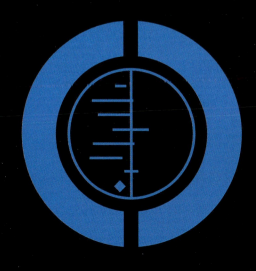

Sir Iain Chalmers
Health Services Researcher

In 1992 the first Cochrane Centre was opened in Oxford, in the UK, "to facilitate systematic, up-to-date reviews of randomized controlled trials of health-care." A year later a decision to form The Cochrane Collaboration was taken at a meeting (the 1st Cochrane Colloquium) convened by the Centre. An account of the background and early history of The Cochrane Collaboration was published in 1998.[1] Thousands of individuals have contributed to its success, and I hope that many of them will record their recollections. The purpose of this personal memoir is to reflect on the prehistory of the first Cochrane Centre.

THE PRE-HISTORY OF THE FIRST COCHRANE CENTRE

I became interested in evaluating the effects of health-care in 1969 and 1970, while working for the United Nations in a Palestinian refugee camp in the Gaza Strip. It gradually dawned on me there that some things I had been taught in medical school were probably lethally wrong.[2] This came as a very sobering realisation: how could it be that health professionals acting with the best of intentions could do more harm than good to those who looked to them for help?

After a couple of years in Gaza I returned to Britain, to train in obstetrics, in Cardiff, the capital city of Wales. As a junior obstetrician I was confused by the conflicting opinions of senior doctors about when and how to intervene in pregnancy and childbirth. In 1972, however, a very readable little book[3] came to my rescue.[4] *Effectiveness and Efficiency: Random Reflections on Health Services* (Cochrane 1972) had been written by Archie Cochrane, the director of the Medical Research Council Epidemiology Unit in Cardiff.

Archie's book and his subsequent friendship made me a lifelong sceptic about therapeutic claims unsupported by reliable evidence. It helped me to understand why some forms of research – particularly randomized controlled trials (RCTs) – were likely to generate more reliable information than others. In addition, I could identify strongly with Archie's commitment to the decent principle of equitable access to (effective) health-care, and his emphasis on the need to provide humane and dignified (and thus effective) *care* when no effective *cure* was available.

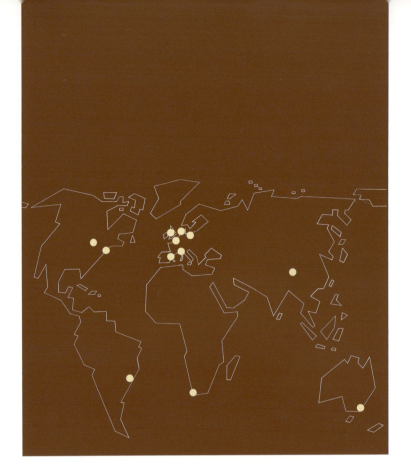

COCHRANE CENTRES

Australasian Cochrane Centre Clayton, Victoria, AUSTRALIA	Iberoamerican Cochrane Centre Barcelona, SPAIN
Brazilian Cochrane Centre São Paulo, BRAZIL	Italian Cochrane Centre Milano, ITALY
Canadian Cochrane Centre Hamilton, Ontario, CANADA	Nordic Cochrane Centre Copenhagen, DENMARK
Chinese Cochrane Centre Chengdu, Sichuan, CHINA	South African Cochrane Centre Cape Town, SOUTH AFRICA
Dutch Cochrane Centre Amsterdam, THE NETHERLANDS	UK Cochrane Centre Oxford, UK
German Cochrane Centre Freiburg, GERMANY	United States Cochrane Center Providence, USA

After discussions with one of Archie's young colleagues – David Bainton – I decided to go with David to the London School of Hygiene and Tropical Medicine and the London School of Economics to learn more about evaluating health-care, by attending a masters degree course in social medicine. The first year of the course, which was the creation of Jerry Morris, was the most stimulating twelve months of formal education I had ever experienced, partly because we were actively encouraged to challenge authority! The second year of the course involved doing research at the Department of Medical Statistics at the Welsh National School of Medicine, in collaboration with two statisticians (Robert Newcombe and Hubert Campbell) and two obstetricians (Alec Turnbull and James Lawson), to assess the effects of obstetric care.[5-8] Although we had access to a wonderfully rich database of observational data – the Cardiff Births Survey - the main lesson I learned was that it was impossible, without randomisation, to be confident that our analyses had controlled all the relevant biases sufficiently to allow us to draw confident conclusions about the effects of care.

(...) The critical step forward which brought an experimental approach into clinical medicine can be variously dated. As previously mentioned I personally like to associate it with the publication in 1952 by Daniels and Hill[1]. At any rate there is no doubt that the credit belongs to Sir Austin Bradford Hill. (...) (My pet idea is that there should be a 'Bradford' awarded to the best medical statistical paper of the year!) (...)*

Sir Austin Bradford Hill

SYSTEMATIC SEARCHES FOR REPORTS OF CONTROLLED TRIALS

Through David Bainton I came to know Archie Cochrane as a friend and mentor, and, as a result of his influence and the influence of his book, I started in 1974 to search systematically for reports of controlled trials. Archie tried to help this endeavour by seeking funding support from the Nuffield Provincial Hospitals Trust and the Milbank Memorial Fund. I think that his lack of success may have been one of the factors that prompted his now famous call for a critical summary, updated periodically, of all relevant RCTs.[9] In spite of the lack of formal funding, however, it was possible to make some progress in developing a register of perinatal controlled trials.[10] Steve Pritchard, a librarian at the Welsh National School of Medicine, designed a MEDLINE search for RCTs, and a few generous volunteers – including a general practitioner, Ann McPherson, and my wife, Jan – began the task of handsearching journals for relevant reports. A few years later the Maternal and Child Health Division of WHO provided funds to support handsearches of scores of journals. This helped to create a register that was used by Kay Dickersin and her colleagues to reveal the limitations of MEDLINE searches.[11]

---

1. Daniels M, Hill AB. Chemotherapy of pulmonary tuberculosis in young adults. An analysis of the combined results of three Medical Research Council trials. BMJ 1952; I:1162.

* Cochrane AL. Effectiveness and Efficiency. Random Reflections on Health Services. London: Nuffield Provincial Hospitals Trust, 1972. (Reprinted in 1989 in association with the BMJ, reprinted in 1999 for Nuffield Trust by the Royal Society of Medicine Press, London).
Reproduced with permission from the BMJ Publishing Group and the Royal Society of Medicine Press.

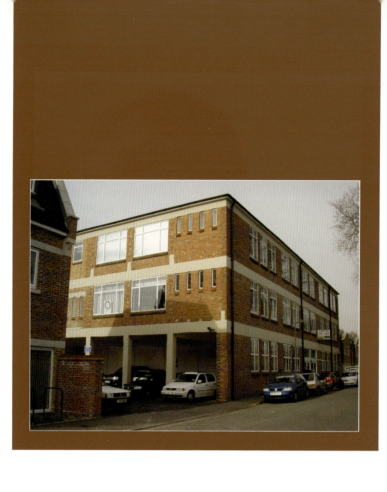

Summertown Pavilion in Oxford, where the first Cochrane Colloquium was held in 1993, and is still now the home of the UK Cochrane Centre.

In the mid-1970s, women in the UK were beginning to criticise the maternity services,[12] and researchers who agreed with many of their criticisms were preparing a book entitled *Benefits and Hazards of the New Obstetrics*.[13] One of the editors, Martin Richards (a professor of psychology in Cambridge), invited me to prepare a chapter on causal inference in obstetric practice. This showed the wide variation in obstetric intervention rates within and across countries, indicating that uncertainties must exist about the circumstances in which interventions did more good than harm.[14] In 1976, while working on this chapter, I outlined in a letter to Martin a plan for addressing these uncertainties in a systematic review of controlled trials in pregnancy, childbirth and early infancy. The plan suggested that it would be worth exploring whether the results of similar trials could be combined to yield statistically more robust estimates of treatment effects.

In 1978, an institutional base to develop these ideas became available when I was asked by the Department of Health to establish a national perinatal epidemiology unit in Oxford. The same year an opportunity arose to test my tentative plans when I was invited to review evidence of the effects of alternative ways of monitoring fetal wellbeing during labour for the European Congress of Perinatal Medicine in Vienna. After I had identified the four relevant RCTs (one of which had not been published), I contacted the investigators for clarifications and additional information, and assembled the data. Klim McPherson, a medical statistician in Oxford, helped me with the analysis. This suggested that the distribution of 13 cases of neonatal convulsions among just over 2 000 babies was unlikely to reflect chance: compared with intermittent auscultation, continuous fetal heart rate monitoring with an option to assess fetal acid-base status seemed to reduce the rate of convulsions.[15] This observation informed the design of a randomized trial involving over 13 000 mothers and their babies, which confirmed the effect suggested by the meta-analysis.[16]

Cochrane Centre Directors meeting in San Antonio, USA, 2000.

From L to R:
Margaret Haugh (France),
Jimmy Volmink (South Africa),
Andy Oxman (Norway),
Martin Offringa (Holland),
Chris Silagy (Australia),
Xavier Bonfill (Spain),
Kay Dickersin (USA),
Youping Li (China),
Gerd Antes (Germany),
Cynthia Mulrow (USA),
Peter Gøtzsche (Denmark),
Lúcia Christina Iochida (Brazil),
Philippa Middleton (Australia),
Elena Telaro (Italia),
Monica Kjeldstrøm (Denmark).

At bottom:
Jini Hetherington (United Kingdom),
Melissa Ober (USA).

ASSEMBLING A PREGNANCY AND CHILDBIRTH SYSTEMATIC REVIEW TEAM

From that year on, a team began to emerge, coordinated from the National Perinatal Epidemiology Unit, for taking forward the plans for a systematic review of the effects of care in pregnancy and childbirth. The first key members to join with me in the team were Murray and Eleanor Enkin – an obstetrician and a library assistant, respectively - from McMaster University in Canada. They coded over 3 500 reports of RCTs, subsequently made publicly available in an indexed bibliography.[17]

As this raw material for systematic reviews emerged, Murray Enkin and I drew on it to edit a book on the effects of antenatal care.[18] Because the book was well received, we were encouraged to embark on a far more ambitious project, and recruited another key member of the team, Marc Keirse, a Belgian obstetrician working at Leiden in the Netherlands. With administrative support from Jini Hetherington and Sally Hunt, and computing support from Malcolm Newdick and Mark Starr, Murray, Marc and I set about extending the team to involve about a hundred contributors, to prepare systematic reviews on most aspects of care during pregnancy and childbirth.

In the 1980s there was a rapid growth in the application of scientific principles to the process of synthesizing the results of clinical research. These syntheses were mainly in the fields of cancer and cardiovascular disease, along with our work in the perinatal field. One of the perinatal reviews[19] was an early version of the meta-analysis that subsequently formed the basis of the logo of The Cochrane Collaboration (http://www.cochrane.de/cochrane/cc-broch.htm#LOGO). This activity began to throw up methodological challenges that had not been dealt with by traditional approaches to reviewing research evidence. Publication bias was one of these

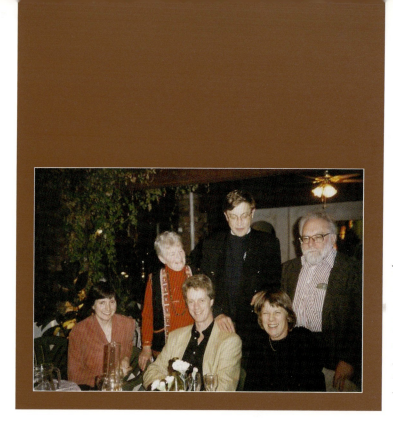

The editorial team of the first Cochrane Collaborative Review Group - Mary Renfrew, Eleanor Enkin, Jim Neilson (subsequently Co-Chair of The Cochrane Collaboration), Marc Keirse, Jini Hetherington and Murray Enkin.

challenges, and Jini Hetherington and I became involved in investigations of this phenomenon in collaboration with Kay Dickersin and Curt Meinert at the Johns Hopkins School of Public Health, and Tom Chalmers at the Mount Sinai Medical Center in New York.[20, 21]

By 1987, the compendium of systematic reviews of the effects of care in pregnancy and childbirth was beginning to take shape, and Murray, Marc and I spent May of that year working on the manuscripts at the Rockefeller Foundation's Study Centre in Bellagio, on Lake Como in Italy. While there, we met Kenneth Warren, the director of the Foundation's medical programme. When he learned that we wanted to ensure that the results of our research were disseminated to women using the maternity services, Ken provided a grant to support the preparation of a paperback summary of our findings. Later that year, our work was greatly helped by Andy Oxman, a masters student (already qualified as a physician), who had designed at McMaster University what was probably the first course on research synthesis for health professionals.[22]

Participants at the 1st Cochrane Colloquium. Oxford (UK), October 1993.

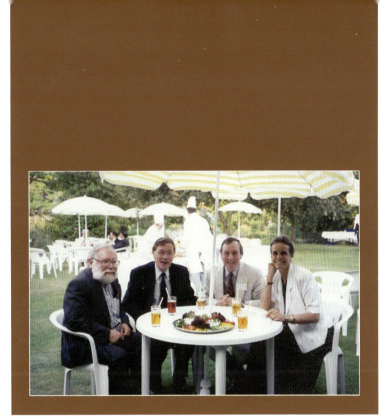

Murray Enkin, Marc Keirse and Iain Chalmers, the editors of ECPC, GECPC and ODPT, with Jan Chalmers.

PUBLISHING SYSTEMATIC REVIEWS ON PAPER AND ELECTRONICALLY

The pregnancy and childbirth books – a 1500-page, 2-volume monster entitled *Effective Care in Pregnancy and Childbirth (ECPC)*[23] and a 370-page paperback summary called *A Guide to Effective Care in Pregnancy and Childbirth (GECPC)*[24] – were published in 1989, the year after Archie Cochrane's death.[25] When it became clear that the project would be completed, we asked Archie to contribute a Foreword for *ECPC*. We were pleased that he withdrew "the slur of the wooden spoon" which he had previously awarded to obstetrics for being the medical specialty that had the worst record of rigorous evaluation of its work.[9] But we were even prouder when he declared the systematic review of the randomized trials of obstetric practice presented in the book to be "a new achievement" and "a real milestone in the history of randomized trials and in the evaluation of care", which he hoped would be "widely copied by other specialties".[26] In fact, replication was already underway: Jack Sinclair and Mike Bracken, while on sabbatical leave at the National Perinatal Epidemiology Unit in Oxford, had developed their plans for *Effective Care of the Newborn Infant (ECNI)*,[27] which were able to draw on the register of perinatal trials we had assembled for their raw material.

Like many books, ours were out of date in some important respects by the time they were published. Although updating the paperback book was a practical proposition (it is now in its 3rd edition, and has been translated into many languages), nobody had the energy or time for the task of updating the 1 500 pages of the main work. Some years previously, however, in a letter to *The Lancet* in 1986, I had signalled an alternative response to Archie's challenge to publish periodic updates of systematic reviews of RCTs.[28] This had been conceptualised on a Sunday afternoon walk in Oxford with Muir Gray, a public health doctor. We had discussed how electronic media might be exploited to make up-to-date information inexpensively available

Drummond Rennie (left), Co-Director of the San Francisco Cochrane Center, and Iain Chalmers (right), Director of the UK Cochrane Centre, reading the Chinese Journal of Evidence-Based Medicine at the 10th Cochrane Colloquium in Stavanger (Norway), 2002.

in remote parts of the world (we used Juba, in the south of Sudan, as our example). The systematic reviews that were then being prepared for the pregnancy and childbirth books seemed ideal candidates for piloting this idea.

Malcolm Newdick and Mark Starr did the programming necessary to assemble and display all the hundreds of analyses being prepared for the books. At the end of 1988, these were published electronically, together with structured abstracts, and then regularly updated in an electronic journal called *The Oxford Database of Perinatal Trials (ODPT)*,[29] which also contained the register of controlled trials we had assembled. Between 1988 and 1992, *ODPT* was distributed every six months on floppy diskettes. Under Mark Starr's guidance, *ODPT* evolved first into the *Cochrane Pregnancy and Childbirth Database* and then into the pregnancy and childbirth module of *The Cochrane Database of Systematic Reviews*.[30]

In 1989 and 1990 these three outcomes of our collaborative work – *ECPC*, *GECPC* and *ODPT* – received a good deal of favourable attention.[31] We were particularly pleased by the reception given to our work by women using the maternity services and by the organisations endeavouring to represent their interests. It was even more fortunate that one of the people who approved of our work was Michael Peckham, an oncologist who had been appointed to establish and direct a Research and Development Programme for the National Health Service.[32]

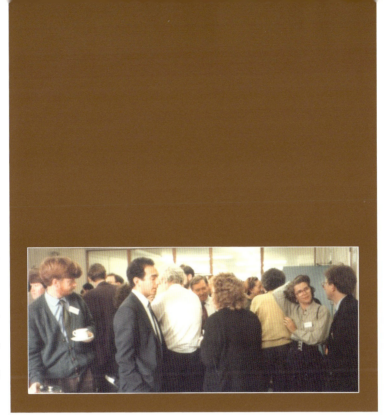

A coffee break during the first Colloquium. L to R: Sally Hunt, Alessandro Liberati, Alejandro Jadad, Muir Gray (from behind), Carol Lefebvre, Doug Altman (from behind), Lelia Duley and Paul Garner.

ENVISIONING A *COCHRANE COLLABORATION*

In May 1991, a few months after Michael Peckham had taken up his post, I was thinking while walking soon after sunrise by the Thames, north of Oxford. It occurred to me that it would be worth attempting to initiate an international collaboration to build on the methods that we had used and explored in the pregnancy and childbirth work, with a view to extending them to other specialties – as Archie Cochrane had hoped would happen. On my return home, I prepared a synopsis of the idea on one side of a sheet of paper, and asked Michael Peckham if I could discuss it with him. A couple of weeks later we met, and he was encouraging. He sent me away to draft a full proposal for 'a Cochrane Centre, to facilitate the preparation, maintenance and dissemination of systematic reviews of randomized controlled trials of health-care'.

Michael Peckham's main advisory committee considered a first full proposal for the Cochrane Centre in October 1991, then a redrafted proposal in February 1992. I gather it received a mixed reception. Some people familiar with the pregnancy and childbirth work knew that there had been some successful pilot experience. Others simply saw the proposal as too risky. Still others thought that it was not worth investing resources to find out what, in theory, was known already. I had applied for 5 years' support, with an external assessment after 3 years. In view of the ambivalence among his advisers, Michael Peckham offered me 3 years' support, with just 20 months to show that progress towards agreed targets was occurring. As a contract researcher, who had never had any job security, this seemed like a risk worth taking. 'The Cochrane Centre' was opened later that year by the minister of health – Tom Sackville - and drawn to the attention of the outside world in editorials published in the *BMJ*[33] and *The Lancet*.[34]

Over the previous two decades, I had come to know many individuals who felt then and continue to feel that the results of research could be exploited more systematically for the benefit of those using and working in health services. During 1992, after the proposal to establish the Cochrane Centre had been given the go-ahead, I contacted many of these colleagues and friends. I thought they should know that the NHS Research and Development Programme had provided an opportunity to show that the vision that we shared could be translated into reality, but that this would not happen without wholehearted, generous-spirited international collaboration. The most important initiative of the first Cochrane Centre was to invite these people to participate in 'a colloquium' to discuss whether, and if so how, an international collaboration could be established to take forward this work. In October 2003, a year after the first Cochrane Centre had opened, they met in Oxford and agreed to establish The Cochrane Collaboration.

ACKNOWLEDGEMENTS

I am grateful to Jan Chalmers, Murray Enkin, Kay Dickersin, Jini Hetherington, Marc Keirse, Andy Oxman, Michael Peckham, Mark Starr and Jan Vandenbroucke for helpful comments on an earlier draft of this memoir, and to the many people who made important contributions to the pre-history of the first Cochrane Centre, particularly Frank Hytten and William Silverman.

REFERENCES:

1. Dickersin K, Manheimer E. The Cochrane Collaboration: evaluation of health-care and services using systematic reviews of the results of randomized controlled trials. Clin Obstet Gynecol 1998;41:315-331.
2. Chalmers I. Why we need to know whether prophylactic antibiotics can reduce measles-related morbidity. Pediatrics 2002;109:312-315.
3. Cochrane AL. Effectiveness and Efficiency: Random Reflections on Health Services. London: Nuffield Provincial Hospitals Trust, 1972.
4. Chalmers I. Foreword to the new edition. In: Cochrane AL. Effectiveness and Efficiency: Random Reflections on Health Services. London: Royal Society of Medicine Press and Nuffield Trust, 1999:xiii-xvi.
5. Chalmers I, Zlosnik JE, Johns KA, Campbell H. Obstetric practice and outcome of pregnancy in Cardiff residents, 1965-1973. BMJ 1976;1:735-738.
6. Chalmers I, Lawson JG, Turnbull AC. Evaluation of different approaches to obstetric care I. Br J Obstet Gynaecol 1976;83:921-929.
7. Chalmers I, Lawson JG, Turnbull AC. Evaluation of different approaches to obstetric care II. Br J Obstet Gynaecol 1976;83:930-933.
8. Newcombe RG, Chalmers I. Changes in distribution of gestational age and birth weight among first born infants of Cardiff residents. BMJ 1977;2:925-926.
9. Cochrane AL. 1931-1971: a critical review, with particular reference to the medical profession. In: Medicines for the year 2000. London: Office of Health Economics, 1979, pp 1-11.
10. Chalmers I, Hetherington J, Newdick M, Mutch L, Grant A, Enkin M, Enkin E, Dickersin K. The Oxford Database of Perinatal Trials: developing a register of published reports of controlled trials. Contr Clin Trials 1986;7:306-324.

11. Dickersin K, Hewitt P, Mutch L, Chalmers I, Chalmers TC. Perusing the literature. Comparison of MEDLINE searching with a perinatal trials database. Contr Clin Trials 1985;6:306-317.
12. Chalmers I. British debate on obstetric practice. Pediatrics 1976;58:308-312.
13. Chard T, Richards MPM, eds. Benefits and Hazards of the New Obstetrics. Clin Dev Med No. 64. London: Spastics International Medical Publications/William Heinemann Medical Books, 1977.
14. Chalmers I, Richards MPM. Intervention and causal inference in obstetric practice. In: Chard T, Richards MPM, eds. Benefits and Hazards of the New Obstetrics. Clin Dev Med No. 64. London: Spastics International Medical Publications/William Heinemann Medical Books, 1977:34-61.
15. Chalmers I. Randomized controlled trials of fetal monitoring 1973-1977. In: Thalhammer O, Baumgarten K, Pollak A, eds. Perinatal Medicine. Stuttgart: Georg Thieme, 1979: 260-265.
16. MacDonald D, Grant A, Sheridan-Pereira M, Boylan P, Chalmers I. The Dublin randomized controlled trial of intrapartum fetal heart rate monitoring. Am J Obstet Gynecol 1985;152:524-539.
17. National Perinatal Epidemiology Unit. A classified bibliography of controlled trials in perinatal medicine, 1940-1984. Oxford: Oxford University Press (for the World Health Organization), 1985.
18. Enkin M, Chalmers I, eds. Effectiveness and Satisfaction in Antenatal Care. Clin Dev Med Nos 81/82. London: Spastics International Medical Publications/William Heinemann Medical Books, 1982.
19. Crowley P, Chalmers I, Keirse MJNC. The effects of corticosteroid administration before preterm delivery: an overview of the evidence from controlled trials. Br J Obstet Gynaecol 1990;97:11-25.
20. Hetherington J, Dickersin K, Chalmers I, Meinert CL. Retrospective and prospective identification of unpublished controlled trials: lessons from a survey of obstetricians and pediatricians. Pediatrics 1989;84:374-380.
21. Chalmers I, Adams M, Dickersin K, Hetherington J, Tarnow-Mordi W, Meinert C, Tonascia S, Chalmers TC. A cohort study of summary reports of controlled trials. JAMA 1990;263:1401-1404.
22. Oxman AD, Guyatt GH. Guidelines for reading literature reviews. CMAJ 1988;138:697-703.
23. Chalmers I, Enkin M, Keirse MJNC, eds. Effective Care in Pregnancy and Childbirth. Oxford: Oxford University Press, 1989.
24. Enkin M, Keirse MJNC, Chalmers I, eds. A Guide to Effective Care in Pregnancy and Childbirth. Oxford: Oxford University Press, 1989.
25. Peto R, Chalmers I. Obituary: Archie Cochrane (1909-1988). Contr Clin Trials 1989;16:193-195.
26. Cochrane AL. Foreword. In: Chalmers I, Enkin M, Keirse MJNC, eds. Effective Care in Pregnancy and Childbirth. Oxford: Oxford University Press, 1989, p viii.
27. Sinclair JC, Bracken M. Effective Care of the Newborn Infant. Oxford: Oxford University Press, 1992.
28. Chalmers I. Electronic publications for updating controlled trial reviews. Lancet 1986;2:287.
29. Chalmers I, ed. The Oxford Database of Perinatal Trials. Oxford: Oxford University Press. 1989-1992.
30. Starr M, Chalmers I. How electronic publishing can help people to do more good than harm in health-care: the story of The Cochrane Library (available at www.update-software.com/history/clibhist.htm).
31. Milbank Quarterly Special Issue. 1993;71:405-532.
32. Peckham M. Research and development for the National Health Service. Lancet 1991;338:367-371.
33. Chalmers I, Dickersin K, Chalmers TC. Getting to grips with Archie Cochrane's agenda: a register of all randomized controlled trials. Br Med J 1992;305:786-788.
34. Sackett D. Cochrane's legacy. Lancet 1992; 340:1131-1132.

Doctor
Xavier Bonfill
Epidemiologist

Dr Xavier Bonfill is Director of the Iberoamerican Cochrane Centre, and a physician at the Hospital de la Santa Creu i Sant Pau in Barcelona. He has been involved in The Cochrane Collaboration since 1994, having been drawn to the challenge of finding workable pathways for the application of the concepts of evidence-based medicine. The fact that the Collaboration was named after Archie Cochrane, whom he admired (although he did not have the chance to meet him personally) because of everything he had read and heard about him, was another important attraction to his involvement in the Collaboration.

THE DEVELOPMENT OF
THE COCHRANE COLLABORATION IN SPAIN AND LATIN AMERICA

ARCHIE COCHRANE, SPAIN AND THE COCHRANE COLLABORATION

The Cochrane Collaboration is an independent, international, non-profit network whose main aim is to prepare, update and disseminate systematic reviews of the effects of health-care interventions. Ten years after its foundation, the first issue of the Cochrane Library 2003,[1] the electronic journal of The Cochrane Collaboration, already contains 1 596 completed systematic reviews and 1 200 review protocols. Although only a proportion of health interventions have so far been covered by systematic reviews, the growth of this database continues, as does the growth of the Collaboration itself. Over 5 000 people around the world collaborate and work in nearly 50 Collaborative Review Groups, in the 13 Cochrane Centres and in the 10 Method Groups. More than 350 000 possible clinical trials, both published and unpublished, have been identified by electronic searches, supplemented by world-wide hand-searching of over 1 500 journals and congress abstracts in different languages.

Despite the possible merit and value of what has been achieved in such a short time, there is still a lot to be done and developed in this project, which the *Journal of the American Medical Association* has compared to the human genome project[2] in its ambition to rewrite medicine, and which the British Medical Journal has encouraged doctors and governments to support.[3]

Archie Cochrane, British doctor and epidemiologist after whom the Collaboration is named, had close ties with Catalonia and Spain which started when he enlisted as a volunteer in the International Brigades in 1936, because he wanted to make a real contribution (*doing something instead of talking about it*, he said) to the fight

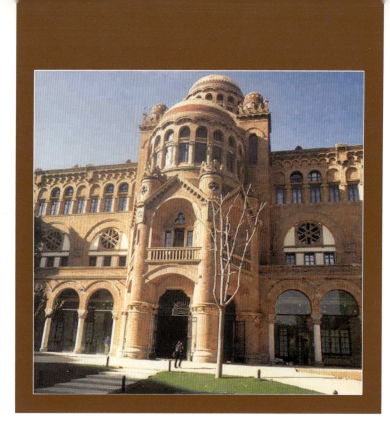

Sant Pau Hospital in Barcelona. The former Convalescence Pavilion now hosts the Cochrane Centre for Spain and Latin America.

for peace and against the totalitarianism threatening Europe at the time. History has proven that those world citizens like Archie Cochrane were right; they are now also considered to be Spanish citizens thanks to the late honour conferred on them by the Spanish Government.

Those of us who have supported The Cochrane Collaboration in Spain have to some extent considered our efforts to be the continuation and embodiment of those democratic ideals held by Archie Cochrane and his generation. With the advent of such principles as democracy, basic rights of freedom of expression and public gathering, universal suffrage and the recognition of Spain's national diversity, putting us on an equal footing with the rest of Western countries, it was then possible and necessary to go beyond the formalities and truly put our basic human rights into practice. One of the most important of these is, without a doubt, the right to health and appropriate and effective health-care.

During the 50s and later, Archie Cochrane was also a pioneer in his efforts to introduce a public health-care system in Great Britain to meet universal rights and needs for health-care. His book *Effectiveness and Efficiency*[4] was influential in arguing in favour of an efficient and equitable public health-care system, and the Spanish edition translated by Joan-Ramon Laporte in 1980,[5] became so popular in Spain that it quickly sold out. Archie Cochrane's visit to Barcelona in 1982 to give a seminar was a significant event as it brought the old international brigadier fighter, now in his final years and an established public figure, into direct contact with the emerging generation of Spanish health-care professionals who would one day become some of the most important experts in the new Spanish health-care system. The recent re-publication of the book in Spanish, thanks to the *Fundación Salud,*

Spanish Advisory Group meeting of the Iberoamerican Cochrane Centre, Barcelona, 2001.

L to R: *Gerard Urrutia, Fernando Carballo, Rafael Gabriel, José Asua, Jesús López Arrieta, Joaquim Camprubí, Manuel Vázquez Caruncho, Eduardo Briones, Xavier Bonfill.*

Innovación y Sociedad,[6] will no doubt give many new readers, the young and not so young, a great opportunity to read a true, world classic in health-care thought. The writings clearly made an impact on an era and on many health-care professionals who have substantially changed their own way of practice. His ideas are still relevant today: published 30 years ago this year, the pages of the first original edition contain reflections and concepts that in following decades have been reformulated and taken further under various names such as clinical epidemiology, health services research, health economics, evidence-based health-care and clinical management.

I would like to highlight the practical activism that characterised the life and work of Archie Cochrane, because this is also the spirit of The Cochrane Collaboration, which has inherited and is continuing his ideas. A vast number of health-care professionals, administrators and politicians share the need to access independent, up-to-date, rigorously-produced information about the effects of health-care. The number of people who want or can actively contribute to the fulfilment of that goal is, however, much lower. We are as yet a far cry from a society whose citizens consider it a fundamental right to be sufficiently well-informed to participate in the clinical and health-care decisions that affect them.

Signature of the Collaborative Agreement between the Program for Clinical Effectiveness and the Iberoamerican Cochrane Centre.

L to R:
Adolfo Rubinstein, Argentina
Xavier Bonfill, Spain
Zulma Ortiz, Argentina.

THE DEVELOPMENT OF THE COCHRANE COLLABORATION IN LATIN AMERICA

The responsibility of pushing forward with The Cochrane Collaboration in Spain was not assumed by the generation that actually met Archie in person during his visit to Barcelona in 1982, but by a later generation. Those pioneers in epidemiology and the public health system in Spain and more particularly in Catalonia, focused their career choices more towards fields related to the planning and organisation of health services and community epidemiology, and less bound to clinical epidemiology and research which were initially The Cochrane Collaboration's most developed areas.

Many varied activities have been undertaken since the creation of the first Spanish Cochrane Centre in 1997, located at the Fundació Parc Taulí in Sabadell, until the 2003 International Cochrane Collaboration Colloquium – organised by the Iberoamerican Cochrane Centre now located in the Hospital de Sant Pau in Barcelona.[7] Particularly noteworthy has been the extension of The Cochrane Collaboration to Latin America where we now have stable support and collaboration from most countries. The editorial centres of two Cochrane Review Groups are based in the Iberian Peninsular: the Lung Cancer Group in Barcelona (Spain), and the Movement Disorders Group in Lisbon (Portugal). In addition, 15 Iberoamericans (nine from Spain, two from Portugal and one each from Chile, Colombia, Cuba and Peru) are members of the editorial teams of various review groups. To date, a notable number of reviews carried out in Iberoamerica have already been published in the Cochrane Library, and more protocols are currently being worked on. This culminated a few months ago in the first publication of an

Iberoamerican Cochrane Centre staff with Peter Langhorne, Chair of The Cochrane Collaboration, at the Cochrane Colloquium, in Lyon, France, 2001.

expanded Spanish version of the quarterly *Cochrane Library*, called the *Cochrane Library Plus*,[8] which is the result of an enormous translating effort undertaken and co-ordinated by the Iberoamerican Cochrane Centre. This is undoubtedly an important step forward in enabling Spanish speaking professionals, and in the near future, the Spanish speaking public, to consult one of the best sources of medical information without language barriers. If various on-going funding initiatives come to fruition, we hope shortly to be able to remove any economic barriers to the Cochrane Library Plus as well.

Extending an influential Cochrane network in Spain and Latin America could have a major impact by encouraging *collaboration* among individuals, groups, institutions, countries and cultures from around the world to tackle some of the main challenges in medicine and public health today in a co-ordinated, professionalised and collective manner. In a world and in a field where teamwork and the division of work are difficult, and where it is sometimes difficult to escape ruthless and often meaningless competition, the formation and development of an open organisation based on universal understanding and transparency, whose aim is solely to be an instrument of transformation, is an extraordinary and quite remarkable achievement.

Moreover, in order to maintain credibility, this has had to be done, and continues to be done, with absolute independence and transparency both of individuals' contributions and funding sources, and in terms of the methodology and analytical systems employed and the strategic partnerships that have been formed. Such a group, made up of a continual turnover of people from a variety of places, can only stay on the right track with crystal clear objectives and working methods, leaving no room for messiahs. The preservation of this transparent, open and diverse spirit without fear of criticism - because it is a stimulus to correct errors and at the same time a source of new collective ideas - is the best guard against succumbing to the temptation of creating a cliquish or even sectarian organisation.

To participate in, support and promote The Cochrane Collaboration is certainly a worthwhile cause. The active and critical spirit and the solidarity of Archie Cochrane lives on in a real way in this project. From Spain and Latin America, we will continue to endeavour to make our contribution. The Cochrane Collaboration can do a lot for us, and we can do a lot for The Cochrane Collaboration.

REFERENCES

1. The Cochrane Library (database on CDROM or Internet). The Cochrane Collaboration; Issue 1. Oxford: Update Software, 2003. Updated quarterly.
2. Bero L, Rennie D. The Cochrane Collaboration. Preparing, Maintaining and Disseminating Systematic Reviews of the Effects of Healthcare. JAMA 1995; 274:1935-1938.
3. Godlee F. The Cochrane Collaboration: deserves the support of doctors and Governments. BMJ 1994;309:969-970.
4. Cochrane A. L. Effectiveness and Efficiency: random reflections on health services. London: The Nuffield Provincial Hospitals Trust, 1972.
5. Cochrane A. Efectividad y Eficiencia. Barcelona: Salvat Editores, 1985.
6. Cochrane A. Efectividad y Eficiencia. Barcelona: Asociación Colaboración Cochrane Española, 2000.
7. Bonfill X, Etcheverry C, Martí J, Glutting JP, Urrútia G, Pladevall M. El desarrollo de la Colaboración Cochrane Española. Med. Clin. (Barc) 1999;112 (Supl. 1):17-20.
8. La Cochrane Library Plus (Internet Database). The Cochrane Collaboration; Issue 1. Oxford: Update Software, 2003. Updated quarterly.

Cartagena de Indias, Colombia.

Sant Pau Hospital, Barcelona in 1930.

THE COCHRANE COLLABORATION IN ITALY

(*)

ALESSANDRO LIBERATI
Italian Cochrane Centre, Mario Negri Institute, Milan, Italy

GIANNI TOGNONI
Consorzio Mario Negri Sud, S. Maria Inbaro (Chieti), Italy

Before the start of The Cochrane Collaboration (CC), Archie Cochrane was known in Italy through his book *Effectiveness and Efficiency: random reflections on health services*. This was very influential within the 'qualified minority' of the scientific community in Italy that were pushing for major changes in the Italian health-care system through the creation of the National Health Service. The Italian translation, however, was first published only in the '80s and then again for the second time in 1999.[1]

Archie did not have many contacts in Italy and did not visit the country often. He was mostly in touch with researchers at the Mario Negri Institute in Milan, a leading research institution that played a pivotal role in the diffusion of the culture of controlled evaluation of drugs.

Archie visited the Institute twice: first in 1977, for a Workshop organized by the World Health Organization's Copenhagen office on the possible criteria and guidelines for drug evaluation. He then returned in 1979 for the second Seminar on Drug Evaluation devoted to systematic reviews of evidence related to cerebrovascular drugs.[2] Iain Chalmers, Charles Warlow and Juan Ramon Laporte were also speakers at this seminar.

Cochrane was asked to participate as a discussant and to act as chair of the final session. On that occasion he showed his ability to intellectually merge two levels of

---

* *Mario Negri Institute, host of the Italian Cochrane Centre.*

*Alessandro Liberati.
Italian Cochrane Centre.*

commitment: a practical one - with the conceptualisation and realisation of important controlled studies - with an intellectual one, committing himself to challenge the medical community to speed up the production and dissemination of information relevant to health-care and services.

Some 'memories' of his appearances in Italy are particularly worth mentioning:

He was surprised that a catholic country that, like those belonging to the 'communist world' should have been intrinsically characterised by a dogmatic outlook, was instead showing an open mind toward clinical trials to the point of being willing to push the market to accept the rules of the scientific method in the form of randomized trials.[3]

When he was invited to comment on the highly complex and pretentious presentation of an Austrian researcher, B. Saletu, on the effects of drugs on EEG as evidence for effectiveness, he impressed the audience, and silenced the presenter, by asking "……. please tell us who pays you?"

During the final round table of the WHO seminar, he started smoking with a smile on his face saying something to the effect: "….You are probably thinking that I am trying to disappoint my good friend Richard Doll (who was sitting beside him). On the contrary I am performing an experiment for him. His data tell us

Staff of the Italian Cochrane Centre.

L to R (top row): *Laura Coe, Vanna Pistotti and Isabella Bordogna.* (bottom row): *Ivan Moschetti, Sabrina Bidoli, Lorenzo Moja, Mariangela Liberati and Alessandro Liberati.*

how to estimate the incubation period for lung cancers caused by cigarettes. My smoking should not harm me as I started smoking at an age that, with respect to the mean life expectancy, shouldn't put me at an increased risk of any tumour".

Meeting him was fun and a great scientific and human experience for young researchers. During dinners in small and smoky restaurants in the suburbs of Milano he loved talking, with humour and enthusiasm, about Britain's passive attitude to the Spanish civil war ('his' Spanish war); his work with miners; and the link between biological and social data (he was writing about the 'French Paradox' in cardiovascular disease at the time).

Acquaintance with him also meant visiting him in his old house in Wales. It had a beautiful stone patio and a swimming pool. In the entrance was a large genealogical tree of his family, which he considered his personal contribution to epidemiology. Because he bore a genetic defect he was unwilling to have children. He also felt that he had been able to stop the transmission of fear. He then loved to explain how his house was an open house for homeless poets and artists and that his job as a retired man was to collect toys that were left around by children.

These are some of the memories of a friendship that became very intense, due to common cultural and political, as well as technical and scientific interests.

THE COCHRANE COLLABORATION IN THE ITALIAN HEALTH SYSTEM

To understand the development of The Cochrane Collaboration in Italy it is good to start with a short account on evidence-based medicine and health-care in this country. These two disciplines (or trends of thoughts, if you like to see them this way) have indeed helped to identify the basic ideas for an effective and sustainable universal health-care system. However, they are now in danger of becoming little more than a popular fashion and trend - a legitimate suspicion given the 'exponential' growth (often acritical) of their supporters and newcomers.[4]

THE NATIONAL HEALTH-CARE SYSTEM IN ITALY

The Italian NHS started 25 years ago, largely influenced by the British one. Unfortunately, this quarter of a century has largely been preoccupied with self-criticism and blame about failures rather than focussing serious efforts to implement reforms as ongoing research projects instead of the replication of models already tested elsewhere.

The large domestic debt in Italy has been the key structural problem that adversely affected the possibility of substantial investments in health-care. But there is no question that Academia has contributed enormously to the inertia that followed the launch of the 1978 health-care reform. It has indeed been a responsibility of many silent opinion leaders that the debate on the Italian NHS has concentrated mostly on financial, structural and organizational problems, rarely raising basic cultural and scientific problems.

These weaknesses are today worsened by the politics of the conservative ruling majority, which is prepared to destroy those basic values that led to the 1978 reform – the concepts of equity and solidarity. It should therefore come as no surprise that health-care in Italy today is a field where the difference between the right and the left political parties is very striking. On the other hand, it is unfortunate that progressive parties have failed to propose new ideas on basic issues for the NHS such as biomedical and health-care research, implementation and monitoring of effective and necessary services and consumers' empowerment on health-care choices. Rather, they consistently concentrate on structural, organizational and financial themes without any attempt to develop a modern social model able to guarantee basic human rights, social solidarity and development.

THE ITALIAN COCHRANE CENTRE AND THE COCHRANE COLLABORATION IN ITALY

The Italian Cochrane Collaboration started its activities in 1994 at the Mario Negri Institute and - as happened in Spain - it was based on the energy and enthusiasm of a younger generation than the one that had brought the themes of controlled evaluation of health-care services to Italy (with particular reference to the rational use of drugs). This happened while institutions and Academia were just

Italian participants at a meeting in Milano, 2002.

becoming aware of the principles of evidence-based medicine, so the newly-founded Cochrane Collaboration faced a difficult time and a great dilemma:

A to follow the footsteps of its stronger siblings - like the Canadian, Australian and Scandinavian Centres - whose main mission was the production of systematic reviews.

B to nurture the systematic development and adoption of evidence-based medicine as the founding principle for the delivery of healthcare, without forgetting that evidence-based medicine itself has profound limitations, especially in terms of the structural imbalance that has led to its focus on therapeutic rather than preventive interventions, and to a concentration on pharmacological rather than non pharmacological interventions.[5]

Two parallel tracks of activities were therefore started.

The first dealt mostly with national and regional institutions of the NHS. Here the CCI tried to launch demonstration projects aimed at raising awareness on the really critical evidence-based medicine themes such as the transfer of information from research to practice, independence of biomedical research, conflicts of interest, ethical implications of research, evidence-based medicine and medical education.

The second was more similar to the work of other Cochrane centres. A network of Cochrane reviewers was created (now over 100 people), mostly affiliated to the Drugs and Alcohol and Multiple Sclerosis Review Groups. Two fields (in the neurological and vaccine area) are also in operation with the support of CCI.

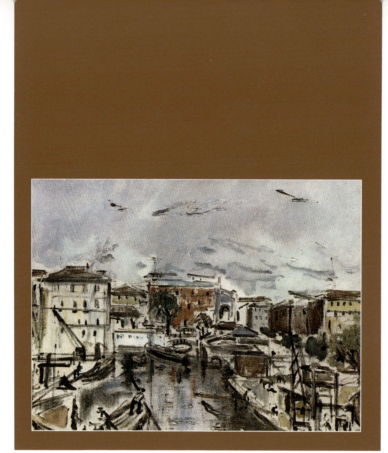

La darsena a Milano by Filippo De Pisis.

So far the Italian contribution to the Cochrane Library amounts to 41 reviews and 48 protocols. A very important event for the young CCI was the VII Cochrane Colloquium (Rome, October 1999), attended by over 1000 people. A four-day discussion took place ranging from methodological issues to the role of consumers in the interpretation, dissemination and use of scientific information.

It is more difficult to assess the CCI's broader cultural contribution to medical education. Seminars, courses and workshops have been organized to this end , in collaboration with health-care institutions, scientific societies and medical schools. The CCI also contributed to the launch of a coordinated initiative among a few Italian medical schools committed to systematic introduction of concepts and practice of development of evidence-based medicine in medical curricula.

It is also worth mentioning the collaboration with the Department for Drug Evaluation of the Ministry of Health. Within the framework of a national program for independent information about drugs, the CCI was appointed as a collaborative institution to translate the book "Clinical Evidence" which was freely distributed to over 40 000 Italian physicians.[6] Also, the Italian version of over 500 abstracts in The Cochrane Library was made available for Italian users on the CCI website.

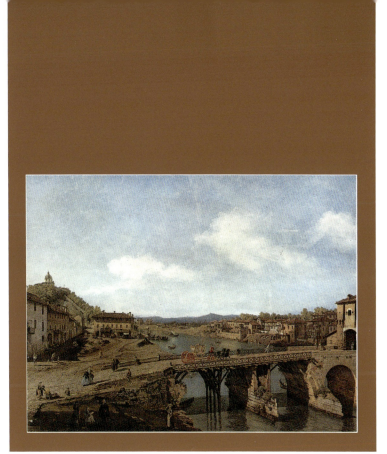

Antico Ponte sul Po a Torino by Bernardo Bellotto (il Canaletto).

CONCLUSIONS

This brief account of the history of the Collaboration in Italy is not meant to be a celebration but rather a reflection on the difficulties in implementing the principles Archie Cochrane fought for: guaranteeing equal access to all truly effective forms of health-care and making clear that efficiency makes little sense without effectiveness.

Much has changed within biomedical research since Archie Cochrane wrote the book mentioned at the beginning of this chapter, especially in terms of quantitative growth and resources required from health-care systems. His message, though, is still of great and compelling interest. Ten years have elapsed since the Collaboration was launched, but it remains to be seen whether its strategy will meet Archie's challenges. This will be widely debated during the Barcelona Colloquium in October 2003, with an open discussion on the cultural, scientific and methodological challenges that the CC must face worldwide.

Only time, of course, will help us to understand whether the efforts of The Cochrane Collaboration have been successful. Yet it is important to stress that it has shown that there is room, and need, for a truly independent scientific initiative. It remains to be seen whether quantifying the limitations of our understanding of what does, and does not, work in health-care will lead to a better and more balanced research agenda.

A better balance is urgently needed, particularly in Italy where - after a short golden season in the '80s - the survival of groups able to undertake and sustain independent research is at high risk. There are currently no national programmes and systematic initiatives to promote innovation, nor to develop health technology assessment or to raise awareness of health-care needs and essential services.

Beside other initiatives, an important role that The Cochrane Collaboration could play in Italy would be to develop an active awareness among consumers' associations, since we are far behind in this respect compared to other countries worldwide.

The Cochrane Collaboration can contribute to this empowerment both through its Consumer Network and by involving consumers' representatives within its review groups. The Cochrane Collaboration has always stressed the importance of active consumer participation in priority setting and to the critical appraisal of biomedical research to patients' needs.

REFERENCES:

1. Cochrane AL. Efficacia ed Efficienza. Riflessioni sui servizi sanitari. Roma: Pensiero Scientifico Editore, 2000.
2. Tognoni G, Garattini S. Drug Treatment and prevention in cerebrovascular disorders. Proc Int Symp, Milan, 1979. Amsterdam: Elsevier/North-Holland Biomedical Press, 1979.
3. Tognoni G, Garattini S. Drug Treatment and prevention in cerebrovascular disorders, Concluding remarks. Proc Int Symp, Milan, 1979. Amsterdam: Elsevier/North-Holland Biomedical Press, 1979.
4. Tognoni G. Prefazione In: La Medicina delle prove di efficacia: potenzialità e limiti della Evidence based Medicine. (Liberati A. Ed) Roma: Pensiero Scientifico Editore, 1997.
5. Garattini S, Liberati A. The risk of bias from omitted research BMJ 2000;321:845-846.
6. Liberati A. Clinical Evidence e la Cochrane Collaboration. In: Clinical Evidence, edizione Italiana. Roma: Ministero della Sanità, 2001.

Milan.
Piazza Duomo

THE COCHRANE COLLABORATION IN GERMANY

(*)

Yngve Falck-ytter
Britta Lang
David Booker
Gerd Antes

German Cochrane Centre

For one who has never met Archie Cochrane personally, it is fascinating to read about his experiences as a prisoner of war. Taken prisoner by the Germans in Crete in 1941, he was later moved to prisoner of war camps in Hildburghausen and Wittenberg-an-der-Elbe in Germany. Although this time must have been painful for him in many respects, it is humbling to see how he stressed the positive experiences when describing, and even joking about, that time. For example, he tells us that this time was his only experience of "patient care", attending to fellow prisoners as a senior medical officer. Epidemics, poor nutrition and the absence of any useful equipment or medications made him rely on fellow prisoners working tirelessly in an uphill battle. His observation of a less-than-expected death rate in such circumstances, and his sense that desperate measures may often have caused more harm than good, led to his now-famous quote when he asked the German Head doctor for more doctors: *No! Physicians are superfluous!* And then he added, *I was furious and even wrote a poem about it; later I wondered if he was wise or cruel; he was certainly right.*[1]

In Cochrane's words his "first, worst, and most successful trial"[2] came from this experience. Since many prisoners developed pitting oedema in their legs, Cochrane hypothesized that the condition was a result of vitamin B deficiency and divided his patients into two groups, adding yeast to the diet of one of these groups. The intervention worked, and he persuaded German army officials at the camp to provide yeast to all inmates.

---

* *Institute for Medical Biometry and Medical Informatics, University Hospital Freiburg, host of the German Cochrane Centre.*

Although these passages from his influential book *Effectiveness and Efficiency: random reflections on health services*[1] are indeed a symbol of reconciliation with the past, other sources clearly illustrate the profound effects of being imprisoned:[3]

I had, in 1949, just about the time I was moving into Rhoose Farm House [his residence for many years], *revisited Germany on an official visit to the West German mines. This I must mention. As the only fluent German speaker in the unit, I was the most obvious person to go, but I found myself more than a little reluctant. There were too many recollections with which I had not come to terms. Finally, however, I recognised that hate was an unproductive emotion and went. I am glad I did. My new associations with Germany led to many valued friendships with German scientists.*

On other occasions, he continued to visit Germany as a consultant on the epidemiology of pneumoconiosis:[3] *It was interesting that soon after this investigation, during a visit to a medical centre in Germany, I was asked to comment on a number of x-ray films of miners, one of which looked typical of Caplan's syndrome. I asked to see the patient and said I thought he would be suffering from rheumatoid arthritis. There was a gasp of disbelief, but when the patient was wheeled in he was such a typical case of rheumatoid arthritis that there was mild applause.*

Later on, in the years from 1970 to 1974, Archie Cochrane repeatedly visited Manfred Pflanz, professor of epidemiology and social medicine in Hannover.[4] Although German scientists such as Professor Pflanz were in close contact with, and clearly influenced by, Anglo-American epidemiologists like Archie Cochrane, the epidemiologists' work did not fall on fertile ground in Germany.[5] Because clinical epidemiology was not considered *true science* for many years, it took the better part of the second half of the last century to establish a basis for a new beginning.

THE COCHRANE COLLABORATION IN GERMANY

In the first half of the nineties, Germany was still isolated from the general discussion about evidence-based medicine. The Cochrane Collaboration, although gaining a presence in neighbouring countries like the Netherlands, was unknown to German physicians and health-care decision-makers alike. In 1996, when care health decision-makers in Germany realised they had not kept pace with concepts such as continuous quality improvement, a growing number of scientists looked for solutions. They quickly realised that research results were not adequately translated into action, and the near non-existence of outcomes and health-services research within Germany made this problem even worse.

In 1995, with the help of the Dutch Cochrane Centre, German scientists became more and more interested in the work of The Cochrane Collaboration. Located in Freiburg, a group of people began a project to systematically identify randomized controlled trials through hand-searching German language journals (under the EU funding scheme BIOMED 1). Building on this experience, this group established the German Cochrane Centre. Funded by the German Ministry for Education and Research with a seed grant, the German Cochrane Centre (GCC) was officially opened in 1998 to serve German speaking countries by supporting Cochrane reviewers. In the following years, activities of German researchers and clinicians within the Collaboration made it possible to establish two Cochrane Collaborative

The team of the German Cochrane Centre.

L to R: Britta Lang (Centre Coordinator), Gerd Antes (Director), Anette Blümle (Trial Search Coordinator), Edith Motschall (Information Retrieval Specialist), Christa Bast (Administrator), Yngve Falck-Ytter (Associate Director), David Booker (Web Site Developer).

Review Groups in 2000: the Metabolic and Endocrine Disorders Group, based in Duesseldorf, and the Haematological Malignancies Group, located in Cologne.

Although evidence-based medicine has been widely discussed in Germany since around 1996, it initially caused more irritation than solutions for pressing problems in the German health-care system. The term, evidence-based medicine, was and still is, frequently misused, and health-care professionals are split between feeling threatened or overly enthusiastic about its potential. Supported by the German Cochrane Centre, this situation led to the creation of the German Network for Evidence-Based Medicine, a collaboration of individuals across many disciplines, professions and organisations interested in evidence-based medicine.[6] The goal was to try to consolidate a previously fractured movement. The Network soon accomplished an important step: to foster a high quality of educational initiatives within Germany, based on a standardised and evaluated national curriculum in evidence-based medicine. This was important, as Germany had only just begun to systematically explore ways to include research evidence in clinical practice guidelines, health technology assessments and patient information.

The German Cochrane Centre has been active in each of these areas since its inception. Because no truly independent health-care organisation exists in Germany, the German Cochrane Centre has increasingly been serving this function, be it to provide sources of evidence through systematic reviews, or to consult in matters of health-care policy. However, since reforming the health-care system in Germany has been an ongoing issue for many years, and the resources of the GCC have often been stretched to their limits.

Even more challenges are ahead. Since funding of the GCC through the German Ministry for Education and Research will end in early 2004, the University of

Freiburg has promised to step in. In addition, although the Cochrane Library is increasingly utilised, German health-care professionals lament the lack of incentives for writing systematic reviews. Efforts, such as improving funding and listing of reviews in the science citation index, will be important in removing barriers for the near future.

Looking back at these exciting, but sometimes strenuous, first five years, we are tempted to debate whether the glass is half empty or half full. Although we believe in the latter, the next five years will certainly be as challenging (and hopefully, as exciting) as the first.

REFERENCES:

1. Cochrane AL. Effectiveness and Efficiency: Random Reflections on Health Services. London: The Nuffield Provincial Hospital Trust, 1972.
2. Cochrane AL. BMJ 1984;289:1726-1727.
3. Source kindly provided by Peter Elwood, MRC Unit, Penarth, UK.
4. Personal communication Ulrich Keil, Professor for Epidemiology and Social Medicine, University of Münster, Germany.
5. Personal communication Elisabeth Pflanz, Freiburg, Germany.
6. http://www.ebm-netzwerk.de

Detail from the City Hall of Freiburg, built in 1558

THE COCHRANE COLLABORATION IN CHINA

NEEDS, CHALLENGES, AND OPPORTUNITIES

YOUPING LI
XIN SUN
JUN LU

Chinese Cochrane Center, West China Hospital, Sichuan University

The first time I heard about Cochrane was on July 28th 1996, when Ming Liu, who had just returned from the UK, told me about the goals of The Cochrane Collaboration. The first time I saw a photo of Archie Cochrane was on 21 August 1997, when Chris Silagy (Australasian Cochrane Centre) made his presentation at the First Workshop of The Cochrane Collaboration of China in Chengdu. The first time I read the book by Archie Cochrane was in June 2001, when Iain Chalmers generously signed and gave it to me at his office in Oxford. Though Archie passed away in 1988, I was always impressed by his thoughts, ideas, special perspectives and legendary life, whose richness encouraged me to read, learn, think, practice and develop.

EFFECTIVENESS AND EFFICACY: THE CORE OF HEALTH SERVICES AND THE NEEDS OF THE CHINESE GOVERNMENT

As the largest developing country in the world, with only 47 dollars per capita available for health-care in 2002, China must provide for the essential health needs of 1.3 billion people and try as far as possible, to reach the level of health services provision achieved in developed countries with many thousands of dollars. In February 1997, we submitted our application to the Ministry of Health to establish the Chinese Evidence-Based Medicine Center (CEBMC) and to develop the Chinese Cochrane Center (ChiCC). To our surprise, two weeks later we received a positive response from Minzhang Chen, the Minister at that time. In July of that year, approval was granted to establish the CEBMC at the first University Hospital of the former West China University of Medical Sciences. We had to register as the Chinese Cochrane Center before the end of 1999.

China was amongst the first developing countries that successfully organized population-based randomized trials. The photographs show a meeting of the steering committee of a vitamin chemoprevention trial for the prevention of esophageal cancer. The study, initiated in 1983 in Huixian, Henan Province, fostered collaboration between Chinese epidemiologists and international scientists coordinated by the International Agency for Research on Cancer.

The Australasian Cochrane Centre, the UK Cochrane Centre and the German Cochrane Centre provided valuable support in technology and human resources for our successful registration and the Chinese Medical Board in New York and AusAid generously gave us set-up funds for the initial operation of the ChiCC. In March 1999 and nine months earlier than planned, the ChiCC was registered as the 15th member of The Cochrane Collaboration, the only one in Asia. Also in July 1999, Youping Li was elected as the member of the fourth Cochrane Collaboration Steering Group, which has enabled her to become involved in the organisation's decision-making processes and has given her the experience to successfully direct the Chinese Cochrane Center. In October 2002, the ChiCC opened a branch centre in Hong Kong.

THE COCHRANE COLLABORATION— A SUCCESSFUL MODEL OF HIGH QUALITY, INTERNATIONAL ACADEMIC COLLABORATION AND EXCHANGE

It was the ideas and early works of Archie Cochrane that led to the formation and cultivation of a group of outstanding experts in evidence-based medicine, including Iain Chalmers and Chris Silagy, and attracted a group of excellent clinical epidemiologists and experts in clinical medicine such as David Sackett and Peter Sandercock. They have worked together with many others to develop the internationally recognised Collaboration, which has successfully:

 attracted thousands of volunteers from all over the world to collaborate in its great vision, practical goals and model of mutual benefit.

Field work in Huixian. Participants in the trial were interviewed, examined and their compliance with the vitamin supplements was carefully monitored. At the end of the trial 98% of the participants underwent esophagoscopy to assess the prevalence of pre-invasive lesions in both treatment arms.

- produced, preserved and disseminated high quality clinical evidence by its in-depth methodological research, rigorous quality control, systematic training, planning and transparent administration.

- enabled the mutual development of The Cochrane Collaboration, clinical epidemiology, and health technology assessment and helped transform traditional medical practice into evidence-based medicine.

- helped decision-making on important health issues in the World Health Organization (WHO), governments, insurance and pharmaceutical companies and research institutes by its high-quality evidence, internationally shared database, qualified staff and comprehensive consultant services.

Because it is a non-profit organisation, it relies on the enthusiastic participation of volunteers and effective international collaboration. These strengths have been fully developed and transformed over the last 10 years to create impressive outcomes in research, administration and management.

EVIDENCE BASED MEDICINE, FROM THE CLASSICAL APPROACH TO ITS BROADEST SENSE- THE NEED IN CHINA.

True evidence-based medicine emphasises the combination of the best available evidence, medical experience and patient values. This concept has been gradually accepted by doctors in developed countries and has helped to change and improve clinical practice. Based on the essence of this movement, a broader evidence-based medicine focuses on not only evidence-based practice but also on a process of

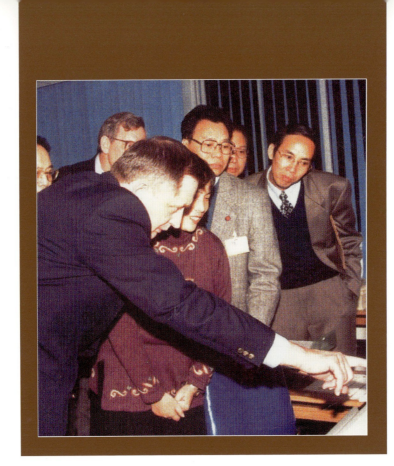

Prof M. Roy Schwarz, Chairman of CMB visiting Chinese Evidence-Based Medicine / Cochrane Center.

updating and full evaluation. Apart from clinical practice, the new broad concept is concerned with contributing to administrative reform, which has been adopted by governments and international organisations.

Minzhang Chen, the previous Minister of Health, first recognised the contribution of evidence-based medicine to health reform in China. He chaired the first steering group of the Chinese Evidence-Based Medicine Center. Jiefu Huang, the current deputy Minister responsible for Science and Technology, chaired the second steering group. The two groups were made up of directors from different departments of the Ministry of Health, the director of the West China Hospital at Sichuan University and the director of the Chinese Cochrane Center. Their responsibilities were to frame the development of evidence-based medicine in China. Members of the group from ministerial departments have been to the UK, South Africa and Denmark to study government evidence-based decision-making and practice. The Ministry of Health and the ChiCC worked together to assess important health technologies such as gene chips and care of the dying patient. As requested, the ChiCC, together with WHO, jointly held two training programmes for health directors, and individually organised training programmes for editors of leading Chinese medical journals. In addition, the State Food and Drug Administration of China and the ChiCC have jointly undertaken an evidence-based evaluation of three categories of medicines in the Essential Drugs List. Since 1999, the State Administration of Traditional Chinese Medicine and the China Academy of Traditional Chinese Medicine have been organising annual high-level workshops to introduce evidence-based medicine into the modernisation of traditional Chinese medicine (TCM) and the development of good clinical practice of TCM. In July 2002, the ChiCC was approved by the Ministry of Education (MOE) to lead a partnership initiative between Fudan University, Sun Yatsen

On 28 December 2002, a conference of Higher Education Press compiling the textbook of Evidence-Based Medicine was successfully held in the Chinese Cochrane Center.

University and the China Academy of Traditional Chinese Medicine in the establishment of the MOE Virtual Co-operation and Research Center for evidence-based medicine. Meanwhile, the MOE gave approval for Sichuan University to commence a course in evidence-based medicine and to enrol postgraduates. The Higher Education Press appointed the director of the ChiCC to be the chief author of an evidence-based medicine course book for medical undergraduates. The Chinese Journal of Evidence-based Medicine, established in June 2001, was approved for publication in October 2002 and was cited in the core scientific journalist, which meant its promotion to the top group of journals in China. There is no doubt that evidence-based medicine is gradually being understood, accepted and valued by the Chinese government, doctors and the public.

EVIDENCE-BASED DECISION-MAKING AND PRACTICE: CHALLENGES AND OPPORTUNITIES

The outbreak of Severe Acute Respiratory Syndrome (SARS) in China and around the world, which began in November 2002, has seriously tested health services in terms of their capacity for emergency response, administration and health service delivery.

The Top Seven Countries/Regions With Most SARS Cases

COUNTRY/REGION	TOTAL	CHINA	HK	TAIWAN	CANADA	SINGAPORE	USA	VIETNAM
CASES	8398	5329	1747	679	213	206	68	63
CURE RATE (%)	65.24	66.77	75.9	20.03	54.46	80.10	/	92.06
MORTALITY (%)	9.20	6.27	16.2	11.93	14.55	15.05	/	7.94

According to WHO, data till 3 June 2003.

Peng Yu, Vice Ministry of MOH (left two) compained with ZHANG Zhao-da, Dean of West China University of Medical Sciences (right one) and SHI Ying-kang, Dean of the First Hospital of West China University of Medical Sciences (left three), visiting the Chinese Evidence-Based Medicine / Cochrane Center.

The different outcomes and speeds of response to an identical epidemic occurring in countries with different economic conditions showed that 1) high-quality problem-based clinical studies, especially prospective clinical trials are most important in health maintenance and protection, and 2) the establishment of an internationally-shared database and central registering system is an urgent priority. The prevention and control of SARS also made us conscious that cost-effectiveness could be achieved only in countries and regions with 1) a good infrastructure, well-organised teams, standardised and advanced emergency systems, and accurate and complete databases; 2) rational allocation and effective use of expensive medical equipment among research institutes; and 3) highly effective responses and health services for emergencies.

In the immediate response to the National Scientific Action against SARS in China, the Chinese Cochrane Center organised teams to write proposals and undertake on-site investigation and data collection. Until now, we have retrospectively investigated and undertaken evidence-based evaluations of clinical studies on aetiology, diagnosis, treatment, prevention and prognosis of acute viral respiratory disease. The review title: 'Chinese herbs combined with western medicine for Severe Acute Respiratory Syndrome (SARS)' has been registered with the Cochrane Acute Respiratory Infections Group. A column in the Chinese Journal of Evidence-based Medicine has been dedicated specifically to publishing a series of articles about SARS and a Clinical Database of SARS Prevention and Control has also been established. We have received visits from officials from central government and regional government and prepared materials as requested by the Ministries of Health and Education. We searched primary and secondary databases, and found that the relevant clinical studies (including Cochrane systematic reviews and clinical trials) in the Cochrane Library were in standard form and of high quality, and that the Cochrane systematic reviews were most frequently consulted.

"Trained for years to be used in seconds." The fact that the ChiCC responded quickly to the SARS outbreak was possible thanks to the accumulation of hard work over the last six years. With the help of The Cochrane Collaboration, especially the Australasian Cochrane Centre and the UK Cochrane Centre, the Chinese Cochrane Center has published 10 systematic reviews and 26 protocols in the

Cochrane Library and a further 41 titles have also been registered. In addition, five health technology assessment reports have been published and 20 titles registered. The Chinese Database of Clinical Trials has collected 15 516 randomized controlled trials, and transferred 1700 to the Cochrane Central Register of Controlled Trials (CENTRAL). The Chinese Cochrane Center also responded to more than a thousand requests for information about clinical trials from 15 countries and helped to perform Cochrane activities in Beijing, Guangzhou, Shanghai and Xiamen. More than one hundred national training programs have been organised to provide training for 4228 medical professionals and 10 373 other audiences.

China is a developing country with the largest population in the world. It is an ancient nation with its own way of thinking and traditional customs. We are confronting many more difficulties than developed countries in getting doctors, other health professionals and the public to understand the philosophy behind the Cochrane Systematic Reviews and The Cochrane Collaboration, and in encouraging them to be not only users but also doers of systematic reviews. Particular barriers include language, knowledge structure, teaching materials, teachers, funding, translation, skill dissemination and instruction in systematic review methodology.

What we can do is to help our health professionals and the public step by step, to know, understand, accept, use, participate and finally to carry out research. Successful evidence-based medicine can only be established based on such a model. At present, training is the biggest difficulty. We need to educate postgraduate health professionals to produce evidence, undergraduates and professionals in training to search and use evidence, managers to make evidence-based decisions and administrators, patients and the public to be well-informed about health services. All this needs staffing, and financial and material support. We will try our best, but we are looking forward to more help from the Collaboration and other Centers.

Although there is a long road ahead of us, we are moving forward step by step.

Professor
Joan Ramón Laporte
Pharmacologist

FUNDACIÓ INSTITUT CATALÀ DE FARMACOLOGIA

Professor of clinical pharmacology at the Autonomous University of Barcelona. In 1984, he published the first Spanish version of Effectiveness and Efficiency. *He is a permanent member of the WHO committee for Essential Drugs. He runs the national registry for unwanted side and adverse effects of medical treatments and has been active in the introduction of the randomized-trials culture in the Spanish medical system.*

OBSERVATIONAL REFLECTIONS OF A CLINICAL PHARMACOLOGIST ON ARCHIE COCHRANE'S LEGACY

In the seventies I stayed at the Mario Negri Institute for Pharmacological Research, in Milan, Italy, for postgraduate training. There I met Gianni Tognoni, a colleague for whom many pharmacologists (and others) feel great admiration, for reasons which are close to those for why we admire Archibald Cochrane. At that time, Spain was still a dictatorship, and for many people, particularly the younger, travelling to any democratic country was a kind of blessing, an opportunity to familiarise oneself with cultural manifestations to which we had no access, simply because in our country they were forbidden. One of my preferred leisure activities was therefore walking into any kind of bookstore. At that time, this was more appealing in a democratic country than in Spain. After returning to Barcelona, I visited Milan at regular intervals and continued with my bookstore raids. In one of them, in 1978, I found a book entitled *L'inflazione medica. Efficacia ed efficienza nella medicina*. Gianni told me about Cochrane's participation in the International Brigades during the Civil War. This made me read the book immediately. Thus, my first contact with Archibald Cochrane was virtual rather than physical.

I personally met Archibald Cochrane for the first time in Milan in May 1979, at a symposium on drug treatment and prevention in cerebrovascular disorders (CVDs). At that time, CVDs were considered "a typically controversial issue ... one of those borderline fields where the questions are far more numerous than the answers". The symposium focused on the pathophysiology, international drug utilization patterns, evaluations of the most commonly used drugs (the so-called cerebral vasodilators), methodological aspects in the clinical evaluation of cerebrovascular disease, and some examples of the first big clinical trials on that issue such as the UK-TIA which were being done at that time.[1]

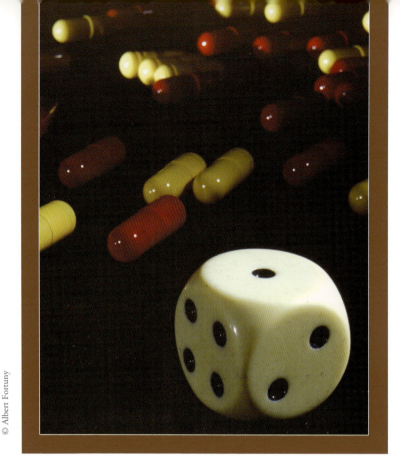

(...) Ethical standards should be the same for therapeutic trials and routine care. (...)*

It was soon apparent that the efficacy of the so-called cerebral vasodilators was at the very least dubious. The proposed mechanisms of action were at best rather imaginative but scientifically unfounded. For each drug, randomized clinical trials were just unavailable or of very poor methodological quality. On the other hand, several studies and data were presented, showing wide international variability in the prescription of these drugs, Southern Europe and Germany showing the highest figures. This reflected international variability at all levels of the therapeutic chain (which is the process describing the fate of medicines in a community – development, registration, other regulatory activities, marketing, distribution, prescribing, dispensing and use of medicines).[2] For example, two of the ten top-selling medicines in Spain, financed through the national health system, were cerebral vasodilators which were not even marketed in the Nordic countries.

In his conclusion at the end of the meeting, in what he described as "the way between retirement and dementia", Cochrane said that the prescribing habits of British GPs (those which in fact ranked among the best in international comparisons of indicators of drug prescribing in CVDs) were a matter of national shame, that he had seen "with growing horror" the evidence about the (in)efficacy of cerebral vasodilators, and that he was shocked by the gross misuse of the double-blind randomized controlled trial. He called on the pharmaceutical industry to put, in their own interest, their money into well planned trials, instead of financing "pseudo-research". He expressed the hope that the Spanish National Health Service might be able "to start with a new list of free drugs", he recommended setting up Ethical Committees in Europe, he called editors and journals to help in distinguishing good research, and he asked for an improvement of education, by teaching students about methods of evaluation, and "by encouraging them always to

* Doll R. Controlled trials: the 1948 watershed. BMJ, 1998; 317: 1217-1220

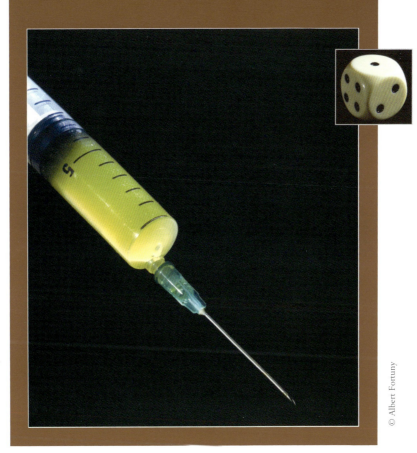

[...] One of the first formal trials to be reported involved the use of streptomycin as a treatment of pulmonary tuberculosis, a topic to which Archie devoted most of his efforts. [...]*

enquire of their elders and betters about the evidence that what they are doing is for the benefit of their patients".

Twenty-five years after, it appears that much has changed.. Is it so?

First, drugs with nil or dubious therapeutic value, although still widely prescribed, have almost disappeared from the national lists of top prescribing medicines. However, these lists are now full of non-first choice and expensive me-too drugs which have found their way in the market to the detriment of less expensive first-choice alternatives. In 2001, of the top five best selling medicines globally, only two were first choice in their class.[4] Although evidence supports thiazide diuretics as the treatment of first choice of hypertension, other non-first choice more expensive drugs are the most consumed. Several non-essential non-innovative drugs have had to be withdrawn from the market because of serious adverse effects, sometimes after millions of people have been exposed to them.[5] In the USA adverse drug effects rank fourth to six in the list of causes of death.[6]

Second, there are still reasons to be shocked by the gross misuse of the double-blind randomized controlled trial. The pharmaceutical industry has certainly put their money into better planned trials, but their methods and objectives are driven mainly by industrial priorities and the fullfilment of regulatory requirements, rather than by a conceptual framework that aims to answer questions that arise in medical practice.[7,8,9] Most clinical trials are designed to evaluate drugs, rather than patients or diseases. They are not generally designed to identify which patients will respond to the drug or those that will develop adverse outcomes. Therapeutic research is mainly oriented towards the fullfilment of regulatory requirements for

* Medical Research Council Streptomycin in Tuberculosis Trials Committee. Streptomycin treatment for pulmonary tuberculosis. BMJ 1948; ii: 769-82

Randomized trials are essential to evaluate the use of non-conventional treatments such as marihuana, sea weed or its chemical components.

regulatory approval of new drugs. The ownership of its results is usually private, with the resulting consequences in terms of data analysis and interpretation,[7,8] secrecy,[10] and publication bias.[11]

Drug regulatory agencies accept placebo-controlled trials as evidence of efficacy of a new drug,[12] as if there was a therapeutic vacuum.[13] But drugs shown to work better than placebo may still be inferior to other drugs for the same indication. On the other hand, drug regulatory agencies accept trials on surrogate endpoints as proof of efficacy. Although potentially useful in the early stages of drug development, these trials do not provide an evaluation of meaningful clinical effectiveness and limit the ability to assess safety because the drug is tested in few people exposed for a short time.[14] The result is that comparative information on the various alternatives for the treatment of a particular disease or risk factor is scarce, while, on the other hand, it would be difficult to find medical reasons for registration of me-too drugs without any demonstrated superiority with respect to already existing drugs.

An additional problem is that while the therapeutic benefit/risk ratio of drugs basically depends on the circumstances in which they are used, national and supranational drug regulatory agencies increasingly tend to assess quality, efficacy and safety as if these were independent of the way and the context where drugs are promoted, financed, prescribed, dispensed and used. The result is that drug- and industry-oriented clinical research and regulation is leading to drug- and industry-driven therapeutic practice.

In fact, the standards on which drug regulatory agencies grant market authorisations for new drugs have been laid down by the International Conference on

Trials, particularly if small, often provide results in the gray zone where clinical judgement, values and opinion still play a role. Meta-analyses and critical reviews are nowadays essential to overcome the limitations of individual studies.

Harmonisation (ICH) of Technical Requirements for Registration of Pharmaceuticals for Human Use, whose secretariat is provided by the International Federation of Pharmaceutical Manufacturer Associations. The ICH has not shown much interest in developing standards for the review of obsolete drugs, the provision of information to prescribers and consumers, the use of international non-proprietary names of medicines, transparency about pricing, international norms to control promotion and advertising, transparency in drug safety monitoring, or access to information.[15]

Third, National Health Systems are increasingly influenced by the pharmaceutical industry, directly or indirectly, through control on the mechanisms of drug selection and purchasing,[16] through direct political influence or even by corrupting prescribers or managers. In the majority of the public health-care systems of the European Union, drugs are reimbursed according to their market value, rather than their therapeutic value, and the result is that new drugs, which tend to be more expensive than old established drugs (and therefore generate more profits), are those most heavily promoted, and product innovation accelerates. The result is that public sector pharmaceutical budgets increase at a pace which is more than double the increase in the total health budget. However, rather than product innovation, medicine needs time for hypothesis testing, verification and acquaintance, and for testing new therapeutic and follow-up strategies.

The marketing budgets of the pharmaceutical industry are enormous, much larger than the research and development costs.[17] The industry has an increasing influence over scientific societies[18] and in continuous medical education,[19] which, in fact, has become a new marketing strategy. It is a failure that health-care systems,

The impact of the pharmaceutical industry in continuous medical education has grown considerably, over and above the role of the University in some countries. Concerns have been expressed on its impact in clinical research and scientific publications.

18th International Papillomavirus Conference. Barcelona, July 21-23 2000.

where decisions are based on knowledge, do not consider continuous education as a strategic priority, and the field has been left to the technology industry. On the other hand, qualitative changes in the promotional activities of pharmaceutical companies are occurring. In 2000, 2 500 million dollars were spent in the USA in direct-to-consumer advertisements of medicines. A recent study by the National Institute for Health-Care Management found that sales of the 50 most advertised drugs accounted for almost half of the 20 800 million dollars increase in pharmaceutical spending.[20]

At a global scale, the Trade-Related Intellectual Property Rights Agreement (TRIPS) of the World Health Organization, which grants patents for a minimum of 20 years, has an important negative impact on the equitable access of populations in less-developed countries to medicines. In industrialised countries, it makes companies concentrate their promotional efforts on the newest and most expensive, but not necessarily better, drugs while they are protected by a patent. The result is that once those involved in drug utilisation are familiar with a new drug – a process which takes years – the interest of the manufacturer for its promotion and clinical research vanishes, and research, promotional messages, and educational activities are filled with the "new" drug.

Indeed, in spite of a number of serious safety problems related with these drugs identified during the eighties and the nineties,[21,22,23] and of various calls and attempts to exclude these and other useless and unsafe drugs from financing,[24,25,26] their financing by the Spanish National Health System was never limited.

Fourth, Ethical Committees have certainly sprouted across Europe, but they have become passive observers, acting as a filter which authorizes but rarely gets

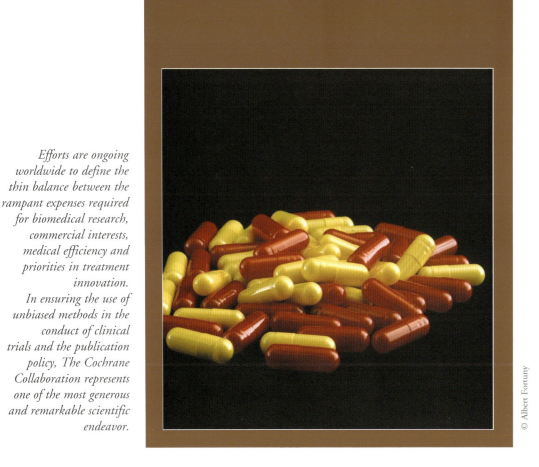

Efforts are ongoing worldwide to define the thin balance between the rampant expenses required for biomedical research, commercial interests, medical efficiency and priorities in treatment innovation.
In ensuring the use of unbiased methods in the conduct of clinical trials and the publication policy, The Cochrane Collaboration represents one of the most generous and remarkable scientific endeavor.

© Albert Fortuny

involved. Their increasing legal and administrative responsibilities (for example, protecting the rights, the safety and the wellbeing of participating subjects and follow up of trials) has not led to their active involvement in research and research policy, and they have instead become passive observers of clinical research, acting as filters which approve, but do not get involved.[27]

Cochrane's principle of equitable access to health-care relies on the availability of good quality systematic information on the effectiveness and cost-effectiveness of health-care interventions. Clinical trials evaluate efficacy in experimental settings and in highly selected populations. The number of participating patients is of the order of hundreds or thousands, thus precluding the identification of adverse effects with an incidence of less than 1 in 1 000. The length of exposure is much shorter than in usual practice, and therefore any effects that appear after a relatively long exposure are unlikely to be identified. Participants usually have a single diagnosis, in contrast with a prevalence of comorbidity in primary health-care of nearly 40%. Patients with potential contraindications are often excluded, thus tending to give a false impression of the benefit/risk ratio. They are generally healthier, younger and of higher social status than the people who will ultimately receive the drug, and they have more accurate and clear cut diagnoses than those in routine practice. As the number of medicines they take is generally more limited than in routine practice, drug interactions are seldom identified.[28] The fundamental differences between randomized trials and routine practice add uncertainty regarding the effectiveness of health interventions. Evaluation of effectiveness in routine practice is therefore needed. The gaps between efficacy and effectiveness on one hand, and between effectiveness and cost-effectiveness on the other, add much difficulty in translating the data into institutional and clinical decisions.

One interesting development of preventive oncology deals with nutrient supplements as chemopreventive agents. These studies are largely inspired by the correlations between diet, diseases and health. Trials including dietary changes at population levels may prove to be one of the limits of randomization.

The aims, methods, ethics and results of clinical research reflect social expectations. Social expectations are shaped according to the dominant social values, and these are strongly influenced by the media and, indirectly, by the most powerful social agents which may exert a strong influence on the media. Unfortunately, clinical research is deeply and increasingly embedded with market values and industrial culture.[29] Research skills have to be built up inside the health system, which is the natural laboratory of clinical pharmacology.[30] The new information technologies may be of great help to set up networks of health professionals, which should monitor what is relevant, feasible, necessary, and effective in therapeutics.[31] Large changes of prescription patterns cannot be achieved by the passive transfer of information, and so a need exists to build up a critical mass of professionals practising in the health-care system and involved in research that should produce knowledge rather than mere information.

The Cochrane Collaboration is an admirable network of thousands of people with experience in evaluating medical research. It would be great to see it widening its scope, and establishing solid collaboration with other institutions and networks, in identifying orphan areas in need of research, and in collaborating with networks of researchers, ethical committees, national regulatory agencies, as well as with WHO and other international organisations.

REFERENCES:

1. Tognoni G, Garattini S (eds). Drug treatment and prevention in cerebrovascular disorders. Amsterdam: Elsevier/North-Holland, 1979.
2. WHO Model List of Essential Medicines, 13rd ed, May 2003. Available at http://www.who.int/medicines/organization/par/edl/edl2003core.pdf
3. Cochrane AL. Concluding remarks. In Ref number 1.

4. Figueras A, Laporte J-R. Failures of the therapeutic chain as a cause of drug ineffectiveness. BMJ 2003;326:895-896.
5. Lasser KE, Allen PD, Woolhandler SJ, Himmelstein DU, Wolfe SM, Bor DH. Timing of new black box warnings and withdrawals for prescription medications. JAMA 2002;287:2215-2220.
6. Lazarou J, Pomeranz BH, Corey PN. Incidence of adverse drug reactions in hospitalized patients. A meta-analysis of prospective studies. JAMA 1998;279:1200-1205.
7. Jüni P, Rutjes AWS, Dieppe PA. Are selective COX 2 inhibitors superior to traditional non steroidal anti-inflammatory drugs? Adequate analysis of the CLASS trial indicates that this may not be the case. BMJ 2002;324:1287-1288.
8. Boers M. Seminal pharmaceutical trials: maintaining masking in analysis. Lancet 2002;360:100-101.
9. Rosser WW. Application of evidence from randomised controlled trials to general practice. Lancet 1999;353:661-664.
10. Anonymous. The tightening grip of big pharma. Lancet 2001;357:1141.
11. Pich A, Carné X, Arnaiz J-A, Gómez B, Trilla A, Rodés J. Role of a research ethics committee in follow-up and publication of results. Lancet 2003;361:1015-1016.
12. Lewis JA, Jonsson B, Kreutz G, Sampaio C, van Zwieten-Boot B. Placebo-controlled trials and the Declaration of Helsinki. Lancet 2002;359:1337-1340.
13. Garattini S, Bertele V. Adjusting Europe's drug regulation to public health needs. Lancet 2001;358:64-67.
14. Psaty BM, Weiss NS, Furberg CD, Koepsell TD, Siscovick DS, Rosendaal FR, Smith NL, Heckbert SR, Kaplan RC, Lin D, Fleming TR, Wagner EH. Surrogate end points, health outcomes, and the drug-approval process for the treatment of risk factors for cardiovascular disease. JAMA 1999;282:786-790.
15. Hodgkin C. International harmonisation – the need for transparency. Int J Risk & Safety in Medicine 1996;9:195-199.
16. Schulman KA, Rubenstein E, Abernethy DR, Seils DM, Sulmasy DP. The effect of pharmaceutical benefits managers: is it being evaluated? Ann Intern Med 1996;124:906-913.
17. Angell M. The pharmaceutical industry – To whom is it accountable? N Engl J Med 2000;342:1902-1904.
18. Anonymous. Just how tainted has medicine become? Lancet 2002;359:1167.
19. Anonymous. Drug-company influence on medical education in USA. Lancet 2000;356:781.
20. Anonymous. DTC ads linked to rising drug costs in US. Scrip 2001;2706/07:18.
21. Laporte J-R, Capellà D. Useless drugs are not placebos. Lessons from cinnarizine and flunarizine. Lancet 1987;1:1324.
22. Capellà D, Laporte J-R, Castel JM, Tristán C, Cos A, Morales-Olivas FJ. Parkinsonism, tremor, and depression induced by cinnarizine and flunarizine. Br Med J 1988;297:722-723.
23. Laporte J-R, Capellà D, Juan J. Agranulocytosis induced by cinepazide. Eur J Clin Pharmacol 1990;38:387-388.
24. Figueras A, Morales-Olivas FJ, Capellà D, Palop V, Laporte J-R. Bovine gangliosides and acute motor polyneuropathy. Br Med J 1992;305:1330-1331.
25. Laporte J-R, Capellà D. Insuficiencia hepática fulminante por bendazaco. Med Clín (Barc) 1995;104:396.
26. Ibáñez L, Ballarin E, Vidal X, Laporte J-R. Agranulocytosis associated with calcium dobesilate. Clinical course and risk estimation with the case-control and the case-population approaches. Eur J Clin Pharmacol 2000;56:763-767.
27. Lucena MI, Tognoni G, Sánchez de la Cuesta F. Comités éticos de investigación clínica: nuevas funciones para un nuevo escenario. Med Clin (Barc) 1999;114:785-790.
28. Stolley PD, Laporte J-R. The public health, the University, and pharmacoepidemiology. In: BL Strom (ed.) Pharmacoepidemiology. Wiley. Chichester, 2000:75-89.
29. Moynihan R, Heath I, Henry D. Selling sickness: the pharmaceutical industry and disease mongering. BMJ 2002;324:886-891.
30. Anonymous. The natural laboratory. Lancet 1986;2:1019.
31. Tognoni G, Bonati M. Second-generation clinical pharmacology. Lancet 1986;i:1028-1029.

ACCORDING TO CARIB MYTHOLOGY, THE SUN, THE MOON AND OTHER HEAVENLY BODIES WERE REGARDED AS HUMAN. EACH HAD SOME SPECIAL RESPONSIBILITY IN ORDERING THE COSMOS. TO SAVACOU, WHO BECAME A BIRD AND THEN A STAR, WAS ATTRIBUTED CONTROL OVER THUNDER AND STRONG WINDS.

THE BIRD IS MY IDEA OF THE CARIB GOD CALLED SAVACOU. SAVACOU WAS THE GOD WHO CAME DOWN TO EARTH AND LOOKED AFTER THE STORMS AND THE SEA. AFTER DOING HIS STINT, AS IT WERE, FOR MANY, MANY YEARS, HE RETURNED TO THE HEAVENS AND BECAME A STAR.

THE 85" HIGH ALUMINIUM SCULPTURE WAS PRESENTED BY RONALD MOODY TO THE EPIDEMIOLOGICAL RESEARCH UNIT OF THE UNIVERSITY OF THE WEST INDIES BY PROFESSOR ARCHIE COCHRANE OF THE SISTER UNIT IN SOUTH WALES. IT IS SITED ON THE CAMPUS AT MONA IN JAMAICA. THE MAQUETTE WAS CAST IN BRONZE FOR ARCHIE WHO COMMISSIONED THE SCULPTURE.

JOE STALKER

* Credit & Legend, see page 326.

BARCELONA, GRANOLLERS, GERNIKA... THE EARLY TRIALS OF A SINISTER SAGA

BARCELONA HOLDS THE UNCERTAIN PRIVILEGE OF BEING AMONG THE FIRST CITIES TO EXPERIENCE AERIAL BOMBING AS PART OF AN INTEGRATED EFFORT TO DEMORALIZE AND TERRORIZE THE POPULATION AND THE ARMY. THE FIRST RECORDED ATTACK IS DATED 9 FEBRUARY 1937. FROM THE 16TH TO 18TH MARCH 1938, AN INDISCRIMINATE BOMBARDMENT TOOK PLACE DOWNTOWN RESULTING IN OVER ONE THOUSAND CASUALTIES. GERNIKA, IN THE BASQUE COUNTRY, FOLLOWED SOON AFTER BARCELONA. IN APRIL 1937, THE VILLAGE WAS SURROUNDED AND ATTACKED FROM ALL SIDES INCLUDING THE AIR IN A BRUTAL DEMONSTRATION OF MILITARY POWER.

AT THE WORLD EXHIBIT OF ARTS AND TECHNOLOGY OF MODERN LIFE, PARIS 1937, THE SPANISH PAVILION OFFERED ARTISTIC CONTRIBUTIONS TO CALL ATTENTION ON THE SUFFERING OF THE CIVIL POPULATION DURING THE WAR. THE MOST DRAMATIC EFFECT WAS ACHIEVED BY THE GIGANTIC PAINTING GERNIKA OF PABLO PICASSO.

IN OUR TIME, WHILE EDITING THIS BOOK, SOPHISTICATED BOMBING OF URBAN AREAS IN BAGHDAD IS TAKING PLACE. NOVEL "PEACE BRIGADES", SOME FROM SPAIN, WENT TO THE WAR IN IRAQ TO ACT AS HUMAN SHIELDS. ANOTHER WAR IS ALSO BEING STAGED IN IRAQ FOR THE HEARTS AND MINDS OF THE PEOPLE: THE INFORMATION FRONT AND THE CLOUDS OF POLITICAL PROPAGANDA TRAGICALLY UP-DATE THE SPANISH SCENARIOS SO POIGNANTLY DESCRIBED BY ORWELL, HEMINGWAY AND, TO SOME EXTENT, ARCHIE COCHRANE. THEY ALL TRIED TO UNDERSTAND THE DEFEAT OF THE POPULAR FRONT AND THE SPANISH REPUBLIC AND POINTED AT THE CRUCIAL ROLE PLAYED BY INTERNATIONAL FORCES AND ALLIANCES.

F. XAVIER BOSCH

RIGHT: *Pablo Picasso in front of a fragment of his masterpiece Gernika.*

© Chim / Magnum Photo

ENTONCES VOLVEREIS.
SERÁ UN REMANSO
SOBRE EUROPA MI PATRIA, Y, SUS ESTRELLAS,
CON LA PAZ MÁS CEÑIDAS SOBRE EL SUELO,
ALUMBRARÁN LAS TUMBAS DE LOS HÉROES.

BARCELONA, VIERNES 28-10-1938
EMILIO PRADOS: "DESPEDIDA A LAS BRIGADAS INTERNACIONALES"

THEN YOU SHALL COME BACK

IT WILL BE PEACE OVER EUROPE, MY LAND

AND ITS STARS, WITH PEACE,

CLOSELY TIED TO THE GROUND,

WILL ENLIGHTEN THE GRAVES OF THE HEROES.

BARCELONA FRIDAY 28-10-1938

EMILIO PRADOS: *FAREWELL TO THE INTERNATIONAL BRIGADES*

* *Credit & Legend, see page 326.*

BARCELONA REMEMBERS THE BRIGADES AND THE CIVIL WAR

Professor
Francesc Bonamusa
Historian

Chairman of Contemporary History at the Autonomous University of Barcelona. He has conducted research and published several books on three areas: social movements, the republic and the Spanish Civil War and states and nations in the contemporary world.

Relevant publications are: *El Bloc Obrer i Camperol (Barcelona 1974), La Huelga General (Barcelona 1989) Historia grafica del Moviment Obrer a Catalunya (Barcelona 1989) Del Roig al Groc, with J Serrallonga, Barcelona 1868- 1871. Quintes i Epidemies (Barcelona 1995); Andreu Nin y el Movimiento Comunista en España (Barcelona 1977), Politica i Finaces Republicanes (1931-1939) (Tarragona 1997) Segona Republica i Guerra Civil (Barcelona 1988), La Europa del Danubio (1815-1918) 2 vols. (madrid 1993) Pueblos y Naciones en los Balcanes siglos XIX-XX . De la Media Luna a la Estrella Roja (Madrid 1998).*

BARCELONA AND THE INTERNATIONALS BRIGADES MEMORY TO THE HOMAGE, 1978-2000

The first homage to the International Brigades in Barcelona was paid on the 28th October 1938. The Brigades were lined up in the Avenue Diagonal to be farewelled in accordance with the mandate of the Society of Nations. While they assembled, they were applauded and strewn with flowers from the multitude that filled the Avenue and crowded onto the balconies. Some brigadiers voluntarily stayed in Spain for a few additional months, witnessing the fall of Catalonia to the fascists and then joining the hundreds of thousands of refugees crossing the French border.

From January 1939, General Franco imposed a harsh dictatorship of political, social and religious repression in Catalonia. Any reference to the International Brigades, other than condemnatory, was prohibited. They were categorized as twentieth century mercenaries, as instruments of international communism, just as the Comintern was accused, of the uprising of Jews and Blacks "against the eternal values of Nation and Country".

It is only after Franco's death and Spain's transition to democracy that we are able to remember the thousands of anti-fascists that came to Spain from around the world to fight for the defence of the Republic and democracy. We remember the names of the Brigades – Lincoln, Garibaldi, Dombrowski, Thailmer, Louise Michel – as some old brigadiers have returned to visit the battlefields where they had fought in Madrid, Guadalajara, Jarama, Brunete, Belchite, Teruel, and the Ebro Battle.

Catalonia held the first open tribute dedicated to those fighters with a session at the conference, "La Guerra Civil a debate" (Debate on the Civil War) organized by the Centre de Treball i Documentació from the 12th to the 16th of June 1978. The session dedicated to the Brigades was held at the Congress Palace in Montjuïc, sponsored by the Ajuntament de Barcelona, (the city hall of Barcelona).

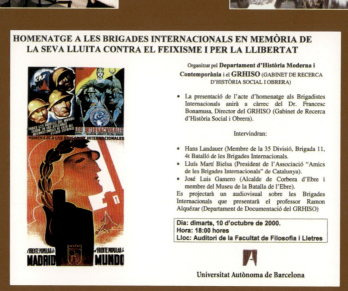

Participating at the conference were historians of the Spanish Civil war, such as the British, Ronald Frazer, Ian Gibson, Robert Marrast and the North American, Herbert R. Southworth, presented by Josep Benet; Professors such as Joaquim Molas and Manuel Aznar; writers and artists such as Joan Oliver, Pere Calders, Avel·lí Artís Gener, Rafael Alberti and Josep Renau; film producers such as Pere Portabella, Antonio del Amo, Carlo Lizzani, or politicians such as Josep Solé Barberà. Author of an extensive work about the Brigades, Andreu Castells, and historian, Francesc Bonamusa, actively participated in the session moderated by Professor Josep Termes. Among the brigadiers, Arthur London ("Gerard"), later a member of the French Resistance, deported to Mauthausen, ex-Vice-Minister of External Affairs of the Czech Social Republic, spoke. Prosecuted and incarcerated by the Stalinist system, he revealed his last experiences in the work "La Confessió", (The Confession) which was made into a film by Costa Gavras with Yves Montad in the leading role. A friend of London, Lisa Ricol, contributed at the conference, and later recorded her experiences, including her time with the International Brigades, in her book "La madeja del tiempo" (The Web of Time). Croatians, Rade Nicolic and Vlaico Begovic, high ranking leaders in the then Jugoslav state, spoke about the activities of numerous Jugoslavians involved in the Brigades. Lastly, there were sessions by a Major of the Spanish militia, Pedro Mateo Merino, Commander of the 35th Division (May-September 1938) and John V. Murra, a prestigious Romanian anthropologist living in the United States where, at that time, he was studying the cultures of the Andes, in particular, the Aztecs. The two, together with London and a few others had formed the commissioner's headquarters of the Brigades in Barcelona. Hundreds of people were present. All seats were taken at the congress centre; many people stood to hear the speakers. A large part of the crowd had lived through the war, many had fought with the brigadiers in

the various Brigades and many, also, had recently been able to return to Catalonia. Men and women of the CNT, the PSUC, the POUM and the ERC contributed their ideas to the debate and relived their differences and their confrontations during the war, especially, in what concerned the Fets (Facts) of May 1937 and its consequences.

Eight years would pass before a public institution in Spain would organize the first homage to the International Brigades. On the 24th of October 1986, the Universitat Autònoma de Barcelona (Autonomous University of Barcelona), honoured the Brigades in an event entitled "Cinquantenari de les Brigades Internacionals" (the fiftyeth anniversary of the International Brigades), attended by six brigadiers. More than a hundred professors and students and the brigadiers gathered in the auditorium of the university. Professor Fransesc Bonamusa opened and closed the ceremony with everyone remembering the poem by Pablo Neruda which was the slogan of the brigadiers, "Per la vostra llibertat i per la nostra", ("For your freedom and for ours"). Professor Ramon Alquézar gave a brief presentation about the organization and activities of the Brigades; J. Sicola spoke in the name of the Coordinadora Catalana d'associacions d'excombatants de la República, (The Catalan coordination of associations of ex-combatants of the Republic), and Professor Empar Tusón introduced the six brigadiers: Eurgenius Szyr, the ex Polish minister; Zofia Saleyen; Karl Kormes and Karl Loesch of the German Democratic Republic; Bengt Sergerson of Sweden and Leo Klaster, from Holland. All of them shared the belief that the Spanish Civil War marked the introduction of World War II. They had all come to Spain with the same objective to fight international fascism. The six brigadiers were invited to dinner by the staff of the University.

Patiente Edney worked as a nurse during the Spanish Civil War. The photograph reflects her reaction at learning that a trip back to the front was also being organized for her on November 1996.

On the fiftieth anniversary of the Civil War, in October 1988, the Catalan coordination of associations of ex-combatants of the Republic, the city of Barcelona and the University of Barcelona organized various ceremonies to honour the International Brigades under the general title of "Jornades internationals per la Pau i la Llibertat 1938-1988", (International Conference for Peace and Freedom 1938-1988). In front of a large representation of brigadiers, the mayor of Barcelona, Pasqual Maragall, unveiled the monument, David and Goliath, in the Rambla de Carmel, just by the tunnel of La Rovira, as a memorial to the International Brigades. The monument made by a North American sculptor, Roy Shifrin, was donated to the City by the "Spanish Civil War Historical Society" (SCWHS) which is a New York organisation sponsored by actors like Woody Allen and Gregory Peck, musicians like Leonard Bernstein, the writer, Norman Mailer, and a Catalan architect, Josep Lluís Sert.

The city hall of Barcelona opened its doors to the brigadiers who were welcomed by the mayor of the city, Pasqual Maragall in the Saló de Cent. A round-table discussion was held at the University of Barcelona entitled "Per la pau, la llibertat i la democràcia" (For Peace, Freedom, and Democracy); the rector Josep Maria Bricall acted as chairman of the discussion where the brigadiers Eugenius Szyr, from Poland; Julius Goldstein from the German Democratic Republic, Colonel Rol Tanguy from France; S.J. Salmann from Israel; Yssopenko from the Soviet Union and Sam Gonshac from the United States, participated. Other presenters included historians Ramon Alquézar and Francesc Bonamusa; writers Montserrat Roig and Manuel Vázquez Montalbán; a member of the Catalan Coordination of Associations of ex-combatants of the Republic, Joan Manuel Paton, and the doctor and surgeon, Moisès Broggi, who had served in the hospitals of the International Brigades.

Eight years later, in November 1996, Barcelona held one of the most emotional and well attended memorials offered by Catalan institutions to honour the brigadiers, in spite of the recently elected Popular Party's contempt of the event. The media exposure was high and many thousands, mainly of young people, gathered at Universitat Autònoma (Autonomous University).

A Document of Tribute was signed by the Ex-President of the Government and Secretary General of the Partido Socialista Obrero Español (PSOE, Spanish Socialist Workers' Party) Felipe González; by the President of the Generalitat, Jordi Pujol; by the Coordinator General of Izquierda Unida (IU, United Left), Julio Anguita, by the Secretary Generals of Comisiones Obreras (CCOO, Trade Union Confederation of Workers' Commissions) the Unión General de Trabajadores (UGT, General Workers' Confederation) and Rafael Alberti, along with more than a hundred politicians, Unions, and recognised intellectuals as a prologue to the arrival of nearly 400 brigadiers and their guests from 35 different countries.

The program for the returning brigadiers involved visits to political institutions and places where they had lived and fought between 1936 and 1938, including a visit to the Parliament in Madrid and the Ministry of Justice where they received a certificate of their Spanish citizenship. Unfortunately, neither the president, nor the first vice-president of the Parliament, Federico Trillo and Enrique Fernández Miranda nor the Minister of Justice, Margarita Mariscal de Gante, all from the Popular Party, welcomed the brigadiers. The brigadiers returned to Albacete, the site of recruitment and training of the International Brigades where the Popular Party's mayor also refused to see them.

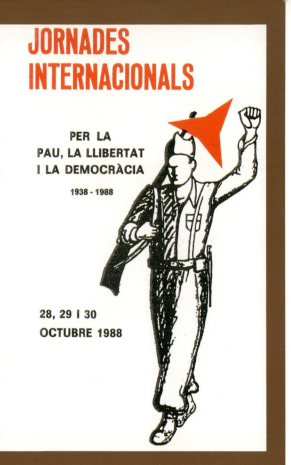

Their visit to Barcelona was very different: the people of Barcelona welcomed the brigadiers with songs and Republican flags and were greeted in the Catalan Parliament by the President of the Generalitat, Jordi Pujol; the president of the Parliament, Joan Raventós, the president of the Delegation of Barcelona, Manuel Royes and the Mayor of Barcelona, Pasqual Maragall.

They toured throughout Catalonia: Girona, Tarragona, Lleida, Vilfranca, Olesa, Esparreguera, Abrera, Sant Esteve de Sesrovires, Castelldefels, Cornellá, Granollers, Badalona, Mataró, Mollerussa, El Prat, Santa Coloma, Tàrrega, Terrassa, and Badalona. At the University Autonoma of Barcelona in Bellaterra, they received an overwhelming welcome by the Gabinet de Recerca d'Història Social i Obrera (GHISCO's) committee formed by Professors Joan Serrallonga, Josep Lluís Martìn, Alejandro Andreassi, Ramon Alquézar and Francesc Bonamusa. At the Facultat de Lletres of the university thousands of people, many young students who were born at the end of the dictatorship and after the death of General Franco, joined to pay tribute to the brigadiers. The ceremony was opened and George Soussenko, a North American from Czechoslovakia, speaking perfect Spanish with an Argentinian accent, reiterated that "we were not mercenaries or paid militants, we didn't want anything in exchange for our help, that's why this tribute, sixty years later, is so unexpected and fantastic." A few short talks followed from the other three brigadiers that were at the table. Russian was mixed with Spanish. The North American brigadier remembered- with a kind of Spanglish- how the big oil companies of his country helped Franco. "Let the women talk", was heard, and the women spoke. The words flowed despite the different languages. Finally, after a pleasant lunch, the brigadiers were escorted to the bus on they way back to Barcelona.

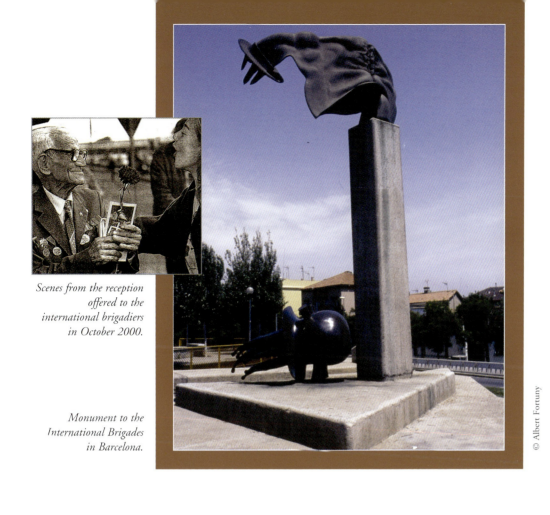

Scenes from the reception offered to the international brigadiers in October 2000.

Monument to the International Brigades in Barcelona.

In the afternoon, they arrived at the sports arena of Barcelona where they took part, between chants and ovations, in a ceremony presented by the North-American historian, living in Barcelona, Gabriel Jackson, the author of a series of well known monographs about the Republic and the Civil War.

In October 2000, a group of brigadiers returned to Spain to be honoured at Albacete. They traveled to Catalonia to visit the towns where they lived during the Ebro Battle, and to the Museum that was inaugurated in remembrance of the battle. They were honoured at the Autonomous University of Barcelona and gathered at Corbera d' Ebre around the monument which was dedicated to them. Present were the Colonel Louis Blesy Granville, former commissioner of the XIV Brigada International and leader of the Association of Spanish Republican Volunteers, the Coronel Henri Tanguy, commissioner of the XIV Brigade and one of the liberators of Paris, and Lise London.

Democratic Catalans, both those who fought in the Civil War and the generations who have come after them, have shown their respect and honour for the men and women of the International Brigades. They were forced to leave Spain in 1938 following the mandate of the Society of Nations in a decision that indirectly favoured the international expansion of fascism.

PER LA VOSTRA LLIBERTAT I PER LA NOSTRA !
FOR YOUR LIBERTY AND FOR OURS!

Barcelona, 15 December 2001

THE DRAMA OF THE COMMON GRAVES AND THE HIDDEN BURIALS,
THE SINISTER STORIES OF "THE DISAPPEARED" AND OF "THE LOST CHILDREN"
REPEATS ITSELF IN SPAIN, LATIN AMERICA, BOSNIA OR CAMBODIA. THE HEALING
PROCESS THAT REQUIRES THE IDENTIFICATION OF REMAINS
AND THE PERSONALIZED BURIAL SEEMS UNAVOIDABLE WHILE THERE ARE
SURVIVORS AND FAMILIES.

F. XAVIER BOSCH, OCTOBER 2003

Credit & Legend, see page 326.

THE LONG LASTING SCARS OF THE CIVIL WAR IN SPAIN

Montserrat Armengou
Journalist

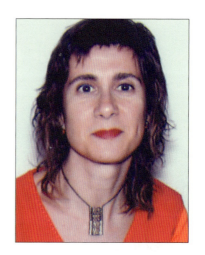

Montserrat Armengou Martín (Barcelona, 1963) is a journalist, currently working at the Catalonian Television (TV3). She is a lecturer at the University Pompeu Fabra in Barcelona and member of the Jury of the Price Europe (Berlin 2002). For the last decade she has specialized in research journalism on the Spanish Civil War and the repression that followed. Examples are "The price of memory", on the late compensation offered to the prisoners; "The alternative radios" on the radio stations that were used during Franco's regime and "The lost children under Franco's regime", unveiling the manuvers to separate children of prisoners from their families. She has received several national and international prices (Montecarlo 2000, National Cultural Price of the Generalitat de Catalunya 2002, Grand Prix FIGRA 2003 and others). Her last documentary "The graves of silence" shows the planning of the terror under Franco's Regime and raises the burning issue of thousands of common graves of innocent civilians executed without trial by fascists squadrons.

TEO, ISABEL AND SUSANNA: AN INTERNATIONAL BRIGADIER, A BRIGADIER OF REMEMBRANCE AND A BRIGADIER OF PEACE

In July 2002, the Asociación para la Recuperación de la Memoria Historica, ARMH (Association for the Recovery of the Historical Memory) obtained authority to open a series of graves in the province of Leon. One in particular, the Piedrafita de Babia, generated great public attention as it was believed that scores of civilian corpses, arbitrary and brutal victims of the repression conducted by pro-Franco troops and the paramilitary Falangists, would be found there. Their methods were familiar: detention and execution without trial of the civilians and the bodies dumped by road sides or in ditches. It is estimated that some 30 000 people disappeared in Spain in this manner. The assassins have never answered for their crimes, not during the dictatorship nor since democracy. The bodies are now being located and given a dignified burial thanks to the persistence and determination of their relatives and survivors, aided by a few associations, who have bravely broken the silence on behalf of the dead: "They will now receive an honorable grave where they will be remembered not as criminals but as defenders of liberty and democracy".

Isabel's kitchen is perhaps the most comfortable room in the house. A precious stone house in Palacios de Sil (province of Leon), that she has not been able to enjoy throughout her many years of political and economic exile. Today, along with the aroma of coffee and toast, a feeling of satisfaction mingles with happiness as the sun shines on the well tended terrace full of flowers. Yesterday, at last, some 65 years after the Falangists had taken them away, the remains of the bodies have appeared: bodies that could well be those of the brother and the brother-in-law of Isabel González. Heaped up, thrown down in any which way, their only common feature a bullet in the head, these bodies have started to appear. Many suspect they are the remains of those taken from their houses one night, never to return. The bodies have been uncovered in a grave, in the ditches beside the highway of

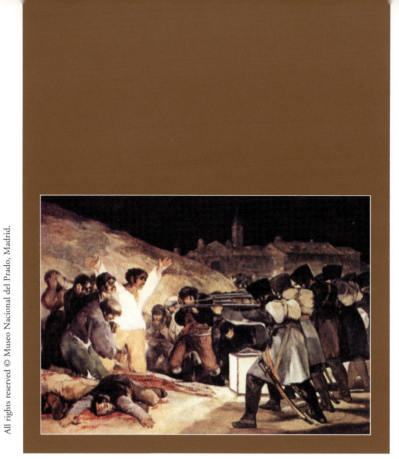

"Francisco de Goya y Lucientes, El Tres de Mayo"

Francisco de Goya y Lucientes (1746-1828) captured in his paintings the full horror of the repression against the civil population that followed the Independence War against France.

Piedrafita de Babia, where local people have always claimed that bodies would be found. Throughout the 40 years of dictatorship and more than 25 years of democracy, no one ever has ever bothered to look. What does now remain are the endless days in which Isabel relentlessly searched for someone who had helped to bury the bodies and who could identify the exact location of the remains. Isabel, a socialist and atheist, and her friend, Asunción Alvarez, political and catholic, united by pain for those missing people, went as far as giving a lawyer a hand-drawn map to be used in the future as proof of the possible place where the remains of their relatives could be found. Democracy had disappointed them so much that they did not believe they would ever be alive to see the day when the graves would be opened. That day had arrived.

At the table, around breakfast, three brigadiers sit. One, a member of the International Brigades, another brigadier for peace and the third brigadier for remembrance. Isabel, who is 85 years old, is the hostess. Her guests are a 90-year-old Frenchman, Teo Francos (who stresses that his last name finishes with an "s") who volunteered in the International Brigades to defend the Republic during the Spanish Civil War and Susanna Lutz, 70 years old. She was a volunteer in the International Civil Service. At the table, also, a group of young people from different countries, known to the town as Brigadiers for Peace, had come to help with exhuming the bodies. Their conversation took place in French, a language that Isabel had to learn in the difficult years as an emigrant in France and Switzerland. They also used the Spanish that Teo had learnt between battles and Susanna had learnt from two women who had been prisoners of war in Segovia. Their stories and testimony inspired her to come to Spain to help to uncover the hidden memories of the past.

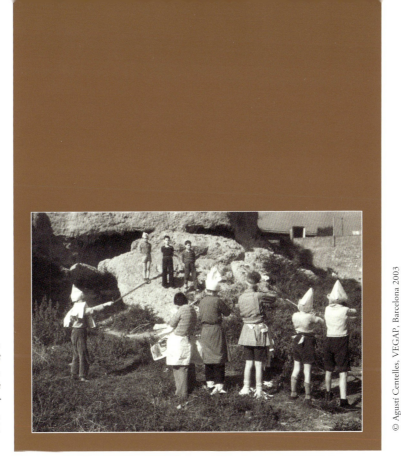

In the Spanish civil war, children were amongst the first victims. The drama has been reproduced over and over again since then. Barcelona, undated.

© Agustí Centelles, VEGAP, Barcelona 2003

–Teo: *This has been a remarkable day for us, especially for you, Isabel. At last we can see the results of what we have all wanted for such a long time. It's and important day for you.*

–Isabel: *I have been fighting for this moment for over 60 years.*

–Teo: *As I have. I started out with the mining revolution in Asturias in 1934, helping people who wanted to cross the border over the Pyrenees and taking them to Paris. Later, I was in the Spanish Civil War. When I returned to France, I was taken prisoner for 14 months in a concentration camp. Later, World War II... I have several bullets in my body! I left home when I was 18 years old and I did not return until I was 32. Now, at my age, I go to schools and talk to make sure that young people don't forget any of this.*

–Isabel: *So that they can learn.*

–Teo: *Yes. So that they can learn, especially the youngest ones. I give talks, as much in France as in Spain. At times my daughter asks me when I am going to stop. And I tell her, I guess the day that my feet go before the rest of me.*

–Isabel: *Really, Teo, just as you said, yesterday was for me the most incredible day that you could imagine. I had so often dreamed of searching for my relatives, and uncovering the dirt with my hands. My obsession has always been to recover the remains of my brother. Well, I imagine that his body will be there since, officially, nobody had ever said anything to us. I never expected that my dreams would become reality. I do not cry easily, but yesterday I was drowning with emotion.*

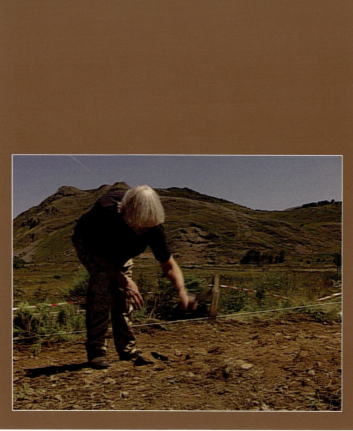

One amongst the many who are still buried in an unknown place is Federico García Lorca, one of the most renowned poets and writers of his generation. He was executed, along with three other persons, in the early morning on 18 or 19 August 1936. His remains are somewhere in a place named Barranco de Viznar in Fuente Grande, near his hometown Granada.

—Susanna: *I understand exactly.*

—Teo: *And here we are, the three of us, fighting for the same thing as these young people who came to help open the graves. That's why they call them —as well as you and Susanna- "Brigadiers for Peace". You are confronted with the same sensation I had 65 years ago, when so many of us foreigners came here with the International Brigades. I now realize that we could not finish the task. And these young people, although they were not witnesses to what happened, are now courageously fighting to understand everything that happened at that time. It was incredibly moving for them when the first bone was found.*

—Isabel: *I fight for them, for the young people. The older people don't want to know anything! Many people have said that I was mad to want to find my brother. Why did I want to stir everything up? I don't want revenge. I don't want to hurt anyone. But, I do want to fight for my rights, to bury my brother and my brother-in-law in an honourable manner and to tell the world that they were not criminals. Their murderers were the criminals. Unfortunately, people have got used to keeping all of this secret.*

—Teo: *It's true. There are young people who are not interested in our past and there are older people who say that 65 years have already passed, and that we should just forget it, and move forward. They say that nothing is gained by digging up the past. On the contrary, we must not forget!*

—Susanna: *It's true as nothing can be learned by forgetting.*

—Isabel: *History repeats itself if you hide it.*

Susana and Theo on the day their recovered the remains of their families and comrades.

–Teo: *And, the only way that the young people can learn the truth is by talking about it, by breaking the silence.*

–Susanna: *A person I knew once said something that made a great impact on me: "Suffering can be forgotten, but you cannot ever forget what caused the suffering. It lives with you forever.".*

That afternoon, the program "30 Minutes" from TV3 (Catalonian Television), broadcast the documentary *The Graves of Silence*, with the presence of the young volunteers participating in the exhumation. During the broadcast, it was mentioned that they would be called brigadiers. Some did not agree with the term as it had military connotations from which they were trying to distance themselves. They preferred to be identified as pacifists. The debate was alive: some said that in the context of 1936, the term brigadiers meant something; others said that we must not forget that the brigadiers were civilians and not soldiers; others felt that the brigadiers should have fought non violently for peace . Finally the discussion came to an end when a young woman from Madrid, Aránzazu, asked "Don't you think it is an honour to be compared to Teo?" Aránzazu's family was one of the defeated; she realized that she had hardly been taught anything about the Civil War at school and she was changed by the fear on the faces of those who approached the grave. She was incredibly moved when Isabel, the Brigadier of Remembrance, thanked her for being at the grave. Aránzazu, the Brigadier for Peace, who admired the international brigadiers, replied, "Thank you for being our memory".

(...) I HAD A YOUNG SOVIET POW PATIENT DYING IN GREAT PAIN. HE WAS MAKING A FEARFUL NOISE IN A LARGE WARD. I HAD NO DRUGS OR SIDE WARD. NO ONE COULD TALK RUSSIAN. IN DESPAIR, AND PURELY INSTINCTIVELY, I SAT ON HIS BED AND TOOK HIM IN MY ARMS. THE EFFECT WAS ALMOST MAGICAL; HE QUIETENED AT ONCE AND DIED PEACEFULLY A FEW HOURS LATTER. I WAS STILL WITH HIM, HALF ASLEEP AND VERY STIFF. I BELIEVE THAT BY PERSONAL INTERVENTION I IMPROVED THE QUALITY OF CARE DRAMATICALLY IN THIS CASE, AND I KNOW IT WAS BASED ON INSTINCT AND NOT ON REASON. I FEEL THEREFORE RATHER DIFFIDENT ABOUT A RATIONAL DISCUSSION ABOUT QUALITY. WE ALL RECOGNIZE QUALITY WHEN WE SEE IT AND PARTICULARLY WHEN WE RECEIVE IT. (...). THE REALLY IMPORTANT FACTORS ARE KINDLINESS AND ABILITY TO COMMUNICATE ON THE PART OF ALL MEMBERS OF THE MEDICAL TEAM. (...)

WE ATTEMPT TO TEACH MEDICAL STUDENTS PSYCHOLOGY AND SOCIOLOGY, BUT WILL WE REALLY MAKE THEM KINDLIER?

ARCHIBALD LEMAN COCHRANE, 1978

* *Credit & Legend, see page 326.*

ARCHIE COCHRANE WISHES YOU WELL ...

OBITUARY
ARCHIE COCHRANE (1909-1988)

SIR RICHARD PETO
Clinical Trial Service Unit, Oxford, UK

SIR IAIN CHALMERS
National Perinatal Epidemiology Unit, Oxford, UK

Archie Cochrane was one of the early enthusiasts both for randomized trials and for the British National Health Service, seeing each as practicable ways of achieving humane ideals. He had the unusual distinction of having done his first controlled trial as a prisoner of war in a German prison camp. (Six of his fellow prisoners to whom a yeast supplement was given recovered rapidly from symptoms of nutritional deficiency, while six apparently comparable controls did not.) More importantly, in prison camp he could not give the treatments that his medical training had recommended for various serious diseases, yet many of his patients recovered anyway. This left him with a strong desire for reliable knowledge as to which treatments really saved lives and which did not. After the war he became a clinical trialist, a respiratory epidemiologist, an MRC unit director and President of the Faculty of Community Medicine. Several obituaries of him have already appeared. Rather than write another that would certainly be no better than that written by Doll, we have decided to abbreviate Archie's own semiautobiographical introduction to his most famous publication, the 1972 monograph entitled "Effectiveness and Efficiency", and to let him share his values and his humour in his own words with the readers of Controlled Clinical Trials.

During the past 40 years randomized trials have become so commonplace that it may now be difficult to understand the enormous enthusiasm they engendered when they were first introduced into clinical medicine by Bradford Hill. Before that time it was obviously possible to recognize reliably any really large effects of treatment - indeed, all of medical practice before 1950 was based on nonrandomized evidence, and much of it was well founded. But thoughtful doctors such as Archie were acutely aware that without randomization there was simply no way to distinguish reliably between the hypothesis that a particular treatment had no material effect on the outcome of disease and the alternative hypothesis that it did have a moderate, yet humanly worthwhile effect. Without something equivalent to proper randomization, it is not possible to allow reliably for the extent to which various characteristics of the patient might affect both the outcome of the disease and the choice of treatment. This remains as true today as it was then, no matter how complicated the adjustments using recorded values of various prognostic features. Because people still do, from time to time, try to reintroduce nonrandomized methods of "efficacy analysis" under one name or another (e.g. historical controls, database analyses, etc.), it is still worth reading the early writings of doctors like Archie who had direct experience of the difficulties of medicine without proper randomization.*

* Reprinted from: Peto R, Chalmers I. Obituary: Archie Cochrane (1909-1988). Contr Clin Trials 1989;16:193-195
Reproduced with permission from Elsevier

KING'S COLLEGE ANNUAL REPORT, OCTOBER 1989

Archibald Leman Cochrane 'was a man with severe porphyria who smoked too much and was without the consolation of a wife, a religious belief, or a merit award – but he did not do too badly'. Thus concludes the short obituary written by Archie himself for the British Medical Journal. The words are characteristic, combining a quizzical self-depreciation and self-regard, an unpompous satisfaction with an adventurous and impulsive life.

Archie was born on 12 January 1909 in the small Scottish town of Galashiels where his great-grandfather and grandfather had been the principal employers at their textile factory, and the Cochranes were leading members of the town's industrial upper-middle-class. There were five other families with whom it was proper for them to relate socially. The family house was Abbotshill, just across the Tweed from Walter Scott's Abbotsford. Archie was the second of four children, brought up in an environment of servants, luxuries and Calvinistic discipline. He acquired a work ethic which persisted throughout his life. Formal education began with governesses who found the young red-head precocious, imaginative and quarrelsome. Then life suddenly changed when Archie's father died in the battle of Gaza. Family circumstances were reduced but Archie could be sent to a preparatory school in North Wales from where he helped the family finances by winning a scholarship to Uppingham. There he pleased the authorities by his success at rugby, cricket, hockey and Eton fives. Perhaps for this reason he suffered less corporal punishment than most. His critical faculties and broad artistic and intellectual interest also developed fast and he lost the religious faith of his upbringing. According to himself, the last straw was a sermon by a muscular Christian on the athleticism of Christ and his probable stroking of the Galilean boat.

From Uppingham, Archie won a scholarship to King's in 1927. He arrived with boundless energy: 'I wanted to learn more science, play rugby, football, golf, tennis, squash; take part in play-reading and debates, act, go to the theatre, talk and argue, ride horses and play bridge'. And he claimed to have involved himself in all these activities without missing a lecture or practical class and he did not fail to get a first in part I of the natural sciences tripos. At his initial interview he admitted an interest in medicine and was firmly told he was at King's to be educated. Nevertheless he studied the usual pre-clinical sciences. While at King's he inherited a small private income on the sale of the family textile business, just before the slump. This degree of independence had an important influence throughout his life. In the short term it enabled him to take two years over part 2 in which he also gained a first despite overwork and nervous exhaustion; and to develop an interest in the ideas of both Marx and Freud. Regretfully, he could find no fellow of the College able or willing to discuss such subjects.

On graduation Archie decided on a quick route to a fellowship by way of the newly developed science of tissue culture, on which he worked under Neville Willmer. But he was inept and impatient at the laboratory bench and soon gave up in favour of studying medicine and psychoanalysis in Berlin, where he was also psychoanalysed himself. He followed his teacher, Theodore Reik, to Vienna and Leyden, acquiring fluent German and a feel for European culture. But he was also increasingly disillusioned by both psychoanalysis and conventional medical training. So he enrolled at University College Hospital, only to complain that there, too the teaching was too dogmatic and evidence too often took the form of 'in my clinical experience'.

King's College main garden, Cambridge, UK Summer 2002.

Archie's interest in politics continued and he debated between the Communist and Labour Parties without joining either. Instead, greatly concerned over the rise of fascism, he joined the first Spanish Medical Aid Ambulance, spent a hair-raising time in Spain, and concluded that 'no one knew how to run a country A revolution'. At one time he was forced to divide the wounded into treatable and untreatable, only to discover that one of the untreatables was an old friend, Julian Bell. He took pains to get a specialist opinion, which confirmed his own.

After a year in Spain, Archie returned to London, qualified as a doctor, and soon (in 1940) joined the Royal Army Medical Corps. Soon, too, he was captured in Crete, an event which he blamed on Evelyn Waugh's map reading. There followed four years as a prisoner of war in Greece and Germany – years of great hardship and privation, during which his medical training and fluent German placed him in an exposed position. At much personal risk he frequently intervened on behalf of fellow prisoners who were being treated with the utmost inhumanity or who desperately needed medical treatment. Often only basic medical skills were called for, but towards the end of the war Archie began to specialise in tuberculosis, most of his patients being Russian, French and Jugoslav prisoners. From his last camp (in East Germany) he was liberated by a lone Russian private on a bicycle. He returned to England and his London flat in very poor health, being suspected of having contracted tuberculosis himself; and became one of the very few officers to be awarded the MBE for services while a prisoner of war. He believed that he was helped to survive those four years by writing poetry and thus externalising his feelings and experiences.

On his return to health and civilian life, Archie took the Diploma in Public Health and then spent a year in America studying the epidemiology of tuberculosis. This was to set him on a path that he was to follow for the rest of his life. On his return to the UK he joined a vigorous, argumentative MRC unit in South Wales under Charles Fletcher, working on pneumoconiosis in the mining villages. Then followed ten years of great productivity. He was specifically concerned with relating the lung condition of miners (through X-ray examination) to the degree of exposure to coal dust. But his interest extended beyond the miners to the populations of which they were part; and beyond pneumoconiosis to anaemia, rheumatoid arthritis, bronchitis and other conditions. The surveys were repeated at ten-year intervals for thirty years and Archie claimed (with a characteristic dig at the medical establishment) to have shown that 'measurements could be made on a population defined geographically with about the same inaccuracy as measurements made in laboratories'. Much of his success depended on his winning the confidence of a very high proportion of the populations concerned.

Despite the handover of his interests in pneumoconiosis research to the National Coal Board, Archie was able to continue his work in South Wales because in 1958 he was appointed to the Chair of Tuberculosis (later, through Archie's persistence, widened to include Chest Diseases) at the Welsh National School of Medicine, Cardiff; and Honorary Director of an MRC Unit of Epidemiology. He did not consider himself to be a great success as head of a university department, having little patience with Senate House manoeuvring and power struggles. Neither did he think of himself as a good teacher, but his kindness and generosity to his students (many from overseas) became proverbial. By now he had moved out of an obscure hotel in Cardiff dockland and had bought a Farm House in Glamorgan where a housekeeper was installed and room found for a succession of colleagues. Here, numerous students were enter-

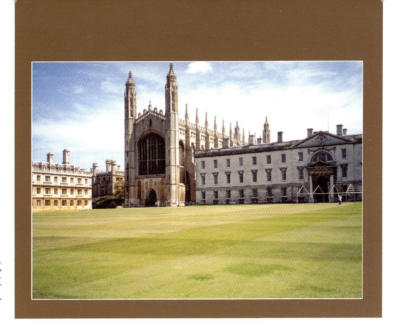

King's College chapel, Cambridge, UK. Summer 2002.

tained in groups of four or five, often perplexed by his unfamiliar style of living. But they enjoyed the swimming pool and occasionally stole the drink.

While maintaining his interest in the populations of the valleys, Archie entered into a second productive period in his professional life. With respect to a wide range of conditions, he asked a vital question: what was the evidence that the accepted mode of treatment did any good? His consequent investigations met with much suspicion and lack of co-operation in the medical world, especially when Archie tried to set up randomized controlled trials. The cry of 'unethical' was often raised. Maybe that cry was directed at Archie personally when he announced the results of a trial of in-patient and home treatment of coronaries. The difference, he announced, was not statistically significant though there was a small numerical advantage in hospitalisation. When cries of 'we told you so' had died down, Archie confessed that he had intentionally reversed the figures which actually favoured home treatment. There was a stony silence.

He even turned his attention to dental treatment, arranging for two dental surgeons to examine the same group of patients and prescribe treatment. He claimed that the only agreement between them was over the number of teeth in each patient's mouth.

Archie was awarded the CBE in 1968 and retired from his Cardiff chair a year later, becoming full-time Director of the MRC Epidemiology Unit. While remaining very closely involved in its work, he also became active on a broader front, including fundamental discussion on the future of the National Health Service and the organisation and funding of medical research. When the new Faculty of Community Medicine was set up in the Royal College of Physicians,

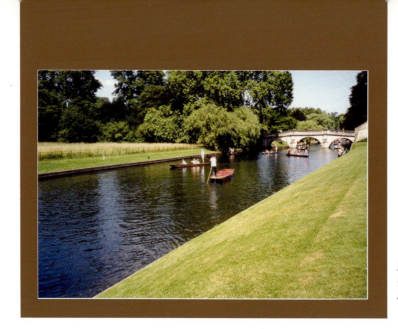

King's College channel, Cambridge, UK Summer 2002.

he reluctantly agreed to become its first president, ('I phoned a lot of friends and they all advised me that I was the best of a bad lot'). Working mainly between 10.00 p.m. and 1.00 a.m. and acquiring a love of whisky at the same time, he wrote *Effectiveness and Efficiency: random reflections on health services* which was translated into four languages and led to a very large number of invitations to travel and lecture. And, not content with these public commitments, he found time to engage in a piece of family research. It started in 1967 when he rescued his very ill sister from a hospital where she was being treated for severe senile psychosis. Archie insisted on further tests and she was found to be suffering from the obscure condition of porphyria, from which she slowly recovered, thanks largely to Archie's devotion. The condition is inherited, so he set about discovering its incidence in his widespread family. His investigations started with a party for all the Cochranes within easy reach, the invitation asking them kindly to supply a specimen of urine and faeces. The survey then became world-wide and, in the end, 152 Cochranes had been traced and warned of the potential danger.

Not content with this very full professional life, and helped by a further family legacy, Archie's move to Rhoose Farm House turned him into a gardener. With his usual energy, enthusiasm and originality, he turned the rough surroundings of the Farm House into a renowned garden which attracted many visitors. And both house and garden provided settings for the collection of modern paintings and sculpture which he bought 'because I liked them and on the whole I think I had good taste.'

After his retirement as Director of the MRC unit, he retained a room and continued working until a short time before his death on 18 June 1988 at the age of seventy-nine. He is remembered as a man of outstanding character; entertaining, stimulating, controversial, no respector of persons, generous, flamboyant, and determined at all times to follow the truth as he saw it.*

* Archie Cochrane. Obituary. King's College Annual Report. October 1989.
Reproduced by kind permission of the Provost and Scholars of King's College, Cambridge.

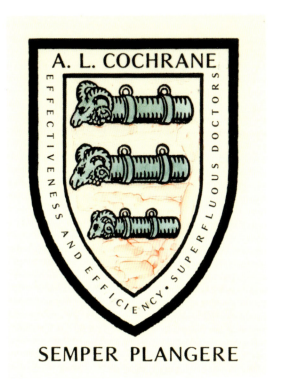

This might be a joke. So far it is not understood.

Joe Stalker

PORTRAIT

Over and above science, politics or being a star lecturer, Archie considered himself as a man professionally devoted to the quality of care at the bedside. Early in life, Archie confronted an imprecise sexual problem that lead him to question, as a young patient, his teachers and colleagues both at home and all the way to Dr Freud's clinic in Austria. There is little doubt that he was not satisfied with the medical answer and some of the attitudes and one could speculate whether this early questioning of medical dogma influenced his life-long attitude to clinical practice. In turn, while in Vienna, he witnessed Nazism in action and that definitely shaped his life to come.

His passionate defence of randomized controlled trials had a solid background, nurtured by the intellect of many fine scientists and colleagues. Verbal ability and a waterproof topic made him both an attractive speaker and a difficult rival. His visceral rejection of medical arrogance and presumption is part of his legacy and a most desirable feature for medical practice. The predictable questions *Why did you not randomize?* and *How can you be sure that you are not doing more harm than good?* could easily summarize his medical battlefront.

Yet he is also remembered, as most of the contributors to this book have shown, by a wealth of human anecdotes, ingenious attitudes and by a recognition of his endurance and courage as a medical practitioner in the extreme circumstances of war and concentration camps. Joining the International Brigades at a very young age is a gesture that aligns Archie with the work of some of the volunteer organizations of our time, very close to the ideas of generosity and rightness.

Archie was a man of family yet a lonely inhabitant of a large farm house in Rhoose. To fill the space and the sound, he was always ready to offer his house and his belongings to friends, guests and even to those he had just met. Several of Archie's friends have made this portrait possible. For the many who did not know him but are familiar with the name, this modest homage should be a fair, although perhaps biased, introduction to the man, and his contributions.

F. Xavier Bosch
Cambridge, UK
July, 2003.

Portrait by Ricard Molas
Barcelona
September, 2003

CREDITS AND LEGENDS FOR INSIDE COVERS

Pages 12-13

Text source: Doll R. Foreword. In: Cochrane AL, Blythe M. One Man's Medicine. An Autobiography of Professor Archie Cochrane. London: BMJ (Memoir Club), 1989.

Pages 24-25

Photograph legend: *Near El Escorial, 1978*.

Pages 88-89

Text source: Cohen D. Archie Cochrane: an appreciation. In: Maynard A, Chalmers I. Non-Random Reflections on Health Services Research. On the 25th Anniversary of Archie Cochrane's Effectiveness and Efficiency. London: BMJ Publishing Group, 1997. Reproduced with permission from the BMJ Publishing Group.

Photograph legend: *Archie is gardening with daughters of the sculptor Peter Nicholas, whose family rented the barn to install his studio and stayed at Rhoose for 20 years.*

Pages 110-111

Text source: Cohen D. Introduction. In: Cochrane AL, Blythe M. One Man's Medicine. An Autobiography of Professor Archie Cochrane. London: BMJ (Memoir Club), 1989.

Photograph legend: *Reproduced by permission of Max Blythe. Archie at Cambridge in the early 1930's.*

Pages 112-113

Text source: Gibson I. The assassination of Federico García Lorca. NY: Penguin Books, 1973.

Photograph legend: *Cerro Muriano (Cordoba front). 5 September 1936. Republican militiaman (Federico Borrell Garcia) at the moment of death. ("The Falling Soldier")*. © Robert Capa / Magnum Photo / Contacto.

Pages 132-133

Photograph legend: *Einstein, Mme Curie and Barsky visiting the recruitment center of the International Brigades at the Union's headquarters in Paris, 18 rue Mathurin Moreau.* Reproduced with permission of Dr Moisès Broggi and Edicions 62, Barcelona, 2003.

Pages 142-143

Photograph legend: *Train transporting wounded Republican soldiers to the rearguard.* Reproduced with permission of Dr Moisès Broggi and Edicions 62, Barcelona, 2003.

Pages 184-185

Text source: Orwell G. *Homage to Catalonia*. London: Penguin Books, 1968. Copyright © George Orwell 1937. Extracts reproduced by permission of Bill Hamilton as the Literary Executor of the Estate of the Late Sonia Brownell Orwell and Secker & Warburg Ltd.

Photograph legend: *On the road from Barcelona to the French border. 25-27 January 1939. After the fall of Barcelona, and with fascist rule over all of Spain clearly imminent, about 500 000 Spanish civilians sought refuge and political asylum in France. France set up camps along the borders in the Pyrénées Orientales region. Catalogne.* © Robert Capa / Magnum Photo / Contacto.

Pages 188-189

Text source: Cohen D. Introduction. In: Cochrane AL, Blythe M. One Man's Medicine. An Autobiography of Professor Archie Cochrane. London: BMJ (Memoir Club), 1989.

Photograph legend: *Archie Cochrane as a prisoner of war. Portrait painted by Spanish prisoner of war named "Basilio" at Elsterhorst, Germany, in 1944. The painting is now in Dorset, home of Joe and Maggie Stalker, where Archie spent his last days.* Reproduced by permission of Max Blythe.

Pages 206-207

Text source: Cochrane AL. Effectiveness and Efficiency. Random Reflections on Health Services. London: Nuffield Provincial Hospitals Trust, 1972. (Reprinted in 1989 in association with the BMJ, reprinted in 1999 for Nuffield Trust by the Royal Society of Medicine Press, London). Reproduced with permission from the BMJ Publishing Group and the Royal Society of Medicine Press.

Photograph legend: *Pit-head of one of the coal mines involved in the study of miners in Wales.* Source unknown.

Pages 230-231

Text source: Archie and the post-man in Villarejo de Salvanés in 1978.

Pages 290-291

Photograph legend: *The Savacou dominated Archie's garden in Rhoose Farm House and travelled with him to Dorset where it continues to protect Archie's family. The making of the sculpture generated long lasting negotiations involving Ronald Moody, the artist, Archie and Bill Miall. Most of it dealt with the length of the legs and the relative position of one to the other.*

Pages 294-295

Photograph legend: *Homage to the International Brigades held at the Autonomous University of Barcelona. Barcelona, 11 November 1996.*

Pages 304-305

Photograph legend: *León (Spain), July 2002.* © Televisió de Catalunya S.A., Reproduced with permission from the program *30 minuts*.

Pages 312-313

Text source: Cochrane AL. Effectiveness and Efficiency. Random Reflections on Health Services. London: Nuffield Provincial Hospitals Trust, 1972. (Reprinted in 1989 in association with the BMJ, reprinted in 1999 for Nuffield Trust by the Royal Society of Medicine Press, London). Reproduced with permission from the BMJ Publishing Group and the Royal Society of Medicine Press.

Photograph legend: *Archie in Grañén in 1978*.

THIS EDITION OF
ARCHIE COCHRANE: BACK TO THE FRONT
HAS BEEN EDITED USING THE TYPEFACES
TRAJAN, GARAMOND AND HELVETICA
BY FOTOCOMPOSICIÓN GAMA
AND PRINTED BY THAU S.L.

NOTE FROM EDITORS

COMMENTS TO THIS WORK AND IDEAS FOR SUBSEQUENT EDITIONS
COULD BE ADDRESSED TO
CRISTINA RAJO / F. XAVIER BOSCH
cris@ico.scs.es